FUNDRAISE PAINLESSLY

How to Earn More Funds

CHIP & RALFIE BLASIUS

Sage
Creek
Press

Traverse City, Michigan

*This book is dedicated to the memory of my father, Bob Macy,
who taught us the meaning of altruism, and to our dear
friend, Lucile Burk, whose 98 years of spunky living inspires us.*

Copyright © 1999 by Chip and Ralfie Blasius

The contents of this book reflects information and experiences gathered by the authors through their many years associated with not-for-profit organizations. The authors make no legal advice express or implied and it is recommended that if there is any question on a particular activity that professional counsel be considered. The authors and publisher disclaim any loss or liability caused by utilizing the information presented herein.

 Published by SAGE CREEK PRESS
121 East Front Street, 4th Floor,
Traverse City, Michigan 49684

Publisher's Cataloging-in-Publication Data
Blasius, Chip and Ralfie.
   Earn more funds : how to earn more funds/
Chip and Ralfie Blasius. – Traverse City, Mich. : Sage Creek Press, 1999.

        p.   cm.

     Includes bibliographical references and index
     ISBN: 1-890394-18-1
     1. Fundraising. 2. Nonprofit organizations.
     I. Blasius, Ralfie. II. Title.
HV41.2 .B53 1998   98-60005
658.152/24 – dc21   CIP

PROJECT COORDINATION BY JENKINS GROUP, INC.

03 02 01 00 * 5 4 3 2 1

TABLE OF CONTENTS

continued on next page

TABLE OF CONTENTS

continued from preceding page

CHAPTER 6—HELPING OTHERS

CHAPTER 7—SENSATIONAL SALES

The first time I sat in the chair of a dunk tank, many thoughts flashed through my mind. I was nervous as I waited for the first successful throw to dunk me. By the time I actually got wet, I was almost relieved. I got over my fear, had great fun, and our group made a lot of money.

As volunteers in varying capacities for over twenty years, my husband and I have done fundraising with many non-profit organizations. We saw the need for a basic resource book for non-profit management and fundraising. Putting our heads together, we combined what we knew and began making notes.

We talked with fundraisers from other groups and found out what projects worked for them and what pitfalls they overcame. We researched fundraising at the library. The deeper we dug, the more ideas we uncovered. The basic framework behind dozens of successful fundraisers emerged.

Throughout this project, we received a lot of valuable advice about fundraising and volunteers. We incorporated much of this information into our book. We'd like to thank everyone who gave us their input.

As you work through the book, you'll meet our mascot, *Ernie Mo Funds*. He's pictured on the title page and on each of the chapter introduction pages. We hope this book will help you earn more funds as his name implies. Raising funds for your non-profit organization is more than just making money; it's an educational experience for all. You'll learn to plan, organize, delegate and beg.

Working on fundraisers teaches everyone in your group to get along with people, to work together and to graciously accept both success and rejection. It helps if you get your members involved with every stage of fundraising, from brainstorming the initial ideas to completing the project.

Learning to fundraise well is like completing a course in human behavior and psychology. You'll learn what works, what doesn't and, most importantly, why. You'll start to understand why people donated or participated in one project and not another.

Keep notes on all fundraising projects you undertake. During a project have in-progress meetings at every stage, from pre-planning to organizing and implementing the project. Remember, people don't plan to fail, they fail to plan. Then review the projects after it is complete. Make notes of successes, failure, and suggestions for next time.

Create a file system for all of your fundraising ideas and information. Begin by jotting down what you already know: Who do you give money to? Why? Who would you never give money to? Why not? What successful fundraisers have you worked on in the past? What made them successful? Write out your own experiences and those of other members.

Gather all this information and keep it in your files. This will help you make even better fundraising decisions and assist your next generation of leaders.

We firmly believe that giving of one's time, resources, and talents through volunteer activity is mankind's sacred duty. Volunteers make things happen. When it comes to performing concrete services to help those in need, non-profit organizations are often more effective than governments.

We dedicate this book to all volunteers and hope our ideas help them fundraise to the best of their ability. When we work to improve the lives of those around us, we also improve our own. As Emerson said, "It is one of the most beautiful compensations of life that no man can sincerely try to help another without helping himself."

> When we work to improve the lives of those around us, we also improve our own. As Emerson said, "It is one of the most beautiful compensations of life that no man can sincerely try to help another without helping himself."

CHAPTER 1
GETTING STARTED

CHAPTER NOTES:

GENERAL GUIDELINES

I started out as a warm corpse in a haunted house. I was scared stiff. When the first customer showed his curious face, I arose and he nearly fainted. I then had a great time and our group scared up some big money.

Fundraising efforts, at their best, enrich both our financial and spiritual coffers. In the following pages we'll help you at every stage, from initial brainstorming to final reports.

A local private high school has held a *Silent Auction* (see page 160) every year since 1980. It is always their largest fundraising event and last year raised $135,000. What's their secret? It's not magic. It's starting with an excellent idea, adding lots of hard work and following the rules of good fundraising.

Most of fundraising is simply applied good common sense. Begin with a sound idea and add all required manpower to transform your idea into action. Next, line up supplies, equipment and facilities, then publicize, publicize and publicize your event some more. Everything is now in place for a great fundraiser!

Let's take a look at the major elements needed to make all your fundraisers successful.

WHO
WHAT
WHERE
WHEN
WHY
HOW

> *Fundraising efforts, at their best, enrich both your financial and spiritual coffers. In the following pages we'll help you at every stage of fundraising, from initial brainstorming to final reports.*

TIMING

Even a sure-fire fundraiser can be ruined by poor timing. Do your homework, then schedule your project for the most opportune time possible.

To avoid conflicts with other popular local events, first check with your local chamber or community calendar, as well as local school calendars. Then just find an open date.

Another approach is to schedule your fundraiser as an addition to a larger, already scheduled local event. For example, setting up your lemonade stand during a local music festival will give you a much larger attendance than just a lemonade stand by itself.

Schedule the event at a convenient time for both your volunteers and the participants. Be considerate of school, work and babysitting schedules.

LOCATIONS

INDOOR: If your project is to be held indoors, ask the following questions:
- *Any rental charge?*
- *Restrictions or rules?*
- *Total crowd capacity?*
- *Do they have the equipment (i.e. kitchen facilities, basketball court, etc.) that you need for your project?*
- *Is it a handy location?*

OUTDOOR: If your project will be held outdoors, consider these questions:
- *If it is public property, are any permits needed?*
- *If it is private property, are there any special regulations?*
- *Do you have a bad weather alternate location or date?*

SUPPLIES

When feasible, ask sponsors to donate supplies. If you can't get donations, ask for a discount or buy from wholesalers.

When approaching a potential sponsor or donor, be polite and courteous at all times. Remember you're asking them to take time out of their busy day to talk to you about a donation. Never waste their time.

Be prepared to give them a

brief recap of your project, as well as some background on your group. Have a specific idea of what you want from them (money, products, services, etc.) If they agree to help you, make detailed notes about all specific arrangements or commitments made. If they can't help you, thank them for their time and move on to your next potential sponsor.

Ask all donors if they want their gift publicized. For various reasons some do not and you need to be sensitive to their wishes. Let your suppliers know if you are tax-exempt or not-for-profit. This helps their tax records as well as yours.

SPECIAL EQUIPMENT

When you need specific equipment for your project, use the following rule of thumb:

Borrow if possible; rent if necessary. Have volunteers and participants bring their equipment when feasible. Buy only if it will be used repeatedly.

MANPOWER

Volunteers are the life force of every fundraiser. Seek volunteers from your group first, then from similar groups. Next, ask supportive family, friends, etc. Many people are willing to help; all you need do is ask.

PUBLICITY

The people coming to your events, buying your goods and services or making outright donations make your fundraiser a success. In order to do

this, they must first know about you and your project. This is where *publicity* is key. Your target market (the people you want to reach) must be aware of

your event as well as when and where it will take place.

There are many ways to get your message out. Some are free; others cost money. Let's review a few:

Start spreading the word first within your organization. As soon as you have decided on a fundraiser and set the date, be sure every member knows about it. Make announcements at all meetings. Keep interest alive through regular progress reports from the project chair.

Send memos, flyers and/or letters to all members in case some missed your meetings. Never let it be said that a group member didn't know about an event you were sponsoring.

To have a successful fundraiser, you need the support of as many hard-working volun-

teers as possible. The project chairperson and helpers can call members and remind them of the event and, while talking, encourage them to volunteer.

After you've generated excitement within your own group about your project, the next step is to move outside your organization. Use every available media form to get your message out to your target market. What follows is a listing of ways to get your message to your target market.

In general, the more ways you give your intended audience information about your upcoming event, the bigger crowd you'll draw!

SPECIAL PUBLICITY ANGLES

What makes your fundraiser unique? Focus on special aspects of your project to create public interest. These angles will also attract the attention of editors and news personnel.

• *Why is it unusual?*
• *What special group will benefit from the project?*
• *Are there any other human interest angles?*
• *Any civic interest angles?*

TELL EVERYONE

Publicize your project among family, friends, business contacts and other interested groups. Call them by phone or send a letter or postcard. If every member of your organization agrees to contact 10 people, you'll have multiplied your contacts ten-fold.

FREE PUBLICITY

Church and school bulletins and newsletters are all good, *free* sources of publicity. Grab attention with your notice (i.e. "Y.G.A.C.W. is coming!"— Youth Group's Annual Car Wash, or "Keep June 9th open...Details next week!")

News releases (see *Sample News Release* on page 47) or public service announcements (PSAs) are other cost-free ways to get your project publicized in various local media: radio, television and the newspaper.

When writing the news release, focus on any original, exciting or unusual human interest aspects of your project. Keep your releases brief, but include all necessary information. Type it, as most editors won't read handwritten releases. List a contact person and phone number.

> When writing the news release, focus on any original, exciting or unusual human interest aspects of your project. Keep your releases brief, but include all necessary information.

If you are producing some kind of good-will service, local newspapers or TV stations may cover the event as a "human interest" story (see *Marketing* on page 44).

Provide this information to all media two to three weeks in advance so they have plenty of time to schedule their announcements of your project.

If your fundraiser is an event of some sort, also send a press release to the editor of the local events section of your paper for possible publication there.

If you have sponsors supporting your event, they may be willing to publicize it within their organization, store, etc. Ask them! If they're large enough to have a print shop, they may be willing to print your flyers or posters. If they can't help with the printing, offer to provide posters and flyers for them to display.

Roadsigns giving the time and location of your upcoming event also help build interest. Check for any local roadside signage ordinances. Place your signs on busy streets and at heavily-traveled intersections.

PUBLICITY FOR A PRICE

Paid ads are feasible when your project is large enough to warrant their expense.

A very effective local multi-media campaign can include newspaper ads, radio and cable TV spots and billboards. You'll need current ratecards (which give their advertising costs) from each of your local media: newspapers, radio and TV stations, so you can plan your advertising buys.

If you're using billboards, they should be up at least two, and preferably three weeks, before the event. Newspaper ads, radio and TV spots should start three or four days before the event and build to a peak on the day of the event.

Well-written, well-designed and well-placed ads and spots are powerful assets for large fundraising projects.

POSTERS

Posters should be neat, bright and easy to read. Artwork adds impact to your message. Use colorful geometric graphics or photos from previous events. Your posters should be informative as well as pleasing to the eye. Be sure to include all pertinent information (who, what, where, when, why and how) on your posters, but keep them looking clean (see *Graphic Design* on page 50).

Contact local businesses to see if they'll let you put your posters in their facilities. Note where you put your posters so you can remove them after the event. Let people know you're grateful for their assistance. Courtesy and good manners alway leave a favorable impression with your supporters.

WHAT TO INCLUDE IN ALL PUBLICITY

WHO: Identify your group.

WHAT: Describe the event; give a brief history of it.

WHERE: Give the location of event. Include directions if it's hard to find.

WHEN: Give the date and time of your event.

HOW: Recap the details of your event.

WHY: How your group will benefit.

Now get busy!

GUIDELINES FOR ALL FUNDRAISERS

A. TIMING

1. Avoid conflicts with other local events *or*
2. Coordinate with them if possible
3. Convenient timing

B. LOCATION

1. Indoor

   Rental fees   *Equipment*
   Restrictions   *Convenience*
   Capacity
2. Outdoor

   Permits/Regulations
   Rain date or alternate location

C. PUBLICITY

1. Within your organization:

   Announcements
   Memos/flyers/letters/phone calls
2. Beyond your organization:

   Posters   *Paid Media (newspapers, t.v., radio)*
   Tell 10 people!   *Free Media (newspapers, t.v., radio)*
   Bulletins and newsletters   *Roadside signs*
3. What to include:

   Who is holding the event   *When it will happen*
   What will happen   *How it will happen*
   Where it will happen   *Why you are doing it*
4. Special angles:

   Unusual project or beneficiary
   Special interest area

D. SUPPLIES

1. Donations   3. Don't forget your courtesy!
2. Wholesalers   4. Tax status

E. EQUIPMENT

1. Borrow
2. Rent
3. Participants bring own

F. MANPOWER

1. Members
2. Family/friends
3. Members of other groups

MAKE AS MANY COPIES OF THIS PAGE AS NEEDED

GOALS & PLANNING

Okay, so a tub of ice did get spilled and some ice cream was left out of the freezer, but nothing serious or long-lasting. In fact, this fundraiser, the most carefully planned of your fundraising career, also ran the smoothest and earned 10% more then your best estimate. Setting goals and planning can pay off big.

Let's start with an overview of the fundamentals of goal-setting, planning and assigning jobs. We have included worksheets to help your group with its decision-making and goal-setting, problem-solving and planning.

GETTING STARTED

Once goals are established, it's easier to make decisions about projects, budgets and the direction your group wants to go.

Without a specific fundraiser in mind, the first thing to do is to set up a committee meeting to generate ideas. By working through this section your committee will develop a clear set of fundraising objectives.

DEFINING OBJECTIVES

One of the most helpful places to begin planning any fundraising activity is by looking at your organization's objectives. For the purposes of this book

> *Written objectives will help you make decisions about which specific fundraising activities best fulfill your organization's mission.*

the terms "objective", "mission" and "purpose" are synonymous. For instance, if your organization is the Red Cross, the objective is to give humanitarian service. The Boy Scouts' mission is to foster good citizenship and outdoor skills in young men. The school band's purpose is to provide aesthetic enrichment and promote musical skills.

The point is this: You must clearly define your organization's objective. Write it down. There may be several different objectives or opinions at this point. That's OK. It doesn't have to be exact. Written objectives help you make decisions about which specific fundraising activities best fulfill your organization's mission.

For example, raffles and

bingo games are not acceptable to the scouting movement and should be avoided by scout fundraisers.

GOALS & PLANNING

After you've defined your objectives, set specific goals to meet with your fundraiser.

One obvious goal is to raise money. The question becomes: How much money? For what purpose do you need the money? How much time do you have? What manpower do you have available? What facilities are available? What previous fundraisers have been done by your organization?

Next, set up your committee meeting and complete the *Planning Worksheet* on page 8.

COMMITTEE BRAINSTORMS

Business managers commonly start new projects with a brainstorming session. An organized brainstorming session with good notes is a very effective starting point for a fundraiser.

Use the following rules for your brainstorming sessions:

1. *Write down all suggestions only once.*
2. *Don't criticize.*
3. *Set a time limit.*
4. *All ideas are good ideas.*
5. *Evaluate later.*

After the meeting, type up your notes and send copies to all committee members. Now the ball is beginning to roll.

PLANNING WORKSHEET

What is the purpose of your organization?_____
_____
_____

Basic goal for fundraising activity_____
_____

Fundraising suggestions_____
_____
_____

Are these fundraisers sensitive to your organization's purpose?_____
_____
_____

Most suitable fundraising activities_____
_____
_____

Labor needed, jobs and hours_____
_____
_____

Resources and facilities needed_____
_____
_____

List all problems anticipated, then list solutions_____
_____
_____

List the steps that need to be taken to complete your fundraiser_____
_____
_____

Anticipated budget_____

MAKE AS MANY COPIES OF THIS PAGE AS NEEDED

RECORDKEEPING

It's October, you're holding your first committee meeting since July. The chairman wants to know why the last check bounced and what happened to the $3,000 you had in January? The Treasurer thinks your summer carnival lost money, he's in a personal crisis and hasn't balanced the checkbook in months. Membership renewals are two months away and your group is in a cash crisis *now*!

New committee members are now nervous and one asks, "How far off budget are we?" You answer in a feeble voice, "We didn't make a budget."

This sad scenario can easily happen to any group that doesn't do enough financial planning and/or keep current records. Establishing a budget and maintaining good records are not impossible feats. And the consequences of not doing so can be dire, as the above situation indicates. Here are a few proven methods your group can use to ensure good records.

FINANCIAL TOOLS

Keeping accurate, current records is a good practice for small non-profit organizations and a must for larger ones. Incorporated non-profit organizations legally must keep complete, accurate records. Good records are an invaluable tool for controlling your organization's finances, preventing financial disasters and, in the long run, realizing your group's goals.

> *Good records are an invaluable tool for controlling your organization's finances, preventing financial disasters and, in the long run, realizing your group's goals.*

Accurate recordkeeping practices make it relatively easy to issue reports (see *Project Planning Guide*, on page 38) for individual events. They also help ensure the future success of your group as a whole. Up-to-date records greatly reduce unexpected financial problems. Once a good recordkeeping system is in place, it takes only a few hours a month to keep a small group's records current. A dependable treasurer who sees the big picture as well as the small details is essential to keep your finances on track.

THE CHECKBOOK

In many organizations the treasurer takes care of the checkbook and all the organiza-

tion's other financial records as well. For a small group this is as easy as maintaining a personal checkbook and household records. A larger, incorporated non-profit group with more complex recordkeeping needs a treasurer with some professional accounting skills.

A small non-profit group with an annual budget of less than $5,000 can get by with a basic checkbook and simple record book to track all the group's financial transactions. For a larger organization, you'll need a business checkbook. Many churches, local government and schools today use a voucher checking system where a numbered, authorized voucher is written before the account is paid. This creates a double tracking system that greatly reduces mistakes. Most groups also have a petty cash system which consists of a cash box with a small amount of cash and a drawer to hold the small purchase receipts.

In addition to the checkbook, your group may find a recordkeeping book, such as a *Dome*™ book, extremely helpful. This book will track your cash and check expenditures and income. It also categorizes your expenditures into specific accounts such as: materials, insurance, interest, rent, dues, utilities, etc. When using a record book, be sure to carry forward running totals of all ex-

continued on page 14

ANNUAL INCOME STATEMENT

Organization Name: _____ For Year: _____

Prepared By: _____ Today's Date: _____

Modify or omit categories as needed.

INCOME:

Membership Dues	$ _____
Pledges/Donations	$ _____
Fundraisers: Service (Gross)	$ _____
Sales (Gross)	$ _____
Events (Gross)	$ _____
Rents/Interests Etc.	$ _____
Grants/Trusts Etc.	$ _____
Other	$ _____
Subtract: Returns or Refunds	($ _____)

TOTAL INCOME ALL SOURCES $ _____

EXPENDITURES:

Wages/Compensation	$ _____
Professional Fees	$ _____
Supplies/Materials	$ _____
Utilities	$ _____
Travel	$ _____
Telephone	$ _____
Postage & Shipping	$ _____
Printing	$ _____
Advertising	$ _____
Rents Paid	$ _____
Depreciation/Depletion Etc.	$ _____
Insurance	$ _____
Other	$ _____
Miscellaneous	$ _____

TOTAL EXPENDITURES (DEDUCT FROM TOTAL INCOME)   ($ _____)

NET INCOME OR (LOSS) $ _____

MAKE AS MANY COPIES OF THIS PAGE AS NEEDED

ANNUAL BUDGET

Organization Name: _____   **For Year:** _____

Prepared By: _____   **Today's Date:** _____

Estimate figures as best you can. Modify or omit categories as needed. Do not include estimated fundraising expenditures.

EXPENDITURES:

Wages/Compensation	$
Professional Fees	$
Supplies/Materials	$
Utilities	$
Travel	$
Telephone	$
Postage & Shipping	$
Printing	$
Advertising	$
Rents Paid	$
Depreciation/Depletion Etc.	$
Insurance	$
Other	$
Miscellaneous	$

TOTAL ESTIMATED EXPENDITURES $ _____

INCOMES:

Membership Dues	$
Pledges/Donations	$
Rents/Interests Etc.	$
Grants/Trusts Etc.	$
Other	$

SUB-TOTAL ESTIMATED INCOME: DEDUCT FROM
TOTAL ESTIMATED EXPENDITURES $ _____

INCOME NEEDED FROM FUNDRAISERS NET OF EXPENSES $ _____

MAKE AS MANY COPIES OF THIS PAGE AS NEEDED

Return of Organization Exempt From Income Tax

Under section 501(c) of the Internal Revenue Code (except black lung benefit trust or private foundation) or section 4947(a)(1) nonexempt charitable trust

Department of the Treasury
Internal Revenue Service

Note: *The organization may have to use a copy of this return to satisfy state reporting requirements.*

OMB No. 1545-0047

1994

This Form is
Open to Public
Inspection

A For the 1994 calendar year, OR tax year period beginning _____ , 1994, and ending _____ , 19 ____

B Check if:
☐ Change of address
☐ Initial return
☐ Final return
☐ Amended return (required also for State reporting)

Please use IRS label or print or type. See Specific Instructions.

C Name of organization

Number and street (or P.O. box if mail is not delivered to street address) | Room/suite

City, town, or post office, state, and ZIP code

D Employer identification number

E State registration number

F Check ▶ ☐ if exemption application is pending

G Type of organization ▶ ☐ Exempt under section 501(c)( ) ◀ (insert number) OR ▶ ☐ section 4947(a)(1) nonexempt charitable trust

Note: *Section 501(c)(3) exempt organizations and 4947(a)(1) nonexempt charitable trusts MUST attach a completed Schedule A (Form 990).*

H(a) Is this a group return filed for affiliates? . . . . ☐ Yes ☐ No

(b) If "Yes," enter the number of affiliates for which this return is filed: . . ▶ _____

(c) Is this a separate return filed by an organization covered by a group ruling? ☐ Yes ☐ No

I If either box in H is checked "Yes," enter four-digit group exemption number (GEN) ▶ ....

J Accounting method: ☐ Cash ☐ Accrual
☐ Other (specify) ▶

K Check here ▶ ☐ if the organization's gross receipts are normally not more than $25,000. The organization need not file a return with the IRS; but if it received a Form 990 Package in the mail, it should file a return without financial data. **Some states require a complete return.**

Note: *Form 990-EZ may be used by organizations with gross receipts less than $100,000 and total assets less than $250,000 at end of year.*

Part I — Statement of Revenue, Expenses, and Changes in Net Assets or Fund Balances

1	Contributions, gifts, grants, and similar amounts received:		
a	Direct public support	1a	
b	Indirect public support	1b	
c	Government contributions (grants)	1c	
d	**Total** (add lines 1a through 1c) (attach schedule—see instructions) (cash $ _____ noncash $ _____)		1d
2	Program service revenue including government fees and contracts (from Part VII, line 93)		2
3	Membership dues and assessments (see instructions)		3
4	Interest on savings and temporary cash investments		4
5	Dividends and interest from securities		5
6a	Gross rents	6a	
b	Less: rental expenses	6b	
c	Net rental income or (loss) (subtract line 6b from line 6a)		6c
7	Other investment income (describe ▶ _____)		7
8a	Gross amount from sale of assets other than inventory	(A) Securities	(B) Other	8a
b	Less: cost or other basis and sales expenses .			8b
c	Gain or (loss) (attach schedule)			8c
d	Net gain or (loss) (combine line 8c, columns (A) and (B))			8d
9	Special events and activities (attach schedule—see instructions):		
a	Gross revenue (not including $ _____ of contributions reported on line 1a)	9a	
b	Less: direct expenses other than fundraising expenses .	9b	
c	Net income or (loss) from special events (subtract line 9b from line 9a)		9c
10a	Gross sales of inventory, less returns and allowances . .	10a	
b	Less: cost of goods sold	10b	
c	Gross profit or (loss) from sales of inventory (attach schedule) (subtract line 10b from line 10a) .		10c
11	Other revenue (from Part VII, line 103)		11
12	**Total revenue** (add lines 1d, 2, 3, 4, 5, 6c, 7, 8d, 9c, 10c, and 11)		12
13	Program services (from line 44, column (B)—see instructions)		13
14	Management and general (from line 44, column (C)—see instructions) . . .		14
15	Fundraising (from line 44, column (D)—see instructions)		15
16	Payments to affiliates (attach schedule—see instructions)		16
17	**Total expenses** (add lines 16 and 44, column (A))		17
18	Excess or (deficit) for the year (subtract line 17 from line 12)		18
19	Net assets or fund balances at beginning of year (from line 74, column (A)) . .		19
20	Other changes in net assets or fund balances (attach explanation) . . .		20
21	Net assets or fund balances at end of year (combine lines 18, 19, and 20) . . .		21

Revenue (left margin label)
Expenses (left margin label)
Net Assets (left margin label)

MAKE AS MANY COPIES OF THIS PAGE AS NEEDED

Form **990** (1994)

Part IV Balance Sheets

Note: *Where required, attached schedules and amounts within the description column should be for end-of-year amounts only.*

		(A) Beginning of year		**(B)** End of year
	Assets			
45	Cash—non-interest-bearing		45	
46	Savings and temporary cash investments		46	
47a	Accounts receivable — 47a			
b	Less: allowance for doubtful accounts — 47b		47c	
48a	Pledges receivable — 48a			
b	Less: allowance for doubtful accounts — 48b		48c	
49	Grants receivable		49	
50	Receivables due from officers, directors, trustees, and key employees (attach schedule)		50	
51a	Other notes and loans receivable (attach schedule) — 51a			
b	Less: allowance for doubtful accounts — 51b		51c	
52	Inventories for sale or use		52	
53	Prepaid expenses and deferred charges		53	
54	Investments—securities (attach schedule)		54	
55a	Investments—land, buildings, and equipment: basis — 55a			
b	Less: accumulated depreciation (attach schedule) — 55b		55c	
56	Investments—other (attach schedule)		56	
57a	Land, buildings, and equipment: basis — 57a			
b	Less: accumulated depreciation (attach schedule) — 57b		57c	
58	Other assets (describe ▶ _____)		58	
59	**Total assets** (add lines 45 through 58) (must equal line 75)		59	
	Liabilities			
60	Accounts payable and accrued expenses		60	
61	Grants payable		61	
62	Support and revenue designated for future periods (attach schedule)		62	
63	Loans from officers, directors, trustees, and key employees (attach schedule)		63	
64a	Tax-exempt bond liabilities (attach schedule)		64a	
b	Mortgages and other notes payable (attach schedule)		64b	
65	Other liabilities (describe ▶ _____)		65	
66	**Total liabilities** (add lines 60 through 65)		66	
	Fund Balances or Net Assets			
Organizations that use fund accounting, check here ▶ ☐ and complete lines 67 through 70 and lines 74 and 75 (see instructions).				
67a	Current unrestricted fund		67a	
b	Current restricted fund		67b	
68	Land, buildings, and equipment fund		68	
69	Endowment fund		69	
70	Other funds (describe ▶ _____)		70	
Organizations that do not use fund accounting, check here ▶ ☐ and complete lines 71 through 75 (see instructions).				
71	Capital stock or trust principal		71	
72	Paid-in or capital surplus		72	
73	Retained earnings or accumulated income		73	
74	**Total fund balances or net assets** (add lines 67a through 70 OR lines 71 through 73; column (A) must equal line 19 and column (B) must equal line 21)		74	
75	**Total liabilities and fund balances/net assets** (add lines 66 and 74)		75	

Form 990 is available for public inspection and, for some people, serves as the primary or sole source of information about a particular organization. How the public perceives an organization in such cases may be determined by the information presented on its return. Therefore, please make sure the return is complete and accurate and fully describes the organization's programs and accomplishments.

MAKE AS MANY COPIES OF THIS PAGE AS NEEDED

penses and income. This makes year-end reports and budget-tracking duties much simpler.

Two systems we've used with success are the *Dome Simplified Monthly Bookkeeping Record*™ book and *Quicken*™ computer software. The Dome book is almost as easy as a checkbook. Keep it current and it's a painless way to track your financial records. This sytem works very well in place of a computer. It is available at major department and office supply stores. The Dome Company also makes a version for both IBM™ and Apple™ computers.

Quicken™ recordkeeping software also works like a check register and can print your checks as well. It's more expensive than a recordkeeping book, but it has significant advantages such as instant report generation, budgeting and separate project breakdowns. It is available for both Apple™ and IBM™ computers.

We're not endorsing either product but we've used them both and they've worked well. There are other good financial recordkeeping products available as well. Focused research in this area will pay long-term dividends to you.

ORGANIZING RECORDS

To be able to most effectively use all the information in your records it's necessary to keep them in a logical system. The first step is to keep your records in a single location. A file box often works well for a small group; larger groups may need a file cabinet or two.

You'll need a separate file for each major source of income or expense (i.e. membership dues, fundraisers, supplies, utilities, etc). Be sure to clearly label each file, so anyone looking through your group's records can easily find the information they need in a timely fashion.

> **A good place to start developing an annual budget is with the previous year's income and expense statements.**

If you end up with a very large file, such as a file for fundraising projects, you'll find it helpful to create a separate fundraising projects section in your system with an individual file for each project you do.

Always keep the original copy of each record. Make *copies* of those records when needed by others. When an invoice comes in, write on it the date it was received, when the invoice is paid along with the check number. Use a numbered receipt book for all cash disbursements.

BUDGET & INCOME STATEMENTS

A budget is an organization's plan to acquire and use resources in a specific period of time. Think of your annual budget as an income statement before the fact. In other words, you start the year with an annual budget then, at year's end, recount it with an income statement. Comparing these two you can point out your successes and failures.

A good place to start developing an annual budget is with the previous year's income and expense statements. Add on all expected cost increases and you now have a projected budget for next year. Annual budgets are also known as operational budgets.

If your group has long-range plans like acquiring a bus, a building, large-scale equipment, etc., you'll need a capital budget. This budget can lay the groundwork for achieving major group goals up to 30 years in the future.

Each budget needs to adapt to change as it occurs. We've included an *Annual Budget Statement* and an *Annual Income Statement* to use as worksheets. Modify them to better suit your unique needs. We've also included *Part 1* and the *Balance Sheet* from *Federal Form 990* to use as worksheets. For a more formal income statement use the *Federal Form 1023 Part IV Balance Sheet* included in *Getting Tax Exempt* on page 25.

Good recordkeeping and budgeting practices establish a firm foundation so your group's goals can be achieved in a timely fashion. Now sharpen your pencil and crack that recordkeeping book!

PROJECT BUDGETS

The trash cans are emptied, the floors mopped and the cleaning crew gone. It's the moment of truth. You and your project co-chair sit at a long table with a couple of stuffed cash boxes and a file of receipts. Soon you know the good news: This fundraiser is a success!

Most small groups don't need elaborate, complicated accounting procedures. They usually appoint a treasurer who handles basic record-keeping, bank accounts and the annual budget. If you have a large group you may want to check into a personal computer with accounting software.

If you need an accountant's advice but don't have the money to hire one, help is available in many communities. Start with your Better Business Bureau and Chamber of Commerce. Ask them if there are any volunteers, groups or classes available to help you with your accounting. You can also contact the group, "Accountants for the Public Interest" (API) for information on help available in your area. See *Appendix B* for address.

PROJECTED BUDGET

Good record-keeping is essential for a successful fundraiser. In the idea and planning stage, your group must first decide

how much money you would like to earn. Then you must decide on what type of fundraiser to do, whether it will be an event (like a car wash) or product sales (selling tins of caramel corn) or whatever.

To help you get an accurate idea of everything involved, work through the appropriate *Projected Budget* forms on the following pages. These forms will help you anticipate all supplies, manpower needs and other expenses that will arise as you produce your fundraising event. We've worked through a couple of examples to show how these forms work in the real world.

Doing a fundraiser projection can also indicate the practicality of meeting your desired income goal. For instance, if you wanted to raise $10,000 on

Keep all of your notes on each project together. Store them in a folder, binder or storage box. This way, the next chairman of the project won't have to repeat your learning curve.

a one-day car wash, with twenty people helping at five dollars per car, it would take 2,000 cars to meet your goal. Not very likely with this crowd. You either need to lower your fundraising goal or get a lot more help with the car wash!

EVENT WORKSHEET

Once you've decided on a fundraising activity, you'll need more specific details about the equipment, supplies and materials needed. This will also help to clearly define the costs involved and the logistics of the fundraiser.

Work through the *Master Event Worksheet* on page 16. Use this along with the earlier forms from Chapter 1 and either the *Service/Event Projected Budget* form on page 19, or your *Product Sales Projected Budget* form on page 21, as a master plan for proceeding with your fundraiser.

INCOME STATEMENT

Fill out the *Project Income Statement* (page 17) after the event is completed. This gives your group information on the "bottom line", or more bluntly, "How much did we make?" Hopefully, you made your projections and more!

NOTE: *Keep all of your notes on each project together. Store them in a folder, binder or storage box. This way, the next project chairman won't have to repeat your learning curve.*

MASTER EVENT WORKSHEET

Organization's Name: _____ Today's Date: _____

Event: _____ Date of Event: _____

Person in charge: _____ Telephone: _____

ITEM NEEDED & DESCRIPTION	DONATED BY	BORROW FROM	BUY AT	COST	WHO WILL PICK-UP & RETURN
				TOTAL	

PROJECT INCOME STATEMENT

Organization Name   **Date of Event:**

Event Name   **Today's Date:**

Person in Charge   **Telephone**

If you have more than 4 revenue sources, combine into categories. Modify or omit categories as needed.

REVENUES EARNED FROM EVENT

1		$
2		$
3		$
4		$

TOTAL REVENUES ALL SOURCES (GROSS PROFIT) $

EVENT COSTS

All Paid Labor	$
Rentals	$
Supplies/Materials	$
Advertising/Printing	$
Telephone/Utilities	$
All Vehicle/Transportation Costs	$
Fees & Licenses	$
Professional Costs	$
Insurance	$
Other Operating Costs	$
Miscellaneous	$

TOTAL COSTS (DEDUCT FROM TOTAL REVENUE)

INCOME (NET PROFIT) $

MAKE AS MANY COPIES OF THIS PAGE AS NEEDED

Smallville Boy's & Girls Club
Organization Name

September 15, 1999
Today's Date:

Car Wash & Wax
Proposed Event

INCOME DESIRED (NET PROFIT) $ 2,500⁰⁰

EXAMPLE

Modify or omit categories as needed.

EVENT COSTS

All Paid Labor	$
Rentals *(Rags, buffers)*	$ 100⁰⁰
Supplies/Materials *(Waxes, sponges)*	$ 100⁰⁰
Advertising/Printing	$ 75⁰⁰
Telephone/Utilities *(Water)*	$ 25⁰⁰
All Vehicle/Transportation Costs	$
Fees & Licenses	$
Professional Costs	$
Insurance *(1 day liability)*	$ 25⁰⁰
Other Operating Costs	$
Miscellaneous *(Pizza & pop lunch)*	$ 25⁰⁰

TOTAL ESTIMATED COSTS (ADD TO INCOME DESIRED) $ 350⁰⁰

TOTAL EVENT GROSS INCOME NEEDED $ 2850⁰⁰

SERVICE/EVENT QUOTA

TOTAL EVENT GROSS INCOME NEEDED (FROM ABOVE) $ 2850⁰⁰

(DIVIDE BY)

PRICE/INCOME PER UNIT (TICKET, PERSON, CAR, ETC.)   *wash/$5 wax/$15 Average*= ÷$ 10⁰⁰

TOTAL DESIRED UNIT SALES (NUMBER OF TICKETS ETC.)   # 285 cars

(DIVIDE BY)

NUMBER OF PEOPLE HELPING/WORKING   ÷# 25

PER PERSON QUOTA (#TICKETS, PERSONS, CARS, ETC.)   # 11 cars

MAKE AS MANY COPIES OF THIS PAGE AS NEEDED

SERVICE/EVENT PROJECTED BUDGET

Organization Name _____   Today's Date: _____

Proposed Event _____

INCOME DESIRED (NET PROFIT) $ _____

Modify or omit categories as needed.

EVENT COSTS

All Paid Labor	$ _____
Rentals	$ _____
Supplies/Materials	$ _____
Advertising/Printing	$ _____
Telephone/Utilities	$ _____
All Vehicle/Transportation Costs	$ _____
Fees & Licenses	$ _____
Professional Costs	$ _____
Insurance	$ _____
Other Operating Costs	$ _____
Miscellaneous	$ _____

TOTAL ESTIMATED COSTS (ADD TO INCOME DESIRED) $ _____

TOTAL EVENT GROSS INCOME NEEDED $ _____

SERVICE/EVENT QUOTA

TOTAL EVENT GROSS INCOME NEEDED (FROM ABOVE) $ _____

(DIVIDE BY)

PRICE/INCOME PER UNIT (TICKET, PERSON, CAR, ETC.)   ÷$ _____

TOTAL DESIRED UNIT SALES (NUMBER OF TICKETS ETC.)   # _____

(DIVIDE BY)

NUMBER OF PEOPLE HELPING/WORKING   ÷# _____

PER PERSON QUOTA (#TICKETS, PERSONS, CARS, ETC.)   # _____

MAKE AS MANY COPIES OF THIS PAGE AS NEEDED

PRODUCT SALES PROJECTED BUDGET

Smallville Boy's & Girls Club
Organization Name

September 15, 1999
Today's Date:

Gourmet Caramel Corn Tins
Proposed Product

EXAMPLE

INCOME DESIRED (NET PROFIT) $ 1,000⁰⁰

Modify or omit categories as needed.

SALES COSTS

All Paid Labor	$
Rentals	$
Supplies/Materials	$ 10⁰⁰
Advertising/Printing	$ 50⁰⁰
Telephone/Utilities	$
All Vehicle/Transportation Costs *(Delivery truck expenses)*	$ 30⁰⁰
Fees & Licenses	$
Professional Costs	$
Insurance	$
Other Operating Costs	$
Miscellaneous	$ 10⁰⁰

TOTAL ESTIMATED COSTS (ADD TO INCOME DESIRED) $ 100⁰⁰

TOTAL SALES GROSS PROFIT NEEDED $ 1,100⁰⁰

PER PERSON SALES QUOTA

TOTAL SALES GROSS PROFIT NEEDED (FROM ABOVE) $ 1,100⁰⁰

(DIVIDE BY)

GROSS MARGIN (PROFIT PER EACH UNIT SOLD)   *$5/sale - $3/cost = $2/profit*   +$ 2⁰⁰

NUMBER OF PRODUCT UNITS NEEDED TO BE SOLD   # 550

(DIVIDE BY)

NUMBER OF PEOPLE SELLING   ÷# 22

PER PERSON SALES QUOTA   # 25 tins

MAKE AS MANY COPIES OF THIS PAGE AS NEEDED

PRODUCT SALES PROJECTED BUDGET

Organization Name

Today's Date:

Proposed Product

INCOME DESIRED (NET PROFIT) $

Modify or omit categories as needed.

SALES COSTS

All Paid Labor	$
Rentals	$
Supplies/Materials	$
Advertising/Printing	$
Telephone/Utilities	$
All Vehicle/Transportation Costs	$
Fees & Licenses	$
Professional Costs	$
Insurance	$
Other Operating Costs	$
Miscellaneous	$

TOTAL ESTIMATED COSTS (ADD TO INCOME DESIRED) $

TOTAL SALES GROSS PROFIT NEEDED $

PER PERSON SALES QUOTA

TOTAL SALES GROSS PROFIT NEEDED (FROM ABOVE) $_____

(DIVIDE BY)

GROSS MARGIN (PROFIT PER EACH UNIT SOLD)   +$____

NUMBER OF PRODUCT UNITS NEEDED TO BE SOLD   #____

(DIVIDE BY)

NUMBER OF PEOPLE SELLING   ÷#_____

PER PERSON SALES QUOTA   #_____

MAKE AS MANY COPIES OF THIS PAGE AS NEEDED

LEGAL & ETHICAL

Legal details and ethical concerns can make or break a project, a budget or an organization. Protect your fundraising efforts and your group's reputation by being aware of the legal and ethical repercussions of your activities. We're going to look at some of the the legal and ethical issues surrounding fundraising for non-profit organizations.

It needs to be pointed out that these are only guidelines. If you think something your organization is doing could be running afoul of government or community regulations, please consult a local professional.

If in doubt, check it out!

LEGAL

TAX EXEMPT: Your charitable organization's tax exempt status is covered by section 501 (c) (3) of the Internal Revenue Code. Generally, charities include: religious, educational, amateur sports, literary, animal/human rights groups, etc.

Small charitable groups with an annual budget of less than $5,000.00 and churches don't need to file with the I.R.S. for exemption. If your organization is chartered through a larger organization your group may already be tax-exempt. Check with your chartering sponsor to find your exact tax status if there is any question. The local I.R.S. office will help you out with any questions, forms and information booklets you may need. See *Appendix B* for additional information sources.

DONATIONS: The I.R.S. allows charitable contributions by individuals, corporations, estates and trusts to be fully tax-deductible if the donor receives nothing in return. To be a deductible contribution, the following basics must be met:

• *Is the donation made to a legally tax-exempt group?*

• *Was the donation made in the taxpayer's tax year?*

• *Is the donation within all charitable deduction limits?*

Goods donated are deductible at "Fair Market Value." For instance, a five-year-old T.V. that cost $400.00 new may be now be worth only about $100.00 as a used donation.

If the donor gets a product or service in return for a contribution, then only part of the donation is deductible. There are government pamphlets available that spell out exactly what portion is deductible. Generally the donor must subtract the "Fair Market Value" of the benefit received and then the balance is deductible. The I.R.S. suggests your organization provide receipts and indicate in writing what portion of the donation is deductible. A good rule of thumb is that for anything over a few dollars, give a receipt or at least ask if the donor would like a receipt.

> *Doing your homework, using common sense and working from a place of personal and group integrity will help you to avoid any negative associations with your organization.*

STATE AND LOCAL LAWS:

There are also regulations that need to be followed on a state and local level. We won't go into depth here, but some of the more common questions you'll want to answer might include:

• *Do you need food permits for food events?*

• *Do you need a state or local sales permit?*

• *Any state or local laws restricting bingo or raffles?*

• *Does your advertising conform to all "Truth in Advertising" laws?*

• *Any regulations restricting or prohibiting soliciting?*

• *Any sales tax questions?*

IF YOU NEED A LAWYER

There are times when your group will need the services of a competent attorney. Hopefully it will be for something pleasant: The legal work for your new building or the estate endowment fund you just received. Some other needs might include: incorporation, legal documents, trusts, taxes, insurance, government compliance and,the unpleasant side, trial work.

Lawyers, like other professionals, specialize in areas of expertise. Some areas include: estate, corporate, tax, copyright, real estate, civil litigation, and criminal. For business needs check with your bar association, chamber or BBB. Some attorneys will work for non-profits at a low or no cost fee. Many items, incorporation for example, have "reasonable and customary" set fees.

We live in a less than perfect world and sometimes just any lawyer won't do. If you find your group a plaintiff or defendant in a civil and/or criminal case, proceed very carefully yet expediently. Some lawsuit examples include: Your hot-tempered coach punches a fan or the treasurer loses $5,000.00 of your money at the track, or someone gets permanently injured at your event. If your group is underinsured and *not* incorporated individual members can be sued.

Honest, competent trial attorneys get their clients the best deals they can. The reason is simple. They put lots of effort into preparing for trial because most civil and up to 90% of criminal cases are settled *before* trial. Opposing forces seeing this kind of preparation work are often more inclined to reach an agreement. It may not be right, but that is the way it is. Inquire, call and research before choosing. Double-check their work. Failure at critical times can result in losing when you should win. Ask about fees: know what to expect. This is a time to definitely "Be Prepared".

• *Any local or state insurance and liability restrictions?*

You can get answers to these and other questions from: your local Better Business Bureau, Chamber of Commerce, your chartering sponsor (if you have one), local government public relations office or your state government public relations office.

CONCLUSION: *When in doubt, check it out!*

ETHICAL

In addition to conforming to all legal restrictions, there are also ethical issues around fundraising for non-profit groups. Many scams are run in the name of charity and the charlatans who run them line their own pockets at the expense of legitimate, worthy causes.

Doing your homework, using common sense and working from a position of personal and group integrity will help you to avoid any negative associations with your organization. These general ethical guidelines will help you keep your group on the straight and narrow.

ETHICAL CHECKLIST

All your fundraisers should:

1. *Be approved by your chartering organizaion.*

2. *Be approved by your members and officers.*

3. *Be consistent with the purpose of your group.*

4. *Meet community standards and approval.*

5. *Be limited in scope and frequency.*

6. *Be fun and educational.*

7. *Maximize the time and energy of everyone involved.*

CHARITY INFORMATION

Potential donors or sponsors have a right to know about your group before they agree to donate services, products, or funds. Your group should be prepared to provide the following information upon request.

1. *Who you are (your organization's full name).*

2. *Where you are based or located.*

3. *Phone number of the person in charge.*

4. *Name of the group leader or president.*

5. *When your group was established.*

6. *The primary purpose of your organization.*

7. *The major programs or services you provide for your members and the community.*

8. *Financial information.*

CONCLUSION: Provide your major supporters with any information they request. Remember them after the event, and thank them for their support. An excellent way to do this is with a thank-you note telling them how the fundraiser went. Patronize their businesses when possible and encourage your members to do the same. Be sure to invite supporters to related events in the future. Overall, just treat your sponsors with the same consideration and appreciation you would like to have extended to you if your roles were reversed.

GETTING TAX EXEMPT

Imagine being exempt from sales, property, local or federal excise and other taxes. Your group could also get non-profit discounts and, possibly, do mailings for 12¢ instead of 32¢ (1995 rates). There are other advantages to having tax-exempt status, for example, being able to assure donors in advance that their contributions are fully tax deductible.

SHOULD YOU APPLY? Even though your organization may not need to file *I.R.S. Form 1023 (Application for Recognition of Exemption)* you may still want to do so. Small charitable groups with gross receipts of $5,000 or less and churches don't need to file. If your organization (a small scout group for example) is chartered through a larger organization, it's probably already covered. Check with your chartering organization and the I.R.S. to determine your status. There are several "peripheral advantages" to becoming formally tax-exempt, including:

   • *Exemption from some state taxes including: sales, local, and personal property*
   • *Tax deductibility of supporter's contributions*
   • *Non-profit discounts*
   • *Exemption from federal unemployment taxes (FUTA)*

   • *Federal corporate tax exemption*
   • *Formal recognition as a non-profit organization*
   • *Prerequisite for non-profit mailing status*
   • *Advantages in soliciting*

> Most supporters are aware of tax deductibility, yet generally are more concerned with what their gifts *do* for your program and the community. Note tax deductibility at the close of your appeal.

   • *Insurance and liability*
   Annual reports must be filed with the I.R.S. and your state government. Many states use a version of Federal Form 990. Contact your state tax office to find out which forms to file.

   The most serious negative, especially with a small group, is that it takes about 100 hours to set up and file your *Application for Recognition of Exemption* with all its recordkeeping and support documents. It takes another 50-100 hours a year to keep all necessary records and file the annual reports.

   APPLYING: To begin, obtain an *Application for Recognition of Exemption* which is governed by Section 501 (c)(3) of the Internal Revenue Code. This small book may be available at your local I.R.S. office. If not, call their *#800 Information and Form Number* in your phone book and request a copy and its support documents. Basic I.R.S. guidelines for filing for exemption are:

   • *Having or applying for a Federal I.D. number*
   • *Incorporating your non-profit group (you can also be a Trust or Association)*
   • *Filing Form 1023 with supporting documentation.*

   To give you an idea of what needs to be done to become exempt, we've included part of the *Federal Form 1023* (pages 25 to 28) as a worksheet. *The Balance Sheet* in *Part IV* (page 28) is also good to use for your group's internal accounting needs, period statements or year-end reports even if you don't file for exemption.

DONATIONS NOTES:

Most supporters are aware of tax deductibility, yet generally are more concerned with what their gifts *do* for your program and the community. Note tax deductibility at the close of your appeal. Also, tell them the amount that is deductible, if your request is for other than cash. Formal recognition also means your non-profit, tax-exempt status is open to government and public scrutiny.

Form **1023**	**Application for Recognition of Exemption**	OMB No. 1545-0056
(Rev. July 1993)	**Under Section 501(c)(3) of the Internal Revenue Code**	Expires 5-31-96
Department of the Treasury Internal Revenue Service		If exempt status is approved, this application will be open for public inspection.

Read the instructions for each Part carefully.
A User Fee must be attached to this application.
If the required information and appropriate documents are not submitted along with Form 8718 (with payment of the appropriate user fee), the application may be returned to you.
Complete the Procedural Checklist on page 7 of the instructions.

Part I   Identification of Applicant

1a Full name of organization (as shown in organizing document)	**2** Employer identification number (If none, see instructions.)
1b c/o Name (if applicable)	**3** Name and telephone number of person to be contacted if additional information is needed
1c Address (number, street, and room or suite no.)	
1d City or town, state, and ZIP code	( )
	4 Month the annual accounting period ends

5 Date incorporated or formed	**6** Activity codes (See instructions.)	**7** Check here if applying under section:
		a ☐ 501(e) **b** ☐ 501(f) **c** ☐ 501(k)

8 Did the organization previously apply for recognition of exemption under this Code section or under any other section of the Code?   . . . .   ☐ **Yes** ☐ **No**
If "Yes," attach an explanation.

9 Is the organization required to file Form 990 (or Form 990-EZ)?   . . . .   ☐ **N/A** ☐ **Yes** ☐ **No**
If "No," attach an explanation (see instructions).

10 Has the organization filed Federal income tax returns or exempt organization information returns?   . .   ☐ **Yes** ☐ **No**
If "Yes," state the form numbers, years filed, and Internal Revenue office where filed.

11 Check the box for the type of organization. BE SURE TO ATTACH A CONFORMED COPY OF THE CORRESPONDING DOCUMENTS TO THE APPLICATION BEFORE MAILING (See **Specific Instructions, Part I, Line 11.**) Get Pub. 557, **Tax-Exempt Status for Your Organization, for examples of organizational documents.**)

a ☐ Corporation—Attach a copy of the Articles of Incorporation (including amendments and restatements) showing approval by the appropriate state official; also include a copy of the bylaws.

b ☐ Trust—Attach a copy of the Trust Indenture or Agreement, including all appropriate signatures and dates.

c ☐ Association— Attach a copy of the Articles of Association, Constitution, or other creating document, with a declaration (see instructions) or other evidence the organization was formed by adoption of the document by more than one person; also include a copy of the bylaws.

If the organization is a corporation or an unincorporated association that has not yet adopted bylaws, check here ▶ ☐

I declare under the penalties of perjury that I am authorized to sign this application on behalf of the above organization and that I have examined this application, including the accompanying schedules and attachments, and to the best of my knowledge it is true, correct, and complete.

Please Sign Here ▶ _____   _____   _____
(Signature)   (Title or authority of signer)   (Date)

MAKE AS MANY COPIES OF THIS PAGE AS NEEDED

Part II	**Activities and Operational Information**

1   Provide a detailed narrative description of all the activities of the organization—past, present, and planned. **Do not merely refer to or repeat the language in the organizational document.** Describe each activity separately in the order of importance. Each description should include, as a minimum, the following: (a) a detailed description of the activity including its purpose; (b) when the activity was or will be initiated; and (c) where and by whom the activity will be conducted.

2   What are or will be the organization's sources of financial support? List in order of size.

3   Describe the organization's fundraising program, both actual and planned, and explain to what extent it has been put into effect. Include details of fundraising activities such as selective mailings, formation of fundraising committees, use of volunteers or professional fundraisers, etc. Attach representative copies of solicitations for financial support.

MAKE AS MANY COPIES OF THIS PAGE AS NEEDED

Part II   Activities and Operational Information *(Continued)*

8 What assets does the organization have that are used in the performance of its exempt function? (Do not include property producing investment income.) If any assets are not fully operational, explain their status, what additional steps remain to be completed, and when such final steps will be taken. If "None," indicate "N/A."

9 Will the organization be the beneficiary of tax-exempt bond financing within the next 2 years? . . . . ☐ **Yes** ☐ **No**

10a Will any of the organization's facilities or operations be managed by another organization or individual under a contractual agreement? . . . . ☐ **Yes** ☐ **No**

  b Is the organization a party to any leases? . . . . ☐ **Yes** ☐ **No**
    If either of these questions is answered "Yes," attach a copy of the contracts and explain the relationship between the applicant and the other parties.

11 Is the organization a membership organization? . . . . ☐ **Yes** ☐ **No**
    If "Yes," complete the following:
  a Describe the organization's membership requirements, and attach a schedule of membership fees and dues.

  b Describe the organization's present and proposed efforts to attract members, and attach a copy of any descriptive literature or promotional material used for this purpose.

  c What benefits do (or will) the members receive in exchange for their payment of dues?

12a If the organization provides benefits, services, or products, are the recipients required, or will they be required, to pay for them? . . . . ☐ **N/A** ☐ **Yes** ☐ **No**
    If "Yes," explain how the charges are determined, and attach a copy of the current fee schedule.

  b Does or will the organization limit its benefits, services, or products to specific individuals or classes of individuals? . . . . ☐ **N/A** ☐ **Yes** ☐ **No**
    If "Yes," explain how the recipients or beneficiaries are or will be selected.

13 Does or will the organization attempt to influence legislation? . . . . ☐ **Yes** ☐ **No**
    If "Yes," explain. Also, give an estimate of the percentage of the organization's time and funds that it devotes or plans to devote to this activity.

14 Does or will the organization intervene in any way in political campaigns, including the publication or distribution of statements? . . . . ☐ **Yes** ☐ **No**
    If "Yes," explain fully.

MAKE AS MANY COPIES OF THIS PAGE AS NEEDED

Part IV   **Financial Data** *(Continued)*

B. Balance Sheet (at the end of the period shown)		Current tax year Date . . . .
Assets		
1 Cash	1	
2 Accounts receivable, net	2	
3 Inventories	3	
4 Bonds and notes receivable (attach schedule)	4	
5 Corporate stocks (attach schedule)	5	
6 Mortgage loans (attach schedule)	6	
7 Other investments (attach schedule)	7	
8 Depreciable and depletable assets (attach schedule)	8	
9 Land	9	
10 Other assets (attach schedule)	10	
11 **Total assets** (add lines 1 through 10)	11	
Liabilities		
12 Accounts payable	12	
13 Contributions, gifts, grants, etc., payable	13	
14 Mortgages and notes payable (attach schedule)	14	
15 Other liabilities (attach schedule)	15	
16 **Total liabilities** (add lines 12 through 15)	16	
Fund Balances or Net Assets		
17 Total fund balances or net assets	17	
18 **Total liabilities and fund balances or net assets** (add line 16 and line 17)	18	

If there has been any substantial change in any aspect of the organization's financial activities since the end of the period shown above, check the box and attach a detailed explanation . . . . ▶ ☐

MAKE AS MANY COPIES OF THIS PAGE AS NEEDED

NON-PROFIT MAILING

Imagine doing all your local mailings for your non-profit organization for less than 12¢ per piece (1995 rates) instead of the usual 32¢. Think of the postage you'll save in just a few mailings!

Depending upon how much pre-sorting you can do and the volume of mail you send, your rates can fall between 6.0¢ and 11.1¢ per letter-sized piece (1995 rates) through the use of *special bulk non-profit organization rates*.

To qualify for the lowest rates, your mail must be bar-coded, pre-sorted and automation compatible. Most small, non-profit organizations don't go to this trouble unless they do frequent, large mailings. However, without too much difficulty or expense, your group could get its average per piece mailing rate down to 7.1¢ or 8.1¢ per piece.

NON-PROFIT MAILING STATUS: There is no charge *to apply* for a non-profit mailing status. You can get all necessary paperwork from the *Bulk Mail* area at your local post office. If your group is planning high volume mailings such as advertising, newsletters, or solicitations, it's well worth your while to investigate non-profit

> *Depending upon how much pre-sorting you can do and the volume of mail you send, your rates can fall between 6.0¢ and 11.1¢ per letter-sized piece (1995 rates) through the use of* special bulk non-profit organization rates.

mailing organization status.

Begin by looking up the *Domestic Mail Manual* (DMM) at your local post office. This manual will give you enough information to decide whether or not your group can qualify for non-profit mailing status.

To qualify, your group should be a federally-recognized, tax-exempt non-profit organization (or be chartered by one) to get these special rates. The federal government subsidizes non-profit mailings from qualifying groups such as church, school and other similar groups. Not all non-profit organizations qualify for these great rates (see *Section B - General Information* to see

which organizations do qualify for these rates).

BULK MAIL: The bulk mail permit now costs $75. This sounds like a lot of money until you calculate how much money your group can save if you qualify for bulk mail rates. If you've ever done any bulk mailing, you know it's a little complicated the first time or two, but once you become familiar with the procedures, it gets a whole lot easier.

U.S. Postal Service employees are generally very helpful and often will walk you through the process the first time. They also have manuals that explain every step of bulk mailing. To simplify matters, consider a good computer labelling program. Some of these programs have built-in barcoding and sorting capabilities that can greatly expedite your bulk mailing procedures. If your mailings are large and frequent, one of these programs would be money well-invested for your group.

For example, if you're mailing 1000 pieces at non-profit bulk rates, your group could save over $200 from the usual 32¢ first-class rate. These greatly reduced postage rates could put direct mail advertising and soliciting within your group's budget.

CARRIER ROUTE PRESORT: If you're willing to do some extra sorting work, you can

continued on page 32

U. S. POSTAL SERVICE
APPLICATION TO MAIL AT SPECIAL BULK THIRD-CLASS RATES

PART 1 - FOR COMPLETION BY APPLICANT   SECTION A - APPLICATION

NOTE: PLEASE READ ALL INFORMATION IN SECTION B ON THE BACK OF THIS APPLICATION BEFORE COMPLETING THE FORM BELOW.

Instructions

A. Be sure that all information entered below is legible so that our records will show the correct information about your organization

B. Show the complete name of the organization in item 1. The name shown must agree with the name that appears on all documents submitted to support this application.

C. A complete address representing a physical location for the organization must be shown in item 2. When mail is received through a post office box, show your street address first and then the box number.

D. The name of the applicant in item 5 must be the name of the individual submitting the application for the organization. The individual must be an officer of the organization. Printers and mailing agents may not sign for the organization.

E. No additional categories may be added in item 6. You must qualify as one of the types of organizations listed in order to be eligible for special rates.

F. Be sure to sign the application in item 12.

G. The date shown in item 14 must be the date that you submit the application to the post office.

NO APPLICATION FEE IS REQUIRED

Please be sure all information is complete.   PLEASE TYPE OR PRINT LEGIBLY

1. Complete Name of Organization

2. Address of Organization (Street, Apt./ Suite No.)   3. City, State, ZIP+4 Code

4. (Area Code)/ Telephone No.
( )

5. Name of Applicant (must represent organization that is applying.)

6. Type of Organization (Check only one. See 'E' above.)

- [ ] (01) Religious
- [ ] (02) Educational
- [ ] (03) Scientific
- [ ] (04) Philanthropic
- [ ] (05) Agricultural
- [ ] (06) Labor
- [ ] (07) Veterans
- [ ] (08) Fraternal
- [ ] (09) Qualified Political Committee

7. Check whether this organization is for profit or whether any of the net income inures to the benefit of any private stockholder or individual.

- [ ] YES
- [ ] NO

8. Check whether this organization is exempt from Federal income tax. (If 'YES', attach a copy of the exemption issued by the Internal Revenue Service which shows the section of the IRS code under which the organization is exempt. If an application for exempt status is pending with the IRS, you must check the 'NO' box.)

- [ ] YES
- [ ] NO

9. POST OFFICE where authorization is requested and bulk mailings will be made (City, State, and ZIP+4 Code of Main Post Office)
NOTE: An authorization may NOT be requested at a station or branch of a post office.

10. If your organization has previously mailed at the special bulk rates, list the post offices where mailings were most recently deposited at these rates:

11. Has your organization had special bulk third-class rate mailing privileges denied or revoked? If you answered "YES", please list the post office (City and State) where an application was denied or an authorization was revoked:
- [ ] YES
- [ ] NO

I certify that the statements made by me are true and complete. I understand that if this application for authorization is approved, it may only be used for our organization's mail at the post office specified above, and that we may not transfer or extend it to any other mailer. I further understand that if this application is approved, a postage refund for the difference between the regular and special bulk rates may be made for only those regular bulk third-class mailings entered at the post office identified above during the period this application is pending, provided the conditions set forth in section 642.4, Domestic Mail Manual, are met.

12. SIGNATURE OF APPLICANT	13. TITLE	14. DATE

Willful entry or submission of false, fictitious or fraudulent statements or representations in this application may result in a fine up to $10,000 or imprisonment up to 5 years or both (18 U.S.C.1001)

PART 2 - POSTMASTER AT ORIGINATING OFFICE
This part should be completed at the time the application is filed with your office

1. Signature of Postmaster (or designated representative)	2. Date application was filed with your office (Round Stamp)

MAKE AS MANY COPIES OF THIS PAGE AS NEEDED

SECTION B - GENERAL INFORMATION

ELIGIBILITY CRITERIA
The special bulk third-class rates may be granted only to:
  a. the eight categories of nonprofit organizations specified in section A, item 6, on the front, and
  b. qualified political committees including the National and State committees of political parties as well as certain named congressional committees.

These organizations are defined in sections 623.23 and 623.3 of the Domestic Mail Manual (DMM), which may be reviewed at the local post office.

A nonprofit organization must be both **ORGANIZED** and **OPERATED** for a qualifying primary purpose that is consistent with one of the types of organizations in 623.23 DMM. Organizations which **incidentally** engage in qualifying activities will not qualify for special rates.

Not all nonprofit organizations may mail at the special rates. Section 623.4, DMM, lists certain organizations, such as business leagues, chambers of commerce, civic improvement associations, social and hobby clubs, governmental bodies, and others, which, although nonprofit, do not qualify for the special bulk rates.

APPLICATION PROCEDURES
  1. Only organizations may apply. Individuals may not apply.
  2. Only the **ONE** category in item 6 which best describes the **PRIMARY PURPOSE** of the organization must be checked.
  3. The application must be **SIGNED** by someone in authority in the organization, such as the president or treasurer. It must not be signed by a printer or mailing agent.
  4. The completed Form 3624 must be submitted to the post office where bulk mailings will be deposited. If the application is approved, the authorization will apply only at that post office.

THE FOLLOWING DOCUMENTS MUST BE SUBMITTED WITH THE COMPLETED APPLICATION:

  a. Evidence that the organization is **NONPROFIT** and that none of its net income inures to the benefit of any private stockholder or individual. Acceptable evidence includes:
   • an IRS letter of exemption from payment of Federal income tax OR,
   • if an IRS exemption letter is not available, a financial statement from an <u>independent</u> auditor, such as a Certified Public Accountant, substantiating that the organization is nonprofit (a statement from a member of the organization is not sufficient.)

  b. Documents which describe the organization's **PRIMARY PURPOSE** such as:
   • formative papers which state the purpose for which the group is ORGANIZED, such as the Constitution or Articles of Incorporation, and
   • materials that show how the organization actually OPERATED during the past 6-12 months and how it will operate in the future, such as bulletins, financial statements, membership forms, publications it produced, minutes of meetings, a listing of its activities.

WHAT MAY BE MAILED
An organization authorized to mail at the special rates may mail only **ITS OWN MATTER** at those rates. It may not delegate or lend the use of its special rate permit to any other person or organization.

COOPERATIVE mailings may be made at the special bulk rates **ONLY** when **EACH** of the cooperating organizations is individually **AUTHORIZED** to mail at those rates at the office where mailings are deposited.

MAKE AS MANY COPIES OF THIS PAGE AS NEEDED

earn a discount off the basic third-class mailing rate. To qualify, the carrier route part of the mailing must contain at least 200 pieces or weigh at least 50 pounds. Pieces must be part of a group of ten or more sorted and sacked to the same carrier route. Groups smaller than ten do not qualify for the lower rates and are called residual pieces.

When you take a presorted mailing to the post office, you'll need to provide the post office a list of the qualifying carrier route presorted pieces and the number of residual pieces per five-digit ZIP code. It can take some time, especially at first, to learn how to produce really cost-effective mailings, but the savings can be substantial. For more information, get a copy of *Third Class Mail Preparation* at your local post office.

BUSINESS REPLY MAIL PERMIT: You may also want to look into a *Business Reply Mail Permit* (BRM). With this permit, you pay only for the mail that's returned to you.

People are more likely to send your group something if you've provided a BRM envelope for their use. Then all they have to do is to enclose their donation, seal it and mail it.

Overall, a BRM is better for your organization because you only pay postage for those pieces that are returned to you. The other alternative, including a self-addressed stamped envelope in each mailing will cost far more because you're paying postage even on those envelopes that aren't returned.

We've included two pages of forms from the *U.S. Postal Service Application To Mail At Special Bulk Third Class Rates* for your use as worksheets. Read these pages very carefully before proceeding.

If you are a chartered organization and your local governing office holds a non-profit bulk permit, you may be able to use their permit. To do this, you'll also need to use

their return address, with a subhead for your return address.

For example, this could work for a scout group that doesn't do enough annual mailings to financially justify the effort. Using your chartering group's permit may also work if your group is not incorporated and/or you don't have formal federal tax-exempt non-profit status.

No matter what your group's situation, every organization can bulk mail and save money through reduced postage costs. The most money on postage will be saved, however, when your group qualifies for non-profit bulk mailing.

No matter what your group's situation, every organization can bulk mail and save money through reduced postage costs. The most money on postage will be saved, however, when your group qualifies for non-profit bulk mailing. All this means is that with some research and development time you will be able to mail to the same sized group for less or reach an even larger group for the same postage costs as before. Either way, you can greatly increase your group's direct mail effectiveness.

CHAPTER 2
BUSINESS STUFF

CHAPTER NOTES:

PUBLIC SPEAKING

You see your neatly-typed speech there on the podium and as you raise your eyes you see the microphone. Looking out over the seated crowd, the conversational buzz stops and they all look back at you. It's time for your first public speech.

Public speaking can be a terrifying ordeal but it need not be. You'll likely make presentations to potential sponsors, donors or members. You may talk about specific projects or the group's ongoing story. With time and some effort, you'll develop higher level oratory skills. The rewards to you and your organization can be great.

> *Public speaking can be a terrifying ordeal but it need not be. ...With time and some effort, you'll develop higher level oratory skills. The rewards to you and your organization can be great.*

SPEECHWRITING: Once you've decided to make a public presentation, you'll need to develop and write a speech. Carefully think through your overall message beforehand. What exactly do you want?

Develop specific facts and ideas and keep them at your fingertips. If you want a sponsor for a particular project, be prepared with a complete overview: its budget, how it will run, volunteers needed, etc.

When seeking donations, have specific dollar amounts, services or products in mind. Don't risk losing a sizeable donation because you didn't have the nerve to ask!

If you are looking for new members, tell them about your group. Give them your mission statement. Show them your successful projects, budget, social activities and goals. Have all of this clear in your mind, and on paper, *before* you begin writing your speech.

Begin by condensing your message into a one-line objective. What exactly do you want your audience to do or think? What do you want to tell them? Answer these questions and you'll have a speech synopsis.

After defining your objective, brainstorm the speech's content. Write a list of all the points you want to cover. When completed, review the list and select those points you wish to develop into your presentation. Make a 3 x 5 index card for each of these points.

Next, do research. In order to speak with confidence and credibility, you must be able to back your statements with facts. Find all the information needed from public libraries and other sources to verify, quantify and/or qualify your main objective. Photocopy all source materials, then condense relevant facts into notes on 3 x 5 index cards. Attach cards to larger sheets, if necessary.

When your research is done, re-read your notes and organize them into groups that follow your speech outline. Begin with your objective. Then go on to supporting points, arranging them in a logical order: by importance, in chronological order or by value. End with a strong conclusion, then restate your main objective.

Following your outline of notes, it's time to write your speech, using whatever technology you're comfortable with: pen and paper, typewriter or word processing equipment.

Many writers speak of the "terror of the blank page" or other writing frights but it's not all that bad. Pros, who must often produce even if the muse is gone, generally write the first paragraph or two or even three before the real beginning appears. Then they toss the first few paragraphs of "junk" and get on to the craft of writing.

Choose short, precise words over long, ponderous ones. If you're unsure how to pronounce a word, look it up!

The first few paragraphs of your speech, called the "lead,"

are incredibly important. Lose your audience now and most never return. Time studies of professional writers show they typically spend up to three-fourths of their writing time on the first three paragraphs alone.

Begin your speech with an anecdote, joke or short story to introduce your topic and main objective. Whatever your lead, make it as attention-grabbing as possible. If you have a new and/or striking statistic or fact, use it now to get your audience's attention. Next, tell them what you're going to speak about.

Now get into the body of your speech, where you introduce all of your relevant points in their logical sequence. At the end, recap your main objective. Always, always, always let your audience know exactly what you want from them: A donation, specific action or change of mind or heart.

Finally, craft the lead to a point of perfection. Be sure your internal logic is working, then correct all grammatical errors. Show the speech to several trusted advis-ors for feedback. Make last minute corrections or additions. Create a clean, double-spaced copy and get ready to speak.

PUBLIC SPEAKING: To present your message in its most positive manner, it's im-portant to be confident. Be well-prepared when you speak, know your material inside and out. Rehearse your speech several times, anticipate questions and think out answers.

Your appearance is very important in public speaking. *Always* dress consistently with your message and audience. Like it or not, first impressions do count.

In most cases, neat, conservative dress is the rule. If you have uniforms or name badges, wear them while speaking. You want to be seen in a positive light.

Present yourself as relaxed and confident; stand straight without rigidity. Make eye contact with people in the crowd, a few seconds at a time, when speaking.

If you fidget, keep all small items off the podium so you won't be able to toy with them. Your audience should focus on you and your message, not the pencil you are tapping. Up until speech time you can keep the butterflies at bay with affirmations, such as:

• *I anticipate a good reception to my message.*

• *I am calm, collected and prepared to give my material.*

• *I am enthusiastic about my speech.*

• *I smile and am confident in my presentation.*

• *My audience responds well to my message.*

Avoid negative, self-defeating thought. Affirm success!

Now let's work on your speaking style. Start with an audio or a video recording of yourself, so you know how you appear when speaking. This will help you to recognize and address any problem areas.

While speaking, breathe deeply and enunciate carefully. If you're not familiar with microphones, practice before your presentation, so you will know how to speak properly.

Smile and use humor when appropriate. After the speech make notes on favorite anecdotes or jokes you found useful.

Always be considerate of your audience. Never, never be late for a speaking date! Everyone appreciates a speaker who knows his information and makes his message direct and brief. Know how much time you're allotted and make every effort not to exceed it.

Stick to your subject; don't wander off on tangents. If your audience will have lots of questions, be sure to leave time for questions and answers at the end, or give them your address and phone number so they can connect with you later.

Lastly, always thank your audience. Let them know you value their time and attention. A follow-up thank-you note may be in order, depending upon your presentation and the people involved. Good manners are always in good taste.

> **The first few paragraphs of your speech, called the "lead," are incredibly important. ...Time studies of professional writers show they typically spend up to three-fourths of their writing time on the first three paragraphs alone.**

MANAGING PROJECTS

Your commitee just voted to set the next fundraising project's major goals and now all you have to do is manage to make it happen. All of this is easier said than done, yet doing it (making the fundraiser actually happen) does not have to be an overwhelming experience.

In business, project management is called the managing and control cycle. It consists of these four interrelated steps:

1. *Setting project goals and planning*

2. *Implementing the plans (organizing and directing)*

3. *Controlling (measuring performance)*

4. *Evaluating differences between planned and actual performance.*

Your fundraising project goals are accomplished by the combined efforts of a number of people. Effective communication and feedback between everyone involved is extremely important.

Several major multi-thousand dollar fundraisers we're aware of ran into last-minute snags because people did not finish their work on time. This often creates unnecessary and expensive log jams. In one case about $15,000 out of an expected $50,000 return was lost due to ineffective communication and feedback.

> **Four steps for managing a project:**
> **1.** *Setting goals and planning*
> **2.** *Implementing plans*
> **3.** *Measuring performance*
> **4.** *Evaluation*

SETTING GOALS: Take a few minutes now to work your way through the *Project Planning Guide* on page 38. This worksheet will take you through each phase of your fundraiser, from initial planning to final project evaluation.

Use this form to help your group stay focused upon the fundraiser's overall purpose. Make sure you keep the form current. At first this may seem a needless use of your time, but as the event draws near, you'll find these ongoing "field notes" will give you better control at each stage of the project.

When you get to question 4 in the Planning section of the *Project Planning Guide*, go to the *Job Worksheet* on page 39 to help you create a detailed list of all the tasks for your project. From there, decide on your supervisory people and, with their input, assign specific tasks and orchestrate a timetable.

IMPLEMENTING PLANS: Once your goals are set and the plans made, implementation is next. This is the real nuts and bolts of the project: what needs to be done, who will do it, when, where and how. This is when you really need to be organized. Be very specific about each person's job and the time frame in which it must be done.

Throughout this cycle, ongoing decisions need to be made and adopted to keep up with what's actually happening versus what your committee thought would happen.

MEASURING PERFORMANCE: You need to keep your goals in mind, but you also have to be flexible in how you achieve those goals. Perhaps your twenty-person group has dwindled down to ten. If so, you'll need to streamline your project so ten people can do it. A smaller success is always better than a larger failure.

EVALUATION: When the fundraiser is over and you've answered all the *Project Planning Guide*'s questions, especially those in the Evaluation section, keep it in your permanent fundraising file for future reference. Also keep your *Job Worksheet* in the same file for a bird's-eye view of the project. The next time you run the same project, the committee involved will be grateful for your notes!

PROJECT PLANNING GUIDE

Project _____ Date _____

Chairman _____ Mailing Address _____ Phone _____

Assistant _____ Mailing Address _____ Phone _____

Helper _____ Phone _____ Job _____ Helper _____ Phone _____ Job

Helper _____ Phone _____ Job _____ Helper _____ Phone _____ Job

INSTRUCTIONS: Use and follow the instructions in this planning guide throughout all phases of your project. Try to answer the questions completely and honestly on a separate sheet of paper and attach. Be specific in your evaluations.

PLANNING:

1. What is the basic purpose for this fundraising activity?
2. How does this project relate to the needs of your organization?
3. What labor will be needed, what jobs, and how many hours to complete your project?
4. List all people involved, their job assignments and duties.
5. List all supplies, materials, resources, and facilities needed.
6. List all problems anticipated and then list solutions.
7. List in specific detail the steps that need to be taken to complete your fundraiser.
8. Work up the project's budget as best you can. Show anticipated income and costs.

IMPLEMENTATION:

1. Record all changes or revisions of the plans as they occur.
2. Record all costs and incomes as they occur.
3. Record the steps taken and the results obtained.
4. Record all of the supplies, materials and resources used.

CONTROLLING:

1. Were people informed of changes as they occurred? (Be specific.)
2. How were anticipated and unanticipated problems handled?
3. Were job assignments and duties completed? Were there any problem areas? How were they resolved?

EVALUATION:

1. In light of problems encountered, what changes would you make if you were running this project again? What additional help could be used next time?
2. Give a condensed evaluation of the project as a whole. Did it meet your goals and did it make a profit? (Be specific.)

MAKE AS MANY COPIES OF THIS PAGE AS NEEDED

JOB WORKSHEET

Project:_____   Date:_____

Use this form for coordinating jobs and deadlines with volunteers. Make a list of all major jobs then estimate deadlines for completing them. Minor jobs would be a sub-set of major tasks and the responsibility of the person in charge who could use this same form and procedure for working up minor jobs and deadlines.

JOB	DEADLINE	PERSON IN CHARGE	PHONE	HELPERS

MAKE AS MANY COPIES OF THIS PAGE AS NEEDED

INSPIRING VOLUNTEERS

The meeting room is filled with enthusiastic volunteers eager to make the upcoming event your best fundraiser ever. Your job is to keep them motivated, efficient and focused on the task at hand. We'll give you skills to deal with problems that arise when managing and motivating volunteers. Believe me, there will be problems!

Keep in mind that everyone involved is donating his or her time to help because they believe in your group, its mission, or because they simply enjoy volunteer work. People have different amounts of time to give and degrees of enthusiasm. It's very important to make the most of what each individual is willing to give. This section helps you do that.

> *People have different amounts of time to give and degrees of enthusiasm. It's very important to make the most of what each individual is willing to give.*

TIME MANAGEMENT

Even for simple fundraisers, it's good to practice some sort of time management. The larger the project the more important a time management system becomes. The basic idea is to avoid wasting time—yours and that of the other volunteers.

Everyone has suffered through at least one interminable three-hour planning meeting that could have been finished in a half hour. When one or two people turn the meeting into a prolonged social

event, everyone else gets bored, frustrated and ready to quit.

One way to keep committee meetings focused is to appoint a committee chairman. This is not necessarily the same as the fundraising project chairman. The committee chairman's job is to see to it that the meeting stays formal and people are informed in advance of any preparations they need to have made before the meeting. The chairman sets a time limit and has a written agenda. The trick is to take care of business first. Then if someone needs to leave, they can. Others can stay and socialize if they want to.

Top business executives use the following rules for keeping board meetings and presentations focused on the issues.

Socializing is saved for after the meeting, not during. It only detracts from everyone's thought process.

TIME MANAGEMENT RULES FOR MEETINGS

1. *Be punctual and be sure you have your facts ready.*

2. *Do quick studies, present only what is neccessary. Details will be assigned.*

3. *Anticipate questions; do your homework.*

4. *Take time to think; don't fill time with idle talk.*

5. *Get to the point and pull others back to the point.*

6. *Know which priorities to pursue.*

7. *Develop a written timetable and a written agenda.*

GOOD TIME MANAGEMENT EQUALS GOOD RESULTS

Now that we have some time management rules for running the meetings, it's time for some suggestions or rules for managing your volunteers' time. These rules are used by successful business people, teachers and sales people. They can apply to people in all walks of life, including the volunteer. After all, we're trying to get the largest fundraising results most effectively.

VOLUNTEER TIME MANAGEMENT

SET PRIORITIES: Prioritize all the steps needed to complete the project or your job in the project. Decide what's most important and do that first. When working on your first priority, avoid interruptions at all costs. Interruptions create procrastination and procrastination is a major thief of your valuable time.

AVOID PROCRASTINATION: People procrastinate because it is a defense mechanism for avoiding an unpleasant task. One way many successful people deal with the fear of an unpleasant task is to do it first. This may sound like a bit of twisted logic at first, but by doing the least pleasant task first, the rest is easier. And you won't waste time worrying about the unpleasant task. Do the worst first and your confidence will soar.

DELEGATE: Know when to ask for help. Encourage your volunteers to request help as soon as they have a problem. If it becomes obvious that you and/or they cannot complete a job, then by all means get help immediately. The mark of a good manager is the ability to delegate effectively. Spread out the workload so no single volunteer, *including yourself,* is overburdened.

KEEP YOUR PERSPECTIVE: Take time to step back a bit and look at what you've accomplished. Get some feedback from other volunteers on the project and decide how best to proceed. Don't be afraid to scrap a bad course of action and start anew.

SHOW YOUR APPRECIATION: Let your volunteers know you appreciate them. No matter how small their contribution, each volunteer is a part of the whole success. Giving praise and thanks will make them, and you, feel good. It also encourages them to continue volunteering. If the project is big enough and your budget will allow it, throw a volunteer appreciation party after your project is over. A pizza and soft drink gathering is a nice gesture that fits almost all budgets.

AVOID RESENTMENT AND ANGER: Someone, somehow, is going to be resentful and angry toward someone else. This is totally unproductive.

The best way to deal with anger is to get it out in the open and resolve the conflict as best you can. If you don't, anger and resentment will undermine the success of your fundraising project. As a last resort, removing the cause of the situation may be necessary. You need to control conflicts objectively, with understanding and compromise, or they'll control you.

AVOID OVERWORKING: If you find that some people involved in the fundraising project are foregoing sleep, proper nutrition, exercise or ignoring their private lives, perhaps it's time you suggest that they need to delegate more and/or slow down a bit. This is often a problem in large, complicated fundraisers. The results are serious: burnout and loss of enjoyment. These problems, if left unchecked, can throw the best of fundraisers off track.

ENJOY WHAT YOU ARE DOING: You're here in the first place because you've made a conscious decision to be here. Enjoy the people in your group, find pleasure in talking to and working with them. Be a good listener and a good teacher. Enthusiasm is contagious. Your job is to make volunteer work as much fun as you possibly can. Happy hands make for quick work.

BURNOUT: It's been said that burnout is the price that has to be paid for doing good. That's hogwash. Burnout is the progressive loss of enthusiasm and enjoyment in what you are doing. When you find yourself angry because you "don't get no respect," and you start to view the members of your organization as ungrateful, self-centered clods, then you are burned out. Other indicators of burnout are: loss of wonder, loss of respect, dread, worry, procrastination and fear.

Avoiding and/or curing burnout is easy to say but hard to do. Don't give in to burnout. Take as long a break as you need, delegate some of the job

> *Enjoy the people in your group, find pleasure in talking to and working with them. Be a good listener and a good teacher. Enthusiasm is contagious. Your job is to make volunteer work as much fun as you possibly can.*

tasks, but don't quit. The trick is to rekindle your wonder and enthusiasm for being there. Enjoy the group you're with, your reasons for being involved with this group and, in general, the subtle yet profound pleasure of being alive. The only real cure is a revitalized attitude.

WORRIERS: There will always be the "worriers." People say, "Oh, this could happen," or "Oh, that could happen." People worry because they are afraid. Unfortunately, they're often afraid of things that haven't happened yet and most likely never will. Worry and fear are the primary reasons for procrastination.

FEAR EQUALS WORRY EQUALS PROCRASTINATION

Worry and fear create an endless loop of negative emotions. In everyday life, negative emotions can kill you. Negative emotions can destroy fundraising projects and create a self-fulfilling prophecy of failure.

Positive emotions, by contrast, make you feel good and help the project go well. This in no way belittles honest concern for unfortunate situations that could arise. But in general, worry is the primary cause of accidents, mistakes, missed deadlines and deadly procrastination.

There is a simple exercise you can do to take the destructive power out of fear and worry. To start, take a sheet of paper and write out all worries and fears. List everything that could possibly go wrong no matter how little, big, or ridiculous it may sound. Try very hard to be completely honest and don't make any judgement or criticism. Then cross out the following:

• *Things that won't happen*
• *Things that can't happen*
• *Things that may not happen*
• *Things that happened in the past but won't happen now*
• *Things that may upset somebody somehow*

What's left are those few things that are likely to go wrong. Now you can write them down and, at the same time, make a list of solutions. This way, no more time will be wasted worrying about something that doesn't deserve worry. "Be prepared," like the Boy Scout motto states. This should kill all worries before they destroy you or your fundraising project.

ENTHUSIASM: Positive thinking is contagious. One of the leader's most important jobs is to instill enthusiasm. Set out to disprove the old cliché, "It's easier said than done," because it is not true. Convince your people that they can do anything they want. Set a new standard of expectation by getting the members involved in the entire process: brainstorming, management, record-keeping and labor for your fundraising project.

People often use excuses when mistakes are made. Show them, by example when possible, that it's easier to take responsibility for their action and simply fix the mistake. When your volunteers start to think, "It's my fault and I'll fix it," they're on the way to a new level of personal responsibility.

The most dangerous handicaps are the self-imposed, mental ones. Usually when people make mistakes or don't complete their job it is because they've made excuses for their procrastination.

ENLIGHTEN THE VOLUNTEERS: Help your people understand that making excuses is pointless. Instead, create an attitude in your group that says: look at it, admit the mistake and fix it now. Soon you'll find more people in your group who can see what really needs to be done, can do it and then move on. One lesson repeatedly preached in business school is that, "Doing nothing is a decision in itself, and is almost invariably the wrong decision."

Be a treasure hunter; do it now!

WHEN SOMEONE FAILS: This is difficult, especially with

> *Help your people understand that making excuses is pointless. Instead, create an attitude in your group that says: look at it, admit the mistake and fix it now. Soon you'll find more people in your group who can see what really needs to be done, can do it and then move on.*

volunteers. "So and so did not get their job done," " I thought somebody else was going to help," or "I didn't know." You'll often find yourself doing a juggling act to correct a serious situation and not let it snowball into a major dilemma.

Try to remain unemotional about the whole situation and treat it simply as an event. Point out that you may be disappointed in someone's behavior or performance, but that doesn't mean you are disappointed in him or her as a person. Here are a few guidelines that should help.

1. *Accept the failure. No excuses, no anger. It's easy to try to blame someone else, but more effective to admit, "It was my fault."*

2. *Help them forgive themselves. Find a new job for them. People fail all the time; that does not mean that they are failed people. Turn it around and help them start anew.*

3. *Look at the lessons for the future. There can be a lot of power in "positive" losing. What did this teach them and how can they profit from it? "Nothing ventured, nothing gained."*

4. *When a situation fails, consider it a signal that it didn't work for that person. Use the failure as an indicator that a new direction is needed.*

WINNING PERFORMANCE: Instill in your volunteers a concept of "winning performance," which boils down to several key ideas. First and

foremost, answer the questions: What is your group's mission? Why are you here as a group? Develop your mission statement, write it down and give everyone a copy. The volunteers and members in your group need to be motivated by the mission of your organization, whatever that might be.

STEP 1: Develop the talents of yourself and other individuals in your group as productive resources. Work to instill the following concepts:

• *Lifelong learning is an investment in oneself*

• *Limits are only mental*

• *People are capable of achieving anything*

• *People are often afraid of their own potential*

STEP 2: Empower others through teamwork. As a group, you should already have a strong concept of teamwork and its benefits. Important points to remember:

• *Give and take feedback with a non-judgmental attitude. When a problem*

arises, criticize the behavior, not the person.

• *Give positive feedback whenever appropriate.*

• *Reward everyone for their efforts.*

STEP 3: Inspire members of your group to be result-oriented. Link fundraiser goals to your group's overall objective. Define short-term goals (i.e., to raise $1000 from this event), intermediate goals (we need $10,000 for this year's budget), and long-term goals (increase the budget and membership by 10% per year).

STEP 4: Some people adapt and learn more quickly than others. They can be very innovative when given a chance. A good volunteer/ fund-raiser has an ability to innovate and change. He sees opportunities in situations the others do not.

STEP 5: Top fundraisers are not born. They're motivated by the group's mission. Goals and plans are temporary means for achieving their mission. They make any job pleasurable and view it as an educational step in their ongoing training for higher accomplishments.

In a survey, people with terminal illnesses were asked to list the two most important things in their lives. The most common responses were:

1. *Spending time with people they love.*

2. *Work they're proud of.*

Use these motivating factors to make all of your group's fundraisers as successful as possible. Let's get busy!

MARKETING

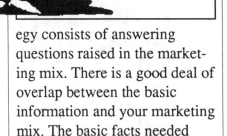

Marketing covers many activities. Basically, marketing is everything involved in delivering your product or service to your customer. As soon as you've defined what you're goals are with this fundraiser, you can define exactly how you'll do this. A good place to start is with the overall marketing mix.

MARKETING MIX

The marketing mix has five elements: product, price, personal selling, promotion and distribution. In college it's the 4 Ps and a D of marketing.

1. PRODUCT-What products, services or events are you using to raise money?

2. PRICE-What are the costs of the product, service or event you're providing? How much do you plan to charge?

3. PERSONAL SELLING-Are you using personal selling? If so, who will do it?

4. PROMOTION-How are you delivering the fundraiser information to your target market?

5. DISTRIBUTION-How will you deliver your product, service or event?

DEFINE INFORMATION

Before you can proceed to methods of promotion you need to set down the basic information about your fundraiser and relate this to the marketing mix.

Planning a marketing strategy consists of answering questions raised in the marketing mix. There is a good deal of overlap between the basic information and your marketing mix. The basic facts needed are: who, what, where, when, why and how. Keep it simple.

WHO-Who are you? Potential customers need to know who they're supporting and what your organization does.

WHAT-What are you selling? Tell about your product, service or event.

WHERE-Where will your fundraiser take place?

WHEN-Give the time and date, or range of dates, for your fundraiser.

WHY-You may want to tell why you're raising money.

HOW-How are you going to deliver your product, service or event to your customers?

TARGET MARKET

Your target market is the group you feel most likely to buy your product or service. This is who you want to reach with your message. Once these people are identified, you can select the best promotional methods and media to reach them.

ADVERTISING, PROMOTION, & PUBLICITY

Promotional messages you pay for are *advertising* and add to your costs. The benefit is the message is completely controlled by your group. *Publicity* is "unpaid for advertising" and is controlled by the media issuing the publicity. You want as much publicity as possible. These kinds of messages are often called public service announcements (PSAs).

NEWS RELEASES

All opportunities for your group to get publicity begin with a *news release*. When writing a news release, focus on any original, exciting or unusual aspects of your project. Study other news releases (also see *Sample News Release* on page 47). Use the "pyramid lead" to present your story: Put the most important facts first, working down to the least important. This method also lets you repeat the important information several times.

Use your group's letterhead or letter-sized white bond paper for your news release. Type it, as most editors won't decipher hand-written releases.

Keep your release factual, timely and brief. Use a catchy

statistic or fact as a starting point. Write short paragraphs and double-space the story.

Date the release with its mailing date. Address it to your contact person by both name and title. Call and get this information if you don't have it.

Charities frequently have trouble getting enough promotional activities done. It's always helpful to ask people in similar organizations how they do their promotional work. They are often willing to let you pick their brains and, at times, even make some copies of their promotional file materials. If you have a large enough budget, consider hiring an advertising professional.

PROMOTIONAL MEDIA SELECTION

You have a wide variety of promotional media to get your message out. Some cost money; others don't. Ultimately, you're limited only by your creativity.

Your local newspaper may run a story about your fundraiser before it happens, like a PSA, and will always take paid ads. Local or area radio and television stations, either commercial, public and/or college, also often run PSAs and most of these will take paid ads, too.

Posters, flyers and leaflets can be produced inexpensively using a typewriter, word processor or computer for the text

and drawings or clip art for illustration. Small quantities can be printed on a copier. Larger numbers can be inexpensively printed by a quick printer.

Most newspapers in larger cities offer some type of "saturation distribution." In our area it's called "Targeted Delivery Service" and with this service we can send flyers announcing fundraisers to specific zip codes, neighborhoods, apartment complexes, etc. to saturate our target market. Using "TDS" we can distribute our flyers to individual carrier routes in lots as small as several hundred, or in a combination of routes in excess of 100,000. Locally, rates range from 10¢ each, for 1-25,000 flyers, to as low as 6¢ each for 250,000+. Check with your local newspaper for similar rates in your area.

> **You have a wide variety of promotional media to get your message out. Some cost money; others don't. Ultimately, you're limited only by your creativity.**

Check with local grocery stores and see if they'll put one of your flyers, called a "stuffer" in this case, in each of their customer's grocery bags. You need to supply the flyers and they often do this for nothing.

In addition, local cable television systems, as part of their franchise agreements, provide a public access channel for locally-produced shows. Often the equipment needed to produce these shows is available free or for a minimal cost. To learn how your group can

produce it's own shows, see *Public Access Television* on page 60 for more details.

There are also billboards, direct mail campaigns, posters, flyers and leaflets to consider as part of your total media mix.

While billboards and direct mail campaigns can be quite effective they can also be too expensive for small events.

DEVELOP A BASIC SCRIPT

If you are planning on using any promotional media or methods, you need to develop a basic written script to work from. Simply take your event information and your marketing mix and write to your intended audience about your event in a simple sentence form. From there you can customize the script to fit the promotional media you want to use.

SCRIPT EXAMPLE

If you want to put out some PSAs on a local radio station telling about your upcoming car wash, your script might sound something like this: "The XYZ School band is holding a car wash on Saturday, May 10, from 10:00 a.m. to 5:00 p.m. in the school parking lot to raise money for new uniforms. For more information, contact Joe Smith, band director, at (list his office phone number here)."

CONCLUSION: At this point you can fill out the *Marketing Worksheet* on page 46 to organize your event's media. Also refer to information in the *General Guidelines* page 3.

MARKETING WORKSHEET

Event: _____ **Date:** _____

Use this worksheet for evaluating your fundraiser's basic information and marketing message. From these you'll decide what promotional media will best reach your target market.

DEFINE TARGET MARKET:

Who and where your prospective customers are_____
_____
_____
_____

DEFINE BASIC INFORMATION:

Who are you?_____

Why are you raising money?_____

What are you selling or asking for?_____

Where will the event be?_____

When will it be held?_____

How much will it cost?_____

BASIC PROMOTIONAL SCRIPT:

Put your basic information in sentence form:_____
_____
_____
_____

APPROPRIATE PROMOTION AND ADVERTISING MEDIA:

1. Personal Selling_____   2. Newspapers_____

3. Magazines_____   4. Radio_____

5. Television_____   6. Outdoor_____

7. Cable Access_____   8. Direct Mail_____

9. Posters_____   10. Flyers & Leaflets_____

SAMPLE NEWS RELEASE

August 20, 1999

Contact: *Jill Smith*
Gotham City Jaycees
1234 Main Street
Gotham City, State Here 46807
(555) 456-7890

FOR RELEASE ON SEPTEMBER 1, 1999

FLIP A CHIP FOR CHARITY

The world record for cow chip tossing, currently at 117 yards, will be under

assault once again at the 12th annual Gotham City Jaycees' cow chip toss, *Flip a*

Chip for Charity. Athletes of all kinds from all over the region will be challenging

the cow chip tossing record on Sunday, September 9, 1999 at 4:00 p.m. at the

Gotham City Soccer Field. For just a one dollar entry fee, each contestant will get

his or her moment in the limelight; a golden opportunity to throw three dry cow

chips onto the field and into the record books (Hey, it could happen). Trophies

will be awarded for both throwing style and throwing distance to the top three

athletes in each category. Proceeds will benefit the Gotham City YWCA's Shelter

for Women and Children. Registration for this year's *Flip a Chip for Charity* will

start at 3:00 p.m. at the soccer field. This event will be held, rain or shine.

For more information, contact Jill Smith, *Flip a Chip For Charity* Chair, at

(555) 456-7890.

* * *

CUTTING & PASTING

Feel free to modify the worksheets and forms in this book to fit the specific needs of your group. Professionals refer to this as cutting and pasting. We've included some cutting and pasting tips to help you create specific master forms from which you can reproduce as many copies as you need for your fundraising project.

It's very helpful to work at an area that has a photocopier. If you don't have access to an office, see if one of your co-leaders has an office you can use or you can go to the local library. If you need several hundred copies of a form, local print shops will often help you with cutting and pasting as a favor for your group and to get your business. A print shop can often do in ten minutes what would take you an hour or two.

To get started, first decide how you need to modify the forms, then gather together the equipment you'll need and head for a photocopy machine. Set up shop on a clean flat table or drafting board. Make a couple of good clean copies of the form you're going to modify then start cutting and pasting. Sometimes you'll need to go through several steps of cut-paste-photocopy and repeat until you get a master form that does everything you want it to. It's not as hard as it sounds and it can even be a lot of fun creating your own forms.

> *Sometimes you'll need to go through a couple steps of cut-paste-photocopy and repeat until you get a master form that does everything you want it to. It's not as hard as it sounds and it can even be a lot of fun creating your own forms.*

EQUIPMENT & SUPPLIES

SCISSORS: Use good, clean paper scissors. These work especially well for larger pieces.

HOBBY KNIFE: This works well for cutting out details, letters, or when cutting inside an area.

RULER: Use for a straight edge and to mark measurements.

DRAFTING TABLE, T-SQUARE & TRIANGLES: These will help you create more professional-looking forms because you'll be able to keep everything lined up while cutting, pasting, placing guidelines, lettering, etc.

BLUE PENCIL: Use a non-reproducing blue pencil (light colored blue), mark softly, and it won't show on most photocopy work. It's a big help for centering and lettering guidelines.

RUBBER CEMENT: Use this traditional graphic arts glue to attach headlines, letters and other graphic elements to the background paper. Use a burnisher (or a large spoon) to smooth down all the elements. Put a piece of tracing paper over the artwork before burnishing so you're less likely to scratch up your master page. Use a rubber cement pick-up to remove any excess. A wadded up piece of tape or a glob of dried rubber cement works fairly well as a pick-up.

TRANSPARENT TAPE: Doesn't usually show on finished forms when photocopied.

WHITE OPAQUE TAPE: Can be typed or written on, or used to block out areas too hard to cut.

ADHESIVE LETTERS: These work well for laying out headlines, dates, prices or whatever. Several styles and sizes are available at most office suppliers or large department stores.

PERSONAL COMPUTER WITH PRINTER: With this set-up, especially with an ink jet or laser printer, your headlines and text will look so good only a pro will see the difference.

By using the forms in this book and modifying them for specific projects with the above tools and techniques, your group's forms will look and work better then ever.

A B C D E F G H I J K L

M N O P Q R S T U V W

X Y Z a a a a b b c c c d

d e e e e e f f g g h i i i i

j j k l l m m m n n o o o

p q r s s t t u v w x y z 1

2 3 4 5 6 7 8 9 0 ! @

$ % & ( ) © = + [ ] { }

" " ' ' ; : ' " , . ?

Sunday Monday Tuesday Wednesday

Thursday Friday Saturday

Photocopy this page to get as many letters as you need for your project, then cut and paste-up the headlines and other type elements you need. You can then enlarge and reduce these type elements on a photocopier to fit your final layouts.

MAKE AS MANY COPIES OF THIS PAGE AS NEEDED

As you walk into the grocery to grab a few items you glance at the bulletin board and a small poster announcing *Troop Seven's Annual All-You-Can-Eat Spaghetti Dinner* catches your eye. You pause for fifteen seconds to read it. Since you had a good time at last year's event, you're favorably inclined to take the family to this year's dinner. You go off and take care of your shopping.

What you didn't notice were three more posters announcing similar fundraising dinners on the same evening. And the reason you didn't see them was because each of them was poorly written and designed and therefore didn't possess enough visual interest to stop your eye as you scanned the bulletin board.

Creating posters, brochures, postcards and newsletters to help find an audience for your events is a challenge that, when

All you can eat of our great Spaghetti, Garlic Bread and Caesar Salads!

Drinks and a great selection of àla carte Desserts, too!

$4 for Adults
$3 for Seniors and Children
Tots under 3 dine free!

STUFF YOURSELF PLEASANTLY!

You can have as much of our great spaghetti, garlic bread and crispy Caesar salad as you'd like this Friday night!

That's right, it's Troop Seven's 4th Annual All-You-Can-Eat Spaghetti Dinner. We start serving promptly at 5:30 p.m. and will do so up until 9 p.m.

Bring the whole family to St. Mary's Church at 907 West Vine Street and join us for a great dinner!

All proceeds go to TROOP SEVEN'S EDUCATIONAL PROJECT FUND

In this poster the headline and the humorous illustration of the eager diner work together to show a prospective customer the main benefit of your fundraiser from his point of view (getting a great and filling meal). Rider heads, in the upper left and right corners add detail to the main sales message. The body copy, under the headline, adds other details and asks for action (...join us for a great dinner!)

Enlarge this poster 180% on a photocopier and you'll have a basic layout for an 8 1/2"x 11" fundraising dinner poster. Just add your own details!

effectively met, can greatly boost your fundraising efforts.

Posters, the very first advertising medium, generally advertise only one event and are designed to make their point quickly. They are posted on bulletin boards and other public sites. Think of *postcards* as small posters you can mail to your various audience lists.

Brochures are unbound pamphlets, usually folded (the tri-fold and 'z' fold are popular formats) and often cover two or more subjects or events in depth. They can be mailed, put in larger packets of information, handed out and put in racks for the public in libraries, businesses or similar places. Include an address panel in your design and you'll end up with a self-mailer, which costs less to mail because it doesn't need an envelope.

A *newsletter* is an ongoing publication that chronicles all the ways your group is fulfilling its mission. For more details about the editorial side, see *Newsletters* on page 56. With the following design guidelines your group can always have hardworking print communications.

Once you've worked out the overall media mix (see *General Guidelines* page 3 and *Marketing* page 44 for details), you're ready to decide what printed pieces you'll use in this campaign. For example, if you're planning an elaborate fundraising dinner just for your active supporters, a postcard in the mail is probably enough. On the other hand, if this is your major money-maker, all-you-can-eat pancake extravagaza, you'll want posters up in as many public places as you can in addition to sending postcards to your active supporters list.

BASIC APPROACH: To begin the overall process, it's good to remember that each printed piece you produce has one essential purpose: to get your message seen by those most likely to act on it in a positive fashion. The most effective way to do this is to present your event in terms that speak to each audience member's own self-interest, i.e. present your event as a benefit to him/her/them. All printed pieces share these common design elements: *headline, copy* and *illustrations.* Some pieces can have additional elements such as a *coupon* in a brochure or tear-off *phone number tabs* on posters.

Before you can begin to

TYPES OF TYPE!

serif

Times Roman, the typeface on the left, is a serif type because it has small graphic elements added to the ends of it's letterforms. **Helvetica,** on the right, is a san serif type because it does not have those elements. Serif and san serif typefaces are often mixed today and the look can be quite eyecatching if well done. If you want to mix serif and san serif type you can safely use a **Times Roman** and **Helvetica** mix in all cases. There are, of course, tens of thousands of other type combinations but some of them can hurt readability, so be careful. Even pros can have trouble mixing type.

create any specific elements for a printed piece you first need to develop an overall approach to advertising your fundraising event. This is best done with a brainstorming session with your marketing committee. Any approach from serious to silly can be effective if it is appropriate to the specific event. When evaluating your ideas always ask if the idea makes your message more clear and compelling to members of your intended audience. If so, then you are on the right track. If it is a solid idea but doesn't work for this project, save it. Good ideas are almost always used at some time or another.

It is at this stage that major ad agencies and marketing

To begin the overall process it's good to remember that each printed piece you produce has one essential purpose: to get your message seen by those most likely to act on it in a positive fashion.

groups spend a lot of time and with good reason. It is here blockbuster campaigns start. If you come up with the right message and attitude, and reach the right audience at the right time, you'll have a great fundraiser. In our poster example, we decided to use some humor to advertise our dinner with the headline *Stuff Yourself Pleasantly* and a clip art (copyright free) image of an overly eager diner to illustrate it!

CAMERA-READY ART: Camera-ready art is the finished page with all elements *exactly* as they'll be printed. Most printers can provide the design, typesetting and paste-up services to create camera-ready art. Expect to pay from $65 to $95 per page or more. While this is fairly exacting work, it's not rocket science by any means. If your group has enough talented members and equipment to produce good camera-ready art, your printed pieces will work better without costing an arm and a leg.

Today you can create cost-effective yet high quality camera-ready art with desktop publishing technology. An ideal system would include a PC with word processing, graphics and page layout software, a scanner and a laser printer. With this system everything

BROCHURES & THEIR LAYOUT BOARDS

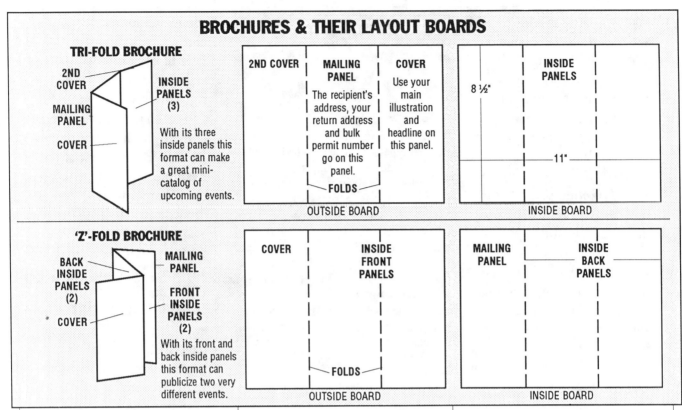

TRI-FOLD BROCHURE

2ND COVER

INSIDE PANELS (3)

MAILING PANEL

COVER

With its three inside panels this format can make a great mini-catalog of upcoming events.

2ND COVER	MAILING PANEL	COVER
	The recipient's address, your return address and bulk permit number go on this panel.	Use your main illustration and headline on this panel.

FOLDS

OUTSIDE BOARD

	INSIDE PANELS	
8½"		

11"

INSIDE BOARD

'Z'-FOLD BROCHURE

BACK INSIDE PANELS (2)

MAILING PANEL

COVER

FRONT INSIDE PANELS (2)

With its front and back inside panels this format can publicize two very different events.

COVER	INSIDE FRONT PANELS

FOLDS

OUTSIDE BOARD

MAILING PANEL	INSIDE BACK PANELS

INSIDE BOARD

after basic design sketches is done on a screen and the camera-ready art is printed out as one piece per page.

A PC with word processing software and a printer is a great leap beyond a typewriter because it automates preparation of *bodycopy* (stories and ad copy) and *headlines*, which can be further enlarged on a photocopier. With just a typewriter or word processor you'll still produce good-looking headlines and copy. Add a photocopier to make various kinds of illustrations to paste-up into camera-ready art. Without a computer it just takes longer.

Now we'll look at the major elements of all printed pieces.

TYPE: Type is what the pros call the printed word on a page and typefaces are the different specific styles of letterforms. In the English language alone there are over 4,000 different typefaces. Type is a major design element and, when used well, it can bring your message to life on the page. It is a vast field of study and application so we'll just touch on a few basics here. For example, the type you're reading now is a typeface called *Times Roman*. It's 12 points tall (a point is 1/72 of an inch) and set on a 14 point line, which adds 2 points of *leading* or white space between the lines to improve readability. Each family of type comes in a basic variety of styles such as: *regular, bold, italic* and *bold italic*.

Today's desktop publishing software offers even more type varity with *shadows, outlines* and *underlines*. When designing, think of contrast in your type. For example, a poster may use a headline in 48 point bold type, the bodycopy at about 14 point regular, the time and location information in the same size but italic and the group name in 24 point bold.

These type selections are not hard and fast rules. In general, use 3 to 5 style changes per piece. The only real measure of good type is this: Does it put this project in its best light? If so, then you're on track.

HEADLINE: The headline is usually the largest type on the page and is where you present your most compelling benefit to the person who will buy your products or attend your events. Headlines often seem to take inordinate amounts of time to write, but that's okay.

When writing a headline, professional copywriters often try to put themselves inside the head of the person they're trying to reach. From that

NEWSLETTERS & THEIR LAYOUT BOARDS

COVER STYLES

LOGO HERE

HEAD-LINE

HEADLINE

NEWSPAPER STYLE
Uses stories and photos on cover.

LOGO HERE

BLURB BLURB BLURB

MAGAZINE STYLE
Uses full page photo with blurbs to highlight stories.

FOUR PAGE FORMAT (11" X 17")

COVER

PAGE 4	COVER
— 17" —	
— 8 ½" —	— 8 ½" —
MAILING PANEL	11"

OUTSIDE BOARD

PAGE 2	PAGE 3
FOLD	

INSIDE BOARD

This format is a logical first expansion step from a one page newsletter. In addition this format is the basic building block for newsletters over 8 pages. In this case each 11" x 17" sheet becomes a 4 page signature.

SIX PAGE FORMAT (11" X 25 ½")

COVER

PAGE 5	PAGE 6	COVER
	MAILING PANEL	

OUTSIDE BOARD

PAGE 2	PAGE 3	PAGE 4
— 25 ½" —		
— 8 ½" —	— 8 ½" —	— 8 ½" —
11"	FOLDS	

INSIDE BOARD

This is the largest practical newsletter format to fit on one sheet. Both these formats can be folded to 5 ½" x 8 ½" for mailing.

---

perspective, they come to an understanding of what will most motivate that person to act. Headlines are sometimes written during a brainstorming session and when most people around the table have a good emotional reaction to a specific headline, you're getting your message in a compelling form.

The headline is your first written communication with your intended audience and, done right, will lead the reader into the bodycopy. Done wrong or ineffectively, your intended audience member may not even see it or if he sees it, may not read it. Either way, he won't get your message.

BODYCOPY: Bodycopy is set in smaller type and takes over where the headline leaves off. Within the copy, mention additional benefits to your intended customer. Note all relevant

details of when, where and how your event will take place. And, *most importantly*, at the end of your copy, ask your potential customer or audience member to buy or attend. Not asking for action is probably one of the more common and crucial copywriting mistakes.

ILLUSTRATIONS: The visual element, one or more illustrations, is the fourth major component. To be most effective in getting your message across, the illustration(s) need to amplify the headline's theme in both content and attitude so these two major elements can create a positive, synergistic impact in the reader's mind.

Illustrations are usually photographs, drawings or other kinds of artwork like a painting or silk-screen print. At the onset of each project, look for graphic elements unique to the

project to illustrate it. Photos from the previous year's event are often available and can be used in a variety of ways. See *How to crop a photo* in this section.

Federal copyright laws make it illegal to directly use a photograph or other illustration that belongs to a magazine, advertiser or other copyright holder without their specific permission. In some cases copyright holders will grant permission to non-profit groups they might favor, but in general using this kind of graphic material can be both time-consuming and expensive.

Even though you can't directly use copyrighted illustrations, you can *borrow* their graphic ideas for use in your own photographs or drawings. You'll find a wealth of good illustration ideas in the magazines, newspapers and other publications now in your home. Study and learn from them.

GETTING IT ALL TOGETHER: After you've gathered all the elements needed for a specific project, you're ready to do the *finished design* and then create *camera-ready art* for the printer. Before you begin doing this, explain any unusual aspects of the project to your printer and seek his input at this time. This can eliminate costly production difficulties later. It is always a good idea to communicate with your printer a week or two before you'll need his services.

DESIGN PROCESS: Stop a minute and remember exactly why you're doing this poster, newsletter or etc. Who do you want to attract and what do you want them to do? With all this firmly in mind again, start the design process with a series of small, quick *thumbnail sketches* that include all the major elements: illustrations, headline and bodycopy.

When one of these sketches catches your attention, make it bigger and refine it. Most pros end the design process with a tight rendition of the design using photocopies of the elements on tracing paper taped over the layout board for the camera-ready art. This greatly eases the production of camera-ready art as well as eliminating the chance of destroying what now are time-consuming or expensive (or both) illustrations, headlines or body copy elements.

When evaluating a design in progress, a second, informed opinion is invaluable. A good rule of thumb to keep in mind is this: If you have to explain the design to someone, it is simply not clear enough yet and needs more development. Pros integrate the major design elements into a cohesive message first, then decide the final page placement.

In the final analysis, there are no absolute design rules to follow. To develop your own design sense, notice what attracts your attention then break those designs down into their components to see how their messages are written and designed. As you gain experience, you will develop your own design sense.

NEWSLETTERS: Newsletters have some unique design considerations because they are periodic publications much like newspapers or magazines. The major editorial difference is that its viewpoint is generally limited to the organization's mission and fulfillment. In addition to its uses as a membership benefit and fundraising

> *When evaluating a design in progress, a second, informed opinion is invaluable. A good rule of thumb to keep in mind is this: If you have to explain the design to someone, it is simply not clear enough yet and needs more development.*

tool, it is helpful to look at your newsletter as the rough draft of your organization's history.

Your newsletter should have a *masthead* or *logo* that remains unchanged from issue to issue. Your newsletter will look more professional if each of your regular departments and columns also has its own unchanging graphic heading, called a *standing head.*

The most effective page layouts are done in a 3 or 4 column format. Consider using a 3 column format for the feature stories, for example, then use a 4 column layout for department or regular columns. These kind of multi-column layouts are more demanding to create, but when illustrated with an appropiate selection of well-cropped photos, they will put your ongoing story in its most compelling form. Make sure each photo has its own caption. It is not uncommon to spend up to four hours per page on design.

To ensure maximun readability of your bodycopy use this guideline: the length of your line should be less (measured in picas) than twice the point size of your type (measured in points). For example, if your bodycopy is set in 10 point type then the line length or column width should be less than 20 picas. Line lengths longer than this make it harder to read.

PRODUCTION & PASTE-UP: If you're using more traditional tools and techniques, the work just takes longer and makes a

HOW TO CROP A PHOTO:

Cropping a photo (or other illustration) lets you focus on the important elements in the image, increasing its overall impact. We do this by eliminating unneeded sections of the photo. In our example the background areas have been cropped out, making the essential elements (the mother and daughter) really stand out. Notice we've cut off the top of the mother's head slightly. This helps create an even greater impact as the reader's mind will automatically add the missing part of her head, thereby making the image seem larger and more immediate.

The photo in our example was scanned into a PC as a grey-scale image at 180 lines of resolution per inch (lpi). The electronic file was then imported into a page layout program where the image was adjusted to more closely match the original photo. It was then electronically cropped and put in final position as a 90 lpi image within the page layout. Then the file (this page) was output as a film negative on a 2540 lpi image-setting computer.

Once you learn to run this equipment, you can scan, adjust and *halftone* a photo in fifteen minutes or less. All photographic and continous tone images like paintings must be halftoned—broken into rows of little dots—so they can be printed. Illustrations without continous tones, like pen and ink drawings, called *line art*, need no halftoning. Desktop technology is

becoming widespread and is one of the most cost-effective ways of improving the overall quality of your printed pieces. This kind of halftone

work done by a traditional printer or film prep house often costs $8 to $15 or more per photo.

A "down and dirty" way to halftone photos is to photocopy them before pasting them in your layout. It's also a good time to crop and size them. Technically you're creating a hybrid halftone. By photocopying a photo several times you'll end up with a striking posterization that works well as the major graphic element in a poster or ad. For realistic photos in your newsletter, photocopy as few times as possible.

Your finished piece will never look any better than your *camera-ready art*. If you're not happy with the art, fix it at this stage. It's unrealistic to expect miracles from your printer.

bigger mess but can be every bit as effective. To begin gathering the tools, see *Cutting & Pasting* on page 48 for the basics. Also get a proportion wheel (available at art supply stores) so you can determine exact enlargements or reductions of different art elements.

If you are going to do an ongoing series of graphic projects, you'll find a hand

waxer (about $50 at a graphic arts supply store) a worthwhile investment. A hand waxer puts a thin layer of pressure-sensitive wax on the back side of design elements. When properly burnished, these elements stay put as well with wax as with rubber cement and are more easily repositioned. Overall, wax is a less messy, more forgiving way to as-

semble camera-ready art.

Always use a T-square and triangle to line up the different design elements. Use a non-reproducible blue pen to make needed marks on the layout. Work as neatly as possible.

CONCLUSION: Putting your group's message before the public in its most compelling form pays short- and long- term benefits to your group!

NEWSLETTERS

You sit nervously while a potentially large sponsor reads your group's latest newsletter. A slow smile breaks out across his face and after a few well thought-out questions, he compliments both your group and its mission. He then writes a large check for your new project. Your newsletter, a well-done effort that reports on your group's mission and the many ways it is fulfilled, was the deciding factor. A professional looking and reading newsletter is more than a source of information for your members, it's also a marketing tool.

GETTING STARTED

Producing a newsletter can be an overwhelming, time-consuming task. To make it a worthwhile undertaking, it must be created in an organized, time-efficient manner. As with all things, planning is the key.

PURPOSE AND AUDIENCE: Why invest the time and money to produce a newsletter? How can it help your group achieve it's mission? What audiences are you trying to reach?

An effective newsletter will inform, entertain, recruit and unite members and sponsors in your common purpose. It will also inform the general public of your organization's goals and calendar of activities.

If you're starting a new publication or extensively changing an existing one, begin with an ad hoc executive committee to define the newsletter's purpose and audience(s). This will help you understand who you're trying to reach and suggest the kind of stories needed to reach them. Identify each audience (members, sponsors, general public, etc.) by their demographics (age, sex, education level, income level and geographic location) as well as attitudes, values and interests.

Newsletters can help market upcoming events as well as create and/or enhance your public image. They should also recognize those who contribute both time and money. By filling your newsletter with unique, valuable information tailored to your members, it also becomes a strong benefit, providing them another incentive to join.

STAFF: Developing a reliable, capable volunteer staff is the crucial key in creating an effective newsletter. Most small organizations can't afford to hire professionals to produce their newsletter. Likewise, expecting a staff person (if you're lucky enough to have one) already burdened with other responsibilities to handle newsletter production is completely unrealistic.

Each newsletter will have its own staff requirements depending on number of pages and frequency of publication. Staff positions to consider include: an *editor* to oversee the production and provide input concerning purpose, direction and story content; one or more *writers* to help generate ideas and write stories; an *art director* or graphic designer to handle overall design, page layout and production of finished art; an *advertising manager* to sell ads, deliver ads to the printer in the right form and then bill the advertisers in a timely fashion; and a *circulation manager* to make sure the finished newsletters reach all your audiences.

If you don't have volunteers with these skills in your organization, you can often recruit capable people from local high school or college journalism,

> *Newsletters can help market upcoming events as well as create and/or enhance your public image. They should also recognize those who contribute both time and money.*

art and business departments.

Once your staff is in place, use the first meeting to determine overall objectives, production concerns and general operating procedures. Specific agenda items for the initial meeting should include defining the newsletter's purposes and audiences, setting a budget (with an all-volunteer staff this budget will cover printing and postage), deciding frequency of publication and pages per issue, creating editorial and advertising policies, a production schedule with printing dates, and methods of distribution.

BUDGET: Once you've defined your purpose, consider the budget. To do this wisely, decide how many pages your newsletter will run (length), how many newsletters you need printed (quantity) and how often (frequency). Most newsletters are published either *bi-annually* (twice a year), *quarterly* (four times a year); *bi-monthly* (six times a year) or *monthly* (12 times a year).

Your budget also sets major production and printing expenditures. Will you use typewriter text for layout and a photocopier for printing or desktop publishing equipment and a commercial printer? What paper stock will you use? Will your newsletter be black and white or use a second color? Will you use photographs?

Discuss these variables with your printer early on, so you can make cost-effective decisions before you start produc-

tion. At the end of these discussions you should end up with a firm quote on the printing costs.

Also consider how you will get your newsletter to your various audiences. If you're using the mail, research bulk mail options (see *Non-Profit Mailing* on page 29).

PRODUCTION SCHEDULE: A production schedule is one of the most important parts of the creation process—even if you don't keep up with it. It provides a map of things to do.

Create a schedule by working backwards through the production cycle. Start with the date you'd like the newsletter out. Then find out how long your printer needs to do his part. Continue in this manner, answering these questions, some of which may not apply:

• *When does it need to be pasted up?*

• *When does the final proof need to occur?*

• *When does the layout need to be finished?*

• *When do the edited copy and ad sizes need to be given to the art director?*

• *When do typesetting, data entry and copy editing need to be completed?*

• *When do the copy, art and photographs need to be ready?*

• *When do advertisers need to be contacted and when do their ads need to be received?*

• *When should an issue's*

editorial planning occur?

Go back and assign start dates to each of these events and you have the beginnings of a production cycle.

Personalize your production when needed. For example, you may need an added proofreading or you may be able to give an artist a bit more time on an illustration if it's delivered in the exact finished size. Parts of the cycle may overlap. For instance, with a large newsletter, you may be pasting up some pages, while proofing and designing others.

The production schedule won't always be met, but it will keep things moving along.

THE PRODUCTION CYCLE

EDITORIAL PLANNING: Good editorial planning requires an editorial grid—a list of all the interest areas to be covered and the specific articles (columns and features) to do this. This grid is your newsletter's skeleton, a "formula" itemizing what's needed each issue.

When filling your grid, consider what makes a story newsworthy: impact, timeliness, prominence, proximity, conflict and the unusual. Most publications have regular columns—articles in each issue—as well as features—or articles that only appear once.

Regular columns may include reports from staff or

> **Good editorial planning requires an editorial grid—a list of all the interest areas to be covered and the specific articles (columns and features) to do this.**

board of directors; minutes from meetings; a calendar of recent, current and upcoming events; a list of volunteers and contributing members; announcements; member/volunteer/staff profiles, etc.

Features are usually one-time articles written in depth. You may limit features as they are time consuming, but each issue should have a "cover story"—special coverage that gives it substance.

Take notes between issues to help remind you of what needs to be included. File monthly reports, etc. to help keep track of other newsworthy items you may want to include.

An editorial grid is essential for planning. It helps an editor quickly see what copy needs to be gathered and when.

ADVERTISING: Selling ads can pay for production costs. In fact, selling ads can make your newsletter a healthy fundraiser.

A cost-benefit analysis will find your break-even point. How much space can you sell to advertisers and profit? That point differs each issue, but more than 50% advertising can increase postage as you may lose non-profit mailing status.

You'll need an established advertising policy before you start selling ads. Are ads paid for when the contract is signed or after the ad is printed? Does the advertiser get a complimentary copy? Does the advertiser supply camera-ready art or will you produce the ad?

Working with your art direc-tor and printer, decide what size ads to sell. Common sizes are full, ½ (vertical & horizontal), ¼ and ⅛ page. You'll need exact dimensions for each ad so camera-ready ads will fit.

After setting sizes, work out prices. Ads are sold by either their page size (full, ½, etc.) or number of column inches. For example, at five dollars a column inch, an advertiser will pay $20 for an ad two inches high and two columns wide (2 x 2 = 4 x $5 = $20). Frequency discounts are often given.

Selling business card-size ads is an effective marketing strategy as most small businesses already have the ad art (their business card). Price these ads competitively.

To create your sales force, find volunteers who can make and maintain business contacts and represent your group. Have them prepare a list of businesses to approach. A good ad prospect has a product or service your readers are *willing and able* to pay for.

Ads are often bought as donations. A noble gesture, but if you deliver live prospects to your advertisers, you'll build a solid, long-term financial base for your newsletter.

When making your prospect list, include the full business name, complete address, phone number and contact name. It's important to talk to the person who handles advertising. If it's a small business, that will likely be the owner or manager.

Initiate contact with a phone call. If you don't know who handles advertising, ask. Speak with them if possible. Explain briefly who you are and the organization you represent.

Explain how they'll benefit selling to your audience. Let them know cost-effective ads are available in your newsletter. In closing, offer to send a letter describing your audience and organization, a page with ad prices, sizes and deadlines (called a "rate card" in the business) and a current issue.

Don't go into a lot of detail —it's not yet time to close the sale. Simply introduce the idea and let them know they can expect something in the mail.

Mail the package in a timely manner—preferably within two days. Also include a simple contract specifying the details of the agreement (see *Ad Sales Worksheet* on page 87).

Call them back three to five days after you've mailed the package to discuss the project. Be prepared to answer questions and close the sale—now is the time to suggest they sign the contract and mail it back.

GENERATING STORIES: While ads are being sold, the editor and writers need to decide how to fulfill the story requirements itemized in the editorial grid. Assign stories to writers based on their interest in that subject. Over a period of time you'll develop a group of writers who each have individual areas of interest and expertise. From time to time you may find a relevant story in another publication. You may be able to publish it, but you first need permission from that publication to reprint.

Using new stories written by involved volunteers creates a unique publication tailored to your organization and audience. However, an inexperienced staff may find the task overwhelming. Here are a few tips to streamline the process.

> **When writing, remember to show, don't tell.** *Help your reader experience the story—not just read about it.*

Make sure each writer understands the story *topic*, *angle* and *length* to be written. Discuss who should be interviewed or what research needs to be done. Give each writer a specific deadline for each story.

There are two basic kinds of stories: news and feature. News stories are focused and to the point—the writer's job is to inform by objectively reporting facts. Feature stories are more descriptive and usually longer. Their purpose is to entertain as well as inform. Your publication will need both.

When writing, ask, "What do I want to say and where does it go?" All stories answer the basic journalistic questions of who, what, where, when, why and how. This information should be organized with the most important material at the story's beginning (called the *lead* by pros). Material that explains and amplifies the lead comes next. Background and secondary information finish off each story. This structure is called an *inverted pyramid.*

The lead is the most important part of the story and should introduce the basic idea or theme. Most news stories use a direct lead—the first paragraph tells you what's most unusual about the story and who's involved. A feature story may use a delayed lead—a descriptive paragraph meant to pique the reader's interest. The main idea of the story is introduced in following paragraphs.

When writing, remember to *show, don't tell.* Help your reader experience the story— not just read about it. For example, instead of writing, "The basketball player was hot and tired," write, "The basketball player walked stiffly as sweat poured from his face."

Whatever you write, make sure it's accurate, clear and fair. Write from first-hand observation whenever you can. When that's not possible, use reliable sources and attribute their statements to them in the story. Seek primary sources (those most familiar with the story) before secondary sources (those who will tell you what they've learned from others).

EDITING COPY: It's an editor's right and responsibility to edit stories for accuracy, style, space and readability.

You'll create a consistent editorial style by using a stylebook, such as the those offered by the Associated Press or New York Times. A stylebook answers questions such as when to use abbreviations, when to spell out numbers, etc.

When editing, check for readability. Do you understand what is being said? Is it clear? Could it be said more clearly? To increase clarity and readability, work with short sentences. A good rule of thumb is to have no more than nine to eleven words per sentence.

Avoid redundancy like the plague. Use headlines and subheads (titles and subtitles) to break up and organize long stories.

To learn about the use of pictures, design, layout and production of finished pages ready for the printer (called camera-ready or mechanical art) see *Graphic Design* on page 50. When your pages are done, it's off to the printer!

DISTRIBUTION: How do you get your newsletter out to your audiences? To start, create a mailing list that includes members, current and potential sponsors, all local media, and important people and businesses in your community. If you are mailing your newsletter, prepare the labels while it's being printed. Have volunteers ready to label and sort according to postal regulations. See *Non-Profit Mailing* on 29 for more details.

CONCLUSION: It will take a few issues to get everyone up to speed. Keep notes as you go and focus on creating systems that work for your organization.

PUBLIC ACCESS TELEVISION

It's nearly eight p.m., you and your family have gathered with some freshly popped corn to watch your group's first public access TV show. More importantly, several thousand others in your city, many who never knew of your group, are also tuned in. Your group and its mission are about to become part of our television culture.

WHAT IS PUBLIC ACCESS TV? Public access started in the early 1970s, when communities were first wired for cable tv. Some lawmakers felt we, the general public, should benefit directly. They decided access to television production and broadcasting would create a wider forum for public debate. This became public access television.

Public access television, then, grows out of our 1st Amendment rights. Today any citizen or non-profit group in a cable system's community can produce a television show for broadcast, using broadcast-quality cameras and equipment, for little or no money.

If a member of your group is adept at video production, you're on your way to making a fundraising documentary. If not, public access stations have staff members to help you produce your show, then when

> *Today any citizen or non-profit group in a cable system's community can produce a television show for broadcast, using broadcast-quality cameras and equipment, for little or no money.*

it's done, broadcast it on your local cable system.

PRODUCING YOUR OWN SHOW: There are few restrictions about what you can put on cable. You cannot do direct fundraising, nor can you broadcast anything libelous or pornographic. Other than that, the sky's the limit.

As an example, let's walk through the process of producing an access tv show about your upcoming festival. First contact your public access station, then you'll have to file a program proposal, a written description of your show.

You'll have an access staff person to help you set up your production. You'll learn your equipment options and get lists of certified camera operators, sound and other technicians you'll need for your show. It will be your job to call and schedule your crew.

The public access station has broadcast-quality equipment to use and, if you want, they also provide tape footage to record your show on. After your show is edited, the station then bulk erases the tapes to use again. Using their tapes eliminates all production costs, but when it's over you have only a copy of the finished show.

On the other hand, if you buy your footage, at the end of the project you'll own the original master and source footage. There are several more ways to use this material. You'll need to give the public access station a dub of your show on their footage to broadcast.

At this point in the process, called *pre-production* by the pros, your plans will be finished, equipment and manpower set and ready to go. Next is *production*, recording the event, followed by *post-production*, the edit process. For a more detailed look at this process, see *Video Shooting & Editing* on the next page.

DISTRIBUTION: If you own your own footage, you now have a lot of options. After the original show is finished, you can sell tapes as fundraising products (some local producers give ten percent of their profits to the station). You can also edit a five or ten minute show to use in meetings. You'll have footage for next year's PSAs and the begining of your group's video archives.

WIDE OR ESTABLISHING SHOT

MEDIUM SHOT

CLOSE-UP

CUTAWAY

HOW A BASIC SEQUENCE WORKS: *In the scene above the man talks to the boy for thirty seconds. Look at the picture and count one-thousand-one, one-thousand-two and so on up to thirty seconds.*

If you're normal, you didn't get past one-thousand-ten before your eyes wandered off. Now look at the sequence of shots starting on the right. Count to one-thousand-five at each then move to the next.

That was a lot easier, right? What we've proved with this little exercise is that it is easier to look at six different images in thirty seconds than to look at one scene for the same time. That's the idea behind the basic sequence—to break up long scenes into several shorter ones. This makes the story more interesting for the viewer. It also lets us, in editing, vary length and emphasis as we desire.

Let's look at this basic sequence, shot by shot, and see how it works.

The first shot is a WIDE or ESTABLISHING SHOT to establish the man, the boy and the great outdoors. Next is a MEDIUM SHOT of the man talking, followed by a reverse shot called a CUTAWAY of the boy listening, then a CLOSE-UP of the man talking, another CUTAWAY and finally a WIDE SHOT at the end.

Your show will have its own mix of these elements.

1

2

3

4

5

6

VIDEO SHOOTING & EDITING

Producing your public access show can be quite an adventure in itself. The pros divide this process into three main steps: *Pre-production*—everything it takes to make sure all the people and equipment show up on the right day to record the show; *production*—videotaping all the footage that will later be edited into your final show; and *post-production*—editing the footage and adding all needed narration, music and graphics to tell your story in an interesting and informative way.

Next we'll look at some basics of video taping and editing the story of your group's next project.

PRODUCTION

It's fifteen minutes before your festival's opening ceremony. The public access volunteer crew, two camera operators and a third person who is both director and sound person are excited and ready to go. Soon they'll create the raw elements of your show: overview scenes, interviews, action sequences and montage elements.

In order to create effective story-telling sequences in the editing process it's imperative the editor(s) have a wide selection of usable video elements. Most scenes consist of wide (or long) shots, medium shots, close-ups and cutaways. Let's go back to our festival example for a minute and see how a typical two-day festival production might work.

At the begining of each day's shooting the director/sound person will give each camera operator a shooting list for the day. The list gives the camera operators a framework for the day's shoot. In these documentary kinds of shoots it is good to leave plenty of flexibility for unexpected events. The director/sound person will work with each camera operator during the day, shooting elements for yet another list. This often consists of interviews with specific people along with other must-get story elements.

When the shoot is over you'll have up to twenty hours of video from your festival in thousands of wide, medium and close-up shots. The production is over and it's on to the post-production and final editing.

POST-PRODUCTION

It is in the edit suite that your show comes together in its finished form. It can take from fifty to eighty hours to turn your raw footage into a dynamic, compelling TV show. If you don't have a group member who is certified on your local public access station's editing suite(s), plan to have a group member working with your public

continued on next page

continued from preceding page
access editor every session. Everyone will be happier at the end and you may gain a valuable ally in your efforts to bring your group's mission to public awareness.

Before you can begin to edit you must know exactly what you have. You do this by logging your tapes. Your public access station probably has a form you can photocopy for logging your tapes. To log a tape, start the tape at zero and record the starting and stopping time, in minutes and seconds (00:00), for each separate scene on the tape. Along the way you can use some visual shorthand to pre-select scenes for the edit process. One local public access producer uses stars to mark scenes: one star, look at again if more is needed later; two stars, has its strong points; three stars, best we've got, let's start here.

By the time the logging is finished, you'll have a clear idea of the show's overall flow and maybe even the opening scenes. You'll also need to outline any narration or other writing needs and get that copy into production. Then it's on with the magic and tedium of video editing.

The basic video editing process is simple. You select all the relevant scenes from your original footage, now called "source tapes," and re-record them in finished sequence on another tape, called "the master tape." This tape is the original recording of your finished show and as such is a very valuable tape.

All this work is done in a room

MONTAGE: *A montage is a series of related shots. Most TV commercials are montages. For a montage to work, each shot should be clearly different in color and composition from the one before it. The montage at the top is very ineffective because all the shots are too similar. The montage above is much more effective because each shot is substantially different.*
DUTCH TILTS: *(Below) Tilting the camera to record a scene is a dynamic way to add visual interest. For reasons lost to time, this is called a DUTCH TILT. It can look good if not overdone.*

filled with source and record decks, switchers and a wide variety of other gear. These rooms are called "edit suites" and it's here that you and your public access editor will create the finished show.

Traditional tape-to-tape editing (most public access editing suites today), has two major edit types. The first, *assemble edits*, adds an entirely new signal (video, audio and control track), obliterating any previous signal. The second, *insert edits* changes video or audio or both but not the control track, which must already be there. Inserts are used to add visual interest and information. For example, while listening to the master of ceremonies make his

opening speech, you would see a wide variety of (inserted) scenes from the opening ceremonies.

The absolute worst thing to do in this kind of editing is break the control track. This creates a magnetic "hole" in your control track that cannot be fixed. Using an assemble edit when you should insert is the most common cause of broken control track.

There are two common editing strategies: The first is to take the new master tape and record a "black burst," an entirely black signal with a one-piece control track, on the tape first then insert edit the whole show. This gives you greater color saturation in the final master tape. The second common strategy is called "butt editing." Here you assemble edit the show's larger scenes together in sequence and then go back and add insert edits of either additional video scenes or narration or music.

With some of the new non-linear desktop video editing suites (basically powerful personal computers with video editing hardware and software) most tape-to-tape limitations are gone. Some of the more popular packages at the moment are the Avid series of suites for Macintosh and the Video Flyer suite, now for Amiga and soon for IBM. Others are coming on the market at a rapid pace and it won't be long before these powerful new tools reach public access television stations.

When you're done with the final insert edit and you've added all titles and credits, you'll have a powerful portrait of your group in action.

CHAPTER 3
SUPER FUNDRAISERS

CHAPTER NOTES:

MEMBERSHIP DRIVES

Why exactly should your group solicit members anyway? The general public remains the least understood source of income for non-profits. Many organizations solicit members without understanding the responsibilities incurred.

A membership drive turns people into non-profit supporters by appealing to their desire to serve a higher cause. The goal is not only to raise money, but to raise people's consciousness and awareness as well. A large show of community support also helps a group get funds from other sources.

A member contributes money, time and support in exchange for a set of benefits. These benefits are *ethereal* (personal satisfaction gained from contributing to a higher cause), *tangible* (discounts for the group's services, premiums, etc.) and *logistical* (a voice in the decision-making process).

When an organization invites members, it creates a constituency entitled to an opinion regarding the organization's overall activities. The organization should be responsive and responsible to this constituency by allowing a legislative voice in major decisions and activities (such as an annual election of Board of Directors.)

Ideally, a check and balance occurs between the membership (or constituency), the staff and the Board of Directors. Each group is equally impor-tant, as each is vital to the organization's survival. An organization should decide if it is willing to take on these responsibilities before inviting members to join.

With many non-profits vying for the support of the general public, which organizations are most successful? Invariably, it's the groups that do the most exciting work, clearly explain their work to the largest number of people and offer attractive benefit packages.

PLANNING YOUR MEMBERSHIP DRIVE

A membership drive is basically a program using a group of volunteers to secure a desired number of new members in a specific time period.

These drives require a vast expenditure of time, energy and money. The only reason to make these investments is the promise of an ample return. At the onset, clearly identify what you want your drive to achieve. Common goals include: 1) To

> *A membership drive turns people into non-profit supporters by appealing to their desire to serve a higher cause. The goal is not only to raise money, but to raise people's consciousness and awareness as well.*

secure new members; 2) To obtain needed funds; 3) To increase public awareness; and 4) To increase the number of people who receive your services and broaden their scope.

Make sure you put these goals in very specific terms, such as: How many new members do you want? How much money do you want to raise? How many of these members do you want turn into active volunteers? What increase would you like in public awareness? Make your goals realistic. When setting goals, consider the success and methods used in past campaigns as well as the state of the economy and your community's frame of mind. (Are you competing for attention with a community-wide crisis or celebration?)

Understand the needs and resources of your organization. Examine your organization's purpose, members, services, major accomplishments, clients, goals, etc. Once you have established reasonable goals, then select the methods you'll use to achieve them.

CREATING COMMITTEES: To get this project going in an organized fashion, categorize different types of responsibilities and create committees to work on each category. Suggested committees can include a *Planning Committee, Prospect Committee, Finance Committee, Promotion/Publicity Committee, Campaign Committee* and a *Volunteer Committee*. You may also need specialized committees due to the unique nature of your drive.

WHEN SHOULD YOUR DRIVE BE HELD? Deciding when your membership drive should take place is crucial to its success. The best time is whenever it's easiest for you to recruit volunteers and contact prospects. This varies from group to group. Early fall and late spring are traditionally good times for drives. Avoid conflicts with national holidays, community events and other large membership drives in your area.

Plan for your campaign to run from 10 days to two weeks. You'll need up to three months of planning and development time, depending on how complex your drive will be and how many people will be involved.

BUDGET: Your group will need to spend some money to achieve your goals. Common costs include graphic design and printing, paid advertising, postage, telephone service, food, prizes and premiums.

A good rule of thumb is to spend 20 to 30 percent of the money you expect to raise for expenses. For example, if you plan to raise $2,000, expect to spend from $400 to $600 to do so (see *Service/Event Projected Budget* on page 19).

Sometimes a corporation will underwrite itemized fundraising expenses. Be prepared to make these requests in a proposal form (See *Grant Writing* on page 71).

CREATING A PROSPECT LIST: Determining your potential donors and creating a prospect list to find them is a crucial step. Most probably, you will be soliciting three different types of members: 1) Past members who've renewed; 2) Past members who have not renewed; 3) People who have never been members.

Each of these categories can be further broken down by income levels, geographic areas, etc. (see *Cash Support* on page 68).

It's important to develop a list of qualified prospects as your drive will only be as successful as your list. Spending time, energy and money soliciting unlikely prospects is an expensive venture.

To avoid this, create a membership profile of the common characteristics of a good prospect. Determine variables such as sex, age, race, occupation, area of residence, education level, interests, political affiliations, religious beliefs, etc.

Once you've defined a good prospect, ask yourself where you can find them. Obtain mailing lists from organizations with similar members or clientele. Approach businesses and

professional groups whose clients or employees would make good prospects. Look for published contributor lists from other organizations. Finally, ask your staff, volunteers, board of directors and others involved with your group for names of people who may be interested in joining. And don't forget to approach your students, clients, etc.

Make sure your list has the prospect's name, address and phone number. Include more information that applies. For example, you may want to know how much members gave in the past and why they quit giving. Or you may want the names of those who referred potential members to you.

Create a recordkeeping process to meet your needs. It can be as simple as an index card for each prospect, filed alphabetically. A computer with database software may be the ideal answer. Whatever you do, make your records accessible from year to year.

CREATING A THEME: Create a theme for your drive by developing a conceptual framework, graphic look and slogan. Make it simple, yet riveting. All membership drive publicity and appeals should then reflect this theme.

CREATE A BENEFIT PACKAGE: Get to know your potential donors well and offer them something they'll value in

> **It's important to develop a list of qualified prospects as your drive will only be as successful as your list.**

exchange for their contribution. There are many creative benefits you can offer even if your funds are limited.

Consider your group's resources and the community you live in. Use this opportunity to expose a large number of people to your services and activities. As a benefit, can you offer a discount on classes, concerts or other events? Can you discount products or arrange to offer a premium?

Create a cross-promotion with other profit or non-profit groups with a similar clientele. See if they'll offer your members a discount on their products or services in exchange for a free ad(s) in your newsletter or event programs. They'll gain increased exposure.

Consider creating a multi-level benefit package, with the number and value of benefits increasing as does the requested contribution. In other words, those who contribute more money get a greater number of more valuable benefits.

In any case, make sure everyone who contributes receives some form of public recognition, such as being listed in your newsletter, concert program, your community's newspaper, etc.

CREATING AN APPEAL: With your theme and benefits package now together, decide the basis of your appeal. Shall you stress the personal benefits, community benefits or a combination thereof?

Always appeal to the com-

mon characteristics of your prospects as you proceed. You may approach each group with a slightly different appeal.

PROMOTION AND PUBLICITY: It's important to tell the community at large about your membership campaign. This will help familiarize those on your prospect list about your organization before you contact them. It will also help generate interest among those *not* on your prospect list, hopefully prompting them to contact you.

Send out news releases, PSAs and posters. Organize special events as part of your publicity campaign. Take full advantage of the media by creating a human interest story that warrants coverage. In all of your publicity, stress the benefits of being a member.

LAUNCHING YOUR MEMBERSHIP DRIVE

Once you've defined goals, prospects, budget, theme, appeal and benefits, you're ready to select the best communication methods. To be most successful, you'll want to implement these communications in a specific sequence.

For example, you may start your campaign by distributing news releases announcing a media-worthy kick-off event.

Follow up with a direct-mail postcard campaign telling prospects that a phone call is coming. Phone each prospect, explain your group and benefit package and ask for a contribution. Don't forget to record

their response!

Next, send a letter with a pledge card and return envelope to collect contributions. After receiving their contribution, send a thank-you letter and, perhaps, a membership card.

There's no end to the possible methods or combinations. Be creative and develop methods that fit your group's resources, budget and objectives.

Regardless of the communication methods you choose, making it all happen takes adequate planning. Think through what you'll need and when, then create a schedule for its preparation. Do you plan to use pledge cards, membership cards, postcards, or a letter with return envelopes? Create training time for your volunteers. For example, if planning a phonathon, practice with some role-playing and a script.

Whatever methods you choose, make the campaign a fun event for all involved. Supply food, contests and prizes as appropriate.

CONCLUSION: Inviting members to join your organization has many benefits. You'll increase public awareness and develop a large base of support among people willing to donate their time and/or money.

In exchange you provide a variety of benefits, including allowing them a voice in decisions facing the organization—usually through monthly or yearly meetings.

Ideally, this relationship is mutually beneficial.

CASH SUPPORT

MEMBERS & BELIEVERS

One area that deserves more attention from most groups is outright cash solicitations. In addition, an important part of your fundraising mission is to promote your organization's purpose to believers as well as members.

Who are your "believers?" They are the people who believe in what your organization does and want it to be successful. Believers will support you with money or donations. Members, on the other hand, actively participate in your group by contributing their time and talent as well as money and donations.

DUES: There are several ways to raise money from your membership. The most widespread way is through membership dues. Dues are a monetary commitment by a member to your organization. Dues are a consistent, dependable source of revenue for your group.

To make the treasurer's job easier, renew memberships at the same time every year so all dues statements can be sent at the same time. Plan your main membership drives to peak with your annual membership renewal. As new members join throughout the year, pro-rate their dues for the months remaining until your annual renewal time.

SETTING DUES: Dues should be sufficient to cover your organization's basic operating

budget for the year. Fundraisers can then be used to generate cash to finance special group events, programs or projects.

The board of directors should set the dues schedule. To help the board set accurate dues, you'll need to start with a basic projected budget for the upcoming year. This budget should include: postage, supplies, meeting expenses, utilities, rents, and other basic costs. See *Annual Budget* page 11 for more details.

Dues should also be set at a level that is reasonable for the majority of your members and comparable to the dues of similar groups. If a few members can't pay because of a hardship, it's better to under-

> *Believers are people who believe in what your organization does and want it to be successful. ... Members, on the other hand, actively participate in your group by contributing their time and talent as well as money and donations.*

write a part or all of their dues rather than to set your overall dues too low. Be sure to build consensus by inviting input from your members when discussing your dues schedule.

If you have different membership levels (i.e. individual, family, student, senior, business, etc.) your dues structure can vary to reflect these various levels. Try to create a dues structure that will ease the financial burden for someone who really wants to be a member but is on a fixed income.

RENEWALS: If your group is small and has regular meetings, renewals can best be handled in person. Use a two-copy receipt book so both the dues-paying member and the treasurer have receipts for all dues paid.

In a larger group, or one without monthly meetings, have the treasurer send renewal statements by mail. Board members can follow up with any needed reminders or phone calls.

FEES: Another way to raise money from your members is through fees charged for services, events, programs, etc. If your group produces public service events, you can give your members a discounted rate for these services. The same goes for programs, seminars, etc. These reduced rate fees will help offset the cost of these events, while still giving your members a price break. It is also more democratic for those members who aren't participating in these particular services or programs.

PLEDGES: Pledges are different from dues. They're additional monies to use for special projects or simply donations in addition to dues. Pledges can be collected monthly or as needed for projects. Churches do well at this type of fundraising.

You'll need to keep consistent, thorough records of all pledges made, received and billed. Ask your most committed members and believers to help out with an additional pledge if they're able to do so.

CASH SOLICITATIONS

Beyond membership dues, fees, and pledges, are a number of ways to solicit cash donations from individuals or businesses who believe in your organization. The five basic methods for soliciting cash are:
- *Door-to-door*
- *Telemarketing*
- *Business*
- *Major supporters*
- *Direct mail*

TIPS ON ASKING FOR CASH: For most people, asking for cash is one of the most difficult aspects of fundraising. You've probably had problems getting members to volunteer to ask for cash. And while asking directly for cash can be uncomfortable, it can also be very effective.

> *To help your members overcome their difficulty asking for money, give the first donation yourself. ... Remind them that the worst that generally happens is simply a polite, "No."*

Get started by putting together a list of potential large donors: past supporters, friends of members, local professionals, businesses and other people who are interested in your group.

Next, write a brief factual biography of each person on the list. This should include information about their job, family, home, education and all else that seems relevant to your group. Rank them in potential giving levels, estimating their giving abilities. If possible, find members who know the prospects on a personal basis and ask him or her to represent your group when asking for the gift.

To help your members overcome their difficulty asking for money, give the first donation yourself. Review parts of chapters 1, 2, and 3 on motivation and sales techniques as well as *General Selling Tips* on page 81. Remind them that the worst that generally happens is simply a polite, "No."

Make sure members are well-prepared with both a receipt book and a copy of your latest newsletter to give to your new donor when they go out to solicit. Everyone should dress nicely and, no matter what the outcome, be courteous!

Thank everyone who donates to your group. A phone call or a card in the mail is always in good taste. Don't delay letting your donors know you appreciate them!

DOOR-TO-DOOR: Group members, dressed in official uniforms and/or equipped with some type of positive identification, go door to door and ask for donations. This method often works best for members' immediate neighbors. This kind of fundraising is often more effective if your organization has a strong, positive public reputation in the neighborhoods where you solicit. Have members work in pairs when they solicit door-to-door and provide them with receipt books so they can write receipts on the spot for all donations.

TELEMARKETING: Telemarketing methods can help in raising cash. Read *Telemarketing* on page 82 for techniques, list development and script ideas for telemarketing.

BUSINESS: Businesses often support organizations that benefit their employees and/or their customers. Ask the following questions to determine which businesses your group can most effectively approach:
- *Where do your members work?*
- *What businesses do your*

members patronize?

• *What businesses does your group patronize?*

• *Who benefits from what you do?*

Have members make lists of businesses that fit the above criteria. Whenever possible, have them include a contact person at each business. Once your list of prospective donors is ready, prepare your information package and get the troops out soliciting.

MAJOR DONORS: A major donor campaign differs from business donations, membership dues and pledges, and should be a separate fundraising effort. This kind of program encourages those who are willing and able to give as much as possible. Make a list of prospects using the criteria outlined in the previous section. Basically, your list should include people who've given before, active members or donors, local professionals and well-to-do individuals who you feel are sympathetic to your group's mission.

DIRECT MAIL: This approach can reach a larger audience than most door-to-door efforts. Be sure to follow all federal and postal direct mail regulations that apply to your type of organization (either for-profit or not-for-profit). You can get direct mail guidelines from the Federal Trade Commission and the US Post Office.

Direct mail generates more donations if you use a pre-paid return envelope. Setting up a *Business Reply Mail* account at the post office will let your group provide a pre-paid return envelope at a lower cost than pre-stamped envelopes because you only pay for those envelopes which actually return. For more details about Business Reply Mail accounts, please see *Non-Profit Mailing* on page 29.

Next, you'll want to create a good, basic direct mail package including a flyer, cover letter and return envelope. For more details see *Graphic Design* on page 50. Be sure to test your mailing on a small scale to check its profitability before doing a massive mailing. This will save you from losing a lot of money on a bad direct mail package or list.

Your group's newsletter should be treated as another kind of direct mail. A good rule of thumb to follow is that whenever you print anything, ask for funds. Your newsletter should go to members, supporters and potential supporters. It keeps them informed of what you are doing and acknowledges their belief in you. Don't forget to sell advertising, if possible, in your newsletter.

UNITED WAY TYPE FUNDING: The two main organiza-tions that do payroll deductions are The United Way, which collects from private business, state, and local government employees, and the CFC (Combined Federal Campaign), which collects from federal employees. If you are thinking about payroll deductions and meet their requirements as a socially beneficial organization, apply with the United Way and/or Combined Federal Campaign. Both distribute funds to qualified local community-oriented non-profit groups.

If you are a chartered organization, make sure your regional sponsor allows United Way type funding.

PAYROLL DEDUCTIONS: If your group doesn't qualify for United Way or CFC funding you can create your own payroll deduction plan. This is a complex way of getting pledges, but for larger community-oriented non-profit organizations, it works very well. Be prepared to do a lot of research and work to create your own payroll deduction federation. There are numerous books written on this topic and the scope of this particular project goes beyond what we can adequately cover here.

There are a number of effective ways to solicit cash donations and adding the right mix of these activities to your overall fundraising efforts is a good idea. So, put on your best outfit, grab the latest newsletter, breathe deep, pause and knock on that door!

> **Your group's newsletter should be treated as another kind of direct mail. A good rule of thumb to follow is that whenever you print anything, ask for funds.**

GRANT WRITING

It took the grant writing duo three months of research, study and writing to prepare the grant application and all its supporting documentation. Then they waited. When they were notified they had been awarded $15,000–all they'd asked for–they were jubilant. A great day for them and their group.

Truth is, most grants are not funded in full. But that's no reason not to explore this important revenue source. Keep in mind the other truth–not all grants take months of research and preparation. Some only require simple applications. Anyone with basic research and writing skills can learn to prepare credible grant applications and proposals.

> **A grant is an award made to a person or organization to help meet general expenses or costs for a specific project. Grants are usually awarded to an organization based on the strength of the proposal or application.**

A grant is an award made to a person or organization to help meet general expenses or costs for a specific project. Grants are usually awarded to an organization based on the strength of the proposal or application. Proposal writing cannot be separated from planning—a proposal is a plan.

Like all good plans, a proposal should explain why, what, where, when, who, how—and how much. It details these in a positive, concise, accurate, believable and clear manner. A good proposal does

this so well, funders then give money or other resources to support the project. Some proposals, called *Project Grants*, seek funds for one-time projects. Others, *General Operating Support* grants *(GOS)* seek funds for ongoing efforts.

It's important to answer questions before you research funding. What is the project's purpose? Its objectives? How much money do you need? What will it be used for?

Most funders fund projects that meet their criteria and help fulfill their missions. Plan some research time to find funding sources most appropriate for your group and its project. (Review *Goals & Planning*, page 7.) Check your local library to see what funding

source information it has. Some libraries have extensive local, state and national information. Others are limited to community funding sources. If your's is limited, it may be worth it for you to go to a larger library. Spend a whole day and take plenty of note paper.

Before going to the library, create a basic form to organize funder facts. Use headings for the funder's name, address, phone number, a contact name, the type of funder (local, corporate, etc.), kinds of grants funded, its priorities, the award dollar range, when grants are due, the recommended process and other needed information.

Small groups generally do not have time to submit applications to every source. Having this information in a systematic fashion lets you to quickly find funding sources most likely to support your organization.

PROSPECTING FUNDING SOURCES

Funds are primarily available to from three different sources: *government* (local, state, national), *corporate giving programs* and *foundations*.

GOVERNMENT: Government grants are available to individuals and organizations on local, state and national levels. Research to find grant programs for your project at your library.

One of the best federal funding resources is the *Catalog of Federal Domestic Assis-*

tance. Other federal resources include the *Federal Register*, published five days a week, and *Commerce Business Daily*, a daily listing of government procurements, potential contracts and awards.

CORPORATE: Corporate giving programs are in-house affairs. They make grants directly to organizations and/or individuals. A good source of corporate giving information is the *Corporate Philanthropy Report*, published by Craig Smith. Also seek local corporate funding opportunities.

Large corporations with a headquarters and several other operating locations often have several giving programs administered through both local and headquarter offices.

Local offices generally give smaller amounts–usually less than $250–to organizations/ projects in their operating location. Approval for these contributions is frequently made through the company's marketing department and may only take a couple of days to process. (However, it's a good idea to start at least six weeks before the funds are needed.)

Requests for these types of funds usually require a one-page letter specifying how much money is being requested, how it will be used and some background informa-tion on the organization.

To approach a company in your area, call their number listed in the phone book and ask the answering receptionist who handles company contributions. Once you are connected, introduce yourself and the organization you are with. Next ask for basic information,

> *Networking is a valuable tool for local fundraising. Find out who in your organization knows community leaders. Get them involved by asking them to sign letters of requests and make follow-up calls.*

such as to whom should the request be directed, what information to include, who makes the decisions and when.

Be sure to verify the company's mailing address (with Post Office Box) and phone number. *Do not* give detailed information about your organization or project unless asked.

Several days after you have sent your request, a follow-up call is in order. When you call, again introduce yourself and the organization you are with. Explain you sent a letter requesting a contribution and ask if it was received. Make yourself available to answer any questions and ask when they expect to make a decision.

Networking is a valuable tool for local fundraising. Find out who in your organization knows community leaders. Get them involved by asking them to sign letters of requests and make follow-up calls.

Once a request is funded, make sure you understand how the company wants to be recognized. Some like to make sure the community knows of their contribution and some would just as soon it not be publicized. Always send a thank-you note thanking the company for their contribution and verifying how the money was spent.

Requests over $250 are often a much more formal process through headquarters. Often awards of several thousand dollars are made to organizations/projects in one of a company's operating locations.

After you find the companies in your area, call or write their headquarters requesting guidelines, applications and/or annual reports. Chances are, you will be asked to complete an application form, provide a narrative with detailed budget information, submit background information on the organization and include your last audited statement.

Often grant materials are only reviewed on a quarterly basis (or less), so plan well in advance. If you are awarded funds, a final grant report is often due at the end of the project. It's important these reports, called *FGRs*, are submitted on time if you want to be considered in the future.

FOUNDATIONS: There are three general types of foundations that give funds to both non-profit groups and individuals: 1) Independent Foundations; 2) Community Foundations; and 3) Company-Sponsored Foundations. (See

Planned Giving, page 75).

The best source for foundation information is The Foundation Center. They publish a number of books including *The Foundation Directory*, the *National Data Book of Foundations*, *A Comprehensive Guide to Grantmaking Foundations*, etc. The Center also publishes guides to funding sources in special fields.

GENERAL RESOURCES: There are also a variety of general resources helpful to those writing proposals. The Grantsmanship Center publishes a free periodical, *The Whole Nonprofit Catalog* and other publications. Taft Publications is a commercial company that publishes a variety of directories, books and periodicals. The *Chronicle of Philanthropy* is another information-rich periodical.

PREPARING YOUR PROPOSAL

Before you prepare a grant for a specific funder be sure to contact that funder. Ask them to send you their guidelines and a grant application.

After you receive their information, review it, then decide if this funder is likely to be interested in your project. Remember, not all funders are interested in all projects.

When you find a good prospect, contact them again. Thank them for their materials. Introduce yourself and let them know you will be submitting a proposal. Describe your project (briefly!) and ask for any feedback/direction they may have. Many want to be part of the preparation process and will give insight on specific concerns and questions.

Follow-up with a letter of intent summarizing your project and advising them you'll soon submit a complete proposal to them.

It's essential each proposal meets the guidelines/criteria of the funder who receives it. Read thoroughly all guidelines, applications and other information available and follow it to the letter. Funders aren't inclined to give you money if you can't follow their directions.

Some funders do not provide guidelines. In these cases, make sure you understand their mission and the types of projects they fund. Use this information as your general guide when writing your proposal.

WRITING YOUR PROPOSAL

Always use positive, assertive language when writing. Leave no doubt about your intentions

> **It's essential each proposal meets the guidelines/criteria of the funder who receives it. Read thoroughly all guidelines, applications and other information available and follow it to the letter. Funders aren't inclined to give you money if you can't follow their directions.**

or methods. Don't say something should or might happen, say it *will* happen.

Different types of proposals require different kinds of information. Know what type of proposal you're writing and make sure you address all relevant issues. A review of *Chapter 1* is helpful now.

The following components are in almost all proposals.

SUMMARY: Your summary should be a persuasive one-page narrative to acquaint the funding source with your project. It should include a *Need Statement, Purpose Statement, Listed Objectives* and *Major Activities*.

BACKGROUND: Every funder wants to know to whom it's giving money. Concisely describe the organization's mission, goals, achievements, history, programs, services, members, clients and other funders. This is where you establish your credibility.

PROBLEM DEFINITION OR NEED: Establishing a credible need is a primary task for grant writers. If a proposed project, service or activity does not yet exist, a specific need must be clearly defined. It's not enough to suppose a need exists–you must document the need then show how your project offers a solution to the need.

Gather information from authoritative sources (letters of support, statistics, etc.) to help define the problem and document the need. Conduct library research and interview local authorities, noteworthy authors and professionals in the field.

PURPOSE AND OBJECTIVES: The overall *Purpose* (goals) of the proposal and the *Objectives* (specific aims) need to be clearly identified. This can be done in the introduction or a separate section titled *Outcome*.

The *Purpose* should clearly and concisely state the proposal's broad goal(s). It should address the stated needs and focus on what will be achieved, the project's benefits. Do not confuse the Purpose with means—Purpose is the intended outcome, not the activity to *achieve* that Outcome.

Objectives further clarify the Purpose. Put them in a numbered list of specific items the program will achieve. State them in measurable terms and include a basis for evaluation.

PROJECT DESIGN: The guts of the proposal, this section describes the project's major activities and how the project will operate.

Start with an overview explaining the philosophy, responsibilities and unique features of the project . Go from the overview to a detailed description of operations.

When describing the major activities of the project, keep in mind the previously stated Purpose, Objectives and Needs. Each and every one of the activities and/or major events should address the Need and achieve your Objectives, thereby fulfilling your Purpose.

Include all pertinent infor-mation. List all participants and explain the methods to be used. Describe the time frame in which the events will occur.

Also explain how the project will be managed. You may need an organizational chart, complete with job descriptions or a project council responsible for administrative policies and management decisions.

It is especially important to describe intended methods of evaluation. This gives the organization and the funder a way to determine the project's success. This will take some research to determine appropriate evaluation methods (Review *Chapters 1* and *2.*).

BUDGET: The Budget section should provide a fiscal explanation that supports the activities described in the Project Design section. Make sure your figures are precise and reasonable. (See *Service/Event Projected Budget*, on page 19.)

Many guidelines ask for estimated expenses in certain categories such as equipment, supplies, travel, personnel, etc.

If appropriate, include an income statement. Showing how a project can generate earned income greatly increases it's credibility. Don't forget to list all in-kind donations. These are the services and resources your group will provide, such as postage, long-distance phone calls, equipment use, etc.

Many funders want to know both how much money you are requesting and how it will be used. Make sure you request the right amount of money for the right reason. Be sure it makes sense in light of the overall budget. Some funders also request a budget narrative—additional paragraphs to further explain budget figures.

REVIEW: After you've written your proposal, review, proof, proof, proof and revise it—several times! Have others review it as well.

THE OVERALL PACKAGE: Check the guidelines again to determine exactly what to include. How many copies are needed? Consider a *Title Page, Table of Contents, Attachments* and a *Cover Letter*.

HOW FUNDERS EVALUATE: Most funders look at the following when evaluating a proposal: Cost-effectiveness/ Impact, Clarity, Completeness, Responsiveness, Consistency, Understanding of Problem and Service Methods, Effectiveness, Efficiency, Accountability and Realism.

WHEN YOUR PROPOSAL IS FUNDED: If your proposal is funded you will receive a letter and a contract. Read the contract carefully, make sure you understand it, then sign it and return it. Include a thank-you note. Follow up with all required final grant reports, etc.

WHEN YOUR PROPOSAL IS REJECTED: If your proposal is rejected, ask for a copy of the critique. Read it to learn what changes can help ensure funding in the future. Send a letter thanking the foundation for their time and consideration.

PLANNED GIVING

The keynote speaker at an endowment seminar related this true story to the audience: In an average city a nice community church had an older widow lady who was an active member of 50 years standing. One day the board was shocked to learn she had donated one million dollars to an international relief organization. Her health was failing and with her needs and those of her heirs provided for she decided to give her surplus cash to charity.

She overlooked the church simply because no one from the church ever asked. This is not to say her money was misspent, but that amount of money set up in a permanent endowment or trust would have helped cover the church's annual budget forever. What made the whole episode more tragic for the church was the fact that they constantly struggled to put on enough small fundraisers to keep their mission alive.

There are times when you'll find these kinds of financial diamonds in your own back yard. For universities, larger churches and large non-profit organizations this is the major

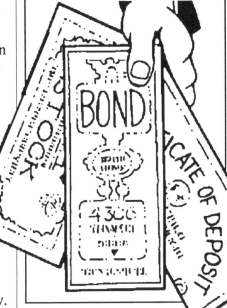

source of operating capital. Universities, for instance, have full-time staff that travel thousands of miles and spend thousands of dollars a year courting alumni on the benefits of setting up trusts, endowments and charitable life insurance for their alma mater. We are talking about *billions* (that's with a B) of dollars here.

> *Universities, for instance, have full-time staff that travel thousands of miles and spend thousands of dollars a year courting alumni on the benefits of setting up trusts, endowments and charitable life insurance for their alma mater. We are talking about billions (that's with a B) of dollars here.*

Now let's look at some basic information about how foundations, endowments, trusts, annuities and charitable life insurance policies work. There are entire volumes on each of these topics at your local library, so we'll only touch on some of the larger, overall

aspects here.

The thing to keep in mind is that some of this type of funding may well be available to benefit you and your non-profit group. Raising funds from these sources is in many ways different and more time consuming than producing traditional fundraising events. The upside of all this is when you're successful in this area you can create financial resources to keep your group in the black for decades into the future. The potential is worth the extra effort.

The more you research these areas, the more confusing it can become. You may encounter contradicting terms and definitions, changing tax laws, dozens of individual variations, different options and so on. After all, we are talking about investment institutions, banks, insurance companies, legal corporations, and tax laws. Please don't get discouraged by this because the common denominator is *very serious* money and a win-win situation for the donor and your organization. Approach this type of giving with persistence and, if needed, professional help.

If you feel one or more of these areas is a potential financial resource for your group, you'll need to do additional research. In general (there are a few exceptions here) your group will need to have I.R.S.

501 (c) tax exempt, non-profit organizational status (see *Getting Tax Exempt* on page 24).

Start at your local library to find out how these different funding programs work and how similar groups have been successful with them. Talk with people from local foundations, bank & trusts and life insurance companies for their suggestions and advice. Contact legal professionals, if you don't have one in your group, to answer your specific questions.

There are also professionals who specialize in obtaining this type of assistance. Their fees are a percentage of the gift. All of them are happy to help you get started. After all, this is their business. Oftentimes, initial consultation and information are free.

They want your potential business, accounts and commissions, so shop and compare. Check references and professional status (BBB, Chamber, etc.). You don't want your account to disappear to Brazil. Additional information sources can be found in *Appendix B*.

ENDOWMENTS:

Foundations give money in two basic ways: grants and endowments. Grants come from their general funds and must meet the criteria of the foundation.

For more information on grants see *Grant Writing* on page 71.

Now let's look at endowments. An endowment is created when a donation is made to a foundation and the donor specifies that the income generated from the donation's investments be paid to a specific organization or group. The assets' principle remains intact until a specific event occurs or perhaps forever.

> **The most likely candidate for your purposes is a community foundation. The United States has over 300 community foundations, so named because they are set up specifically to serve the needs of their community.**

There are several different types of endowments. Let's look at an example of a permanent endowment: Joe and Betty Smith, long-time supporters and members of Maintown's First Street Church, donate $100,000 in securities to Maintown's Community Foundation. An endowment is set up and the church receives all the annual income from the securities, basically, forever.

There are three categories of foundations: corporate, private, and community (a sub-category of government foundations). The most likely candidate for your purposes is a community foundation. The United States has over 300 community foundations, so named because they are set up specifically to serve the needs of their community. Community grants must benefit the community and community endowments

are usually set up to benefit local non-profit organizations.

Minimum account donations to foundations are at least $5,000. The foundation charges an annual fee, generally five to ten percent of the endowment's income, as their service/management fee. If the group designated by the donor folds or goes on to change its mission in a significant way, the foundation can change the endowment to benefit another similar group or a secondary designate. Ask for guidelines and any needed advice from your community foundation. It is their mission to help you.

TRUSTS:

Trust funds are similar in concept to endowment funds. A trust fund can be set up through most major bank and trust companies, security companies or insurance corporations. The financial institution acts as the independent trustee managing the account. Endowments can also be set up in some of the same institutions. Assets used for funding the trust can include: bank accounts, securities, limited partnerships, real estate, I.R.A.s, business interests, life insurance, promissory notes, personal property and qualifying retirement benefits.

There are several types of trusts and a number of ways to set up a specific trust. Two of the more common trusts are the estate trust and the immediate trust (donation).

The basic estate trusts are:

CHARITABLE REMAINDER UNITRUST: This trust fund pays a fluctuating income each year based on a fixed percentage of the market value of the assets. This income is paid to a non-charitable beneficiary for a specific number of years or sometimes the life of the beneficiary. At the end of this period, the trust assets and income are then passed on to the charity named.

CHARITY REMAINDER ANNUITY TRUSTS: The non-charitable beneficiary receives a fixed annual amount for life. Upon death of the beneficiary, the trust passes to the charity.

CHARITY REMAINDER TRUST: The non-charitable beneficiaries receive an income for a set number of years or life. The charity then receives the remaining assets.

IMMEDIATE OR STANDARD TRUST: Another common type of trust is the immediate or standard trust. This trust can be thought of as a donation to the charity of assets (cash, securities or property). This is similar to a specified foundation donation. A gift of assets is made to a trust company with proceeds going to the charity at a specified rate.

The trust company takes a small percentage to manage and disburse the funds. Here's an example of a standard trust: Joe and Betty Smith have $50,000 in certificates of deposit at Maintown's Bank. They transfer these CDs to a trust fund for the Maintown Boys and Girls Club, then interest is paid to the club each year. The Smiths could further specify whether to roll over the CDs at maturity (restricted possession) or allow the club to then take unrestricted possesion.

CHARITABLE LIFE INSURANCE:

Life insurance allows donors to make a significant donation to their favorite charity without depriving the donor's family of any estate assets. There are several advantages to using life insurance for charitable bequests. A few are:

> Decide your campaign goals and get any needed professional help. Many foundations, bank & trusts, legal corporations and life insurance companies will help you create your planned giving program and presentation.

• *If permanent insurance is used, then the gift is self-executing at a specific amount.*

• *State laws limiting certain bequests are avoided.*

• *Tax deductible premiums if the beneficiary is a charity.*

• *The rest of the donor's estate is unaffected.*

• *Life insurance payable to a charity is free from probate, creditors, will contests, etc.*

• *No federal estate tax.*

• *The gift is far greater than the cost of the premiums, especially after taxes.*

There are also many options available through life insurance companies for planned giving. Some involve the use of trusts. Without going into detail (each would take a page) there are:

GRUT, GRAT, and GRIT trusts, living trusts, QTIP trusts, shelter trusts, 2503 (c) trusts, replacement trusts, gift annuities, minor trusts, Clifford trusts and various shelters.

Most are variations of major trusts we looked at earlier. Insurance companies have information for the asking.

CREATING A PLANNED GIVING PROGRAM:

If your committee feels your membership and support base has untapped potential for planned giving, the following ideas should be helpful. Also review chapter 2 and *Membership Drives* on page 65 for ideas.

TARGET MARKET: Identify who is in the best position to consider making an endowment, trust or life insurance donation. Your most likely candidates are wealthier members/supporters, couples without children, senior citizen members, members with grown children, widows and widowers. Also consider a select percentage of the general population (well worth the additional research required).

STRATEGY: Consider your target market mix and how to best reach them: personal calls, visits, newsletters or direct mail. Decide your campaign

continued on page 80

COINS IN A FOUNTAIN

You're standing in a movie theater lobby and you see a wishing well. Your kids have spotted it, too, so you give each of them some change to toss into it. Whether you're doing this for fun, to pass the time before the show or just to amuse the kids—you've also just made a direct donation to the wishing well's sponsor.

Simply put, direct donations are when you solicit money outright. Indirect donations are goods or services donated and then sold to raise money. Many indirect donations are part of larger fund-raisers. For instance, a grocery may donate part of the food for a spaghetti supper you are sponsoring. Let's discuss some donation ideas that have worked for others.

> *Simply put, direct donations are when you solicit money outright. Indirect donations are goods or services donated and then sold to raise money. Many indirect donations are part of larger fundraisers.*

WISHING WELL

Basically, a wishing well is a fancy donation can. Wishing wells can be purchased or you can make your own.

Then find a video rental store, theater, grocery store, gas station or other business with lots of traffic that will let you put your machine at their location. Be sure to attach an attractive sign telling people who benefits from their donation.

One type of wishing well you can buy (check with a coin-

operated equipment dealer for details) is large and funnel-shaped, about three feet across at the top. It is made of fiberglass and has two chutes to insert coins. The coins roll around the funnel like a vortex, (whirl-pool) accelerating as they roll to the bottom and drop through a hole into a collection box.

This machine works with all coins from pennies to half dollars. Kids and adults love to watch the coins go. Sometimes people race each other or feed them through the starting chute in rapid succession. In the right location (theater lobbies are good), this can be a gold mine well worth the several-hundred-dollar price tag of the machine.

SPONSORSHIP

If your group is planning a major trip or event, you may

ask local businesses, church members or the PTA to help support your group by partially funding your undertaking (direct donation). To make their sponsorship a little more attractive, offer gifts (indirect donations) for different levels of giving (a T-shirt for a $20 donation, a dinner for two for a $100 donation, etc.)

After the event, it's nice to show your appreciation by giving a pot-luck dinner for your sponsors. Your group provides the meal and shows pictures or a slide/video presentation of the event. Set up a display table of souvenirs.

GUMBALL OR CANDY MACHINES

This idea has been around for a long time. Kids (and a lot of adults) find gumball or candy machines irresistible. Contact a wholesale store, a wholesale candy supplier or a coin-operated equipment dealer to purchase a machine. Next, find a high-traffic location similar to the wishing well for placement.

Keep the machine stocked with gum or candy that you purchase in bulk. You can sell one or two cents worth of candy or gum for 10 cents, or five cents worth for a quarter. Again, be sure to post a sign indicating who benefits from this indirect donation.

Check your local ordinances, but usually there are no restrictions on these machines.

They may cost about $100, but can generate $10 or more per week on an ongoing basis. If possible, set up a route with a few machines and check them several times per month.

Make sure the business has a member's phone number to call for service if there are any machine problems. In return for allowing you to place a machine, you can hand out their flyers or coupons at your group's social functions. See *Appendix A* for more details.

COIN BOX WITH CANDY

This idea is like the gumball machine and works strictly on donations. Have your members build nice small wooden boxes about the size of a shoebox, with a coin box on one end with a single slot. Put a small padlock on the coin box and fill the rest with assorted small wrapped candies. Make a sign to indicate who benefits from the purchase of the candy.

Place the box in local businesses (much like the gumball or candy machines) near their cash register. Put felt or plastic on the bottom of the box so it won't scratch the countertop.

Put boxes at different locations, checking them every two weeks. Empty the cash box so it doesn't get too full. Leave some candy with the business so they can fill it if it's low.

COIN DROP JAR

Take a large jar (gallon-size or larger) and cut a coin slot in the lid. Glue a shot glass in the bottom of the jar and fill the jar two-thirds full of water. Place it on a counter in a local business. Everyone who drops a coin into the shotglass gets a prize, also donated. Check the jar several times a month to empty the coins and replenish the supply of prizes at the business location. See *Appendix A* for prizes.

POPCORN SALES

There's something about the smell of freshly-popped popcorn that few can resist. Why not cash in on this reaction with a popcorn stand?

This fundraiser takes some prep work: primarily finding a place to have your popcorn stand as well as purchasing

---

LARGE QUANTITY POPCORN RECIPE

- 1 cup popcorn
- ¼- ½ cup oil (or a butter/popcorn oil mix)
- ½ t salt (or popcorn salt mixed)

Sprinkle the salt over the unpopped popcorn before putting it into the hot oil in your machine. Keep about 10 to 20 bags of hot popcorn ahead at all times.

---

your supplies. To actually run the project on a busy day takes only three or four volunteers.

Begin by contacting the manager of a store (building supply stores on Saturdays are a good option) to see if they will allow you to set up a popcorn stand in their store on a given day for specific hours. Explain that you'll provide all the supplies and they will do nothing except provide you a spot and access to electricity.

First and foremost, you will need a commercial-size popcorn machine. You'll also need an extension cord or two and a table. Place a sign or banner at your stand clearly indicating your prices and identifying your group so your customers will know who benefits from the popcorn sales.

Next, line up your supplies. Purchase the popcorn and oil in bulk. Popcorn can be purchased from commercial food suppliers in 10 to 50 pound bags. Oil can be bought in half gallons. A household-sized container of salt should be plenty. Use some butter flavored popcorn oil, or specialty popcorn salt, also purchased in bulk, to add a little zing to your popcorn.

White food bags for your popcorn can be bought in 500-count packages from paper/party goods stores. Lunch bag-size bags or smaller are ideal for popcorn. Price your popcorn according to the bag size. Sell a lunch-bag size of popcorn for about one dollar.

In addition to popcorn, you can sell cold lemonade or soda. Buy these drinks in bulk and sell them by the cup. Be sure you have plenty of ice on hand! Or, simply fill a cooler with cans of drinks, and sell them by the can. Have a trash can for bags and a separate container for recyclable aluminum cans.

This project can be effectively run by three or four volunteers. Two can pop the corn and bag it while the others work as cashiers. If you're

continued on next page

PLANNED GIVING

continued from page 77

goals and get any needed professional help. Many foundations, bank & trusts, legal corporations and life insurance companies will help you create your planned giving program and presentation.

PROMOTION: Why do you need the money? Put together an information packet to explain it all. Tell your organization's story, include budgets, your mission statement, future goals and plans to achieve those goals. Include flyers, booklets and all relevant information from professionals you've consulted with.

HOLD A SEMINAR: Invite everyone who is interested. Line up presenters to cover the areas that will work for you and your audience from endowments, trusts and life insurance. Make the seminar informative and interesting. Present planned giving options. Be sure to cover how these gifts will (or won't) affect remaining assets and always include tax advantages.

Cover your group's mission, future goals and how your attendees can help in the creation of win-win benefits for them and your group. Use handouts, slides, charts, and overheads to show and tell. Have free refreshments and snacks. Set up appointments and follow through. Also don't forget to follow up with people who couldn't attend the seminar but expressed an interest.

This kind of fundraising can take a lot of time to complete but, when successful, these substantial gifts can insure the viability of your group and its mission far into the future.

> *Cover your group's mission, future goals and how your attendees can help in the creation of win-win benefits for them and your group. ... This kind of fundraising can take a lot of time to complete but, when successful, these substantial gifts can insure the viability of your group and its mission far into the future.*

---

continued from preceding page

selling popcorn for more than four hours, break your workforce into shifts, with three or four volunteers per shift.

Now get popping!

RESTAURANT SPONSOR DAY

Ask a local restaurant to sponsor your group for a day, a weekend or a week. This works best if you pick a day or time of the year when the restaurant is usually slow.

Promote the sponsorship period to friends, neighbors, classmates, relatives and others. Typically, you can ask for 10% of all receipts during this period. In return for sponsoring you, your group does all of the bussing, clean-up, etc. during the sponsorship. You could also offer to clean windows, wait tables, fill water glasses and coffee cups.

Or, simply ask the restaurant to give your group 10% of their receipts during a specific period. You'll publicize their sponsorship and generate a lot of business for them.

For example, you could have a *Smith County Youth Fellowship Night* at various local restaurants. Publicize the night well in advance and encourage people to dine at these restaurants on the sponsorship night. This will increase their sales for the night and also net your group 10% of their receipts.

STORE SPONSOR DAY

This idea works in much the same fashion as the restaurant sponsor day. For a set percentage of their receipts for the day, (1 or 2%) your group will provide carry-out service for the grocery. Or they can wash windows, mop floors, etc.

Again, this must be promoted heavily to be successful. Post notices at the store, announce it at meetings and in local newsletters. Encourage friends, neighbors and relatives to do the bulk of their shopping at the sponsoring grocery.

CONCLUSION: These are just a few ways to solicit direct and indirect donations. Use these ideas as a starting point and do some brainstorming with your group. You'll be amazed at the number of donation ideas your group will come up with!

GENERAL SELLING TIPS

These fundamental, time-tested tips will help you and your group sell your fundraisers more effectively. They are designed to help the first-time salesperson get up to speed as well as serve as refreshers for the life-time adult professional. Read and think about each point before you go out to sell.

1. Remember you are selling to a living, feeling person and treat each one as such.

2.. When dealing with people, be honest and treat them with integrity. Your honesty and integrity helps create positive public opinion for you and your group.

3. People love to buy, but hate to be sold to. Avoid hard-sell tactics; help them buy instead. Think of your job as helping your customers feel good about buying from your group.

4. The best salespeople have fun and enjoy selling. They help customers buy.

5. Be conscious, alert and focused on each sale as it is occurring. Do not become a robot repeating a memorized sales pitch word for word. Remember your job is to help your customer feel good about helping your group's fundraising effort.

6. When you get a "no", remember it is only a word. Do not attach any emotions to it. A "no" is just a stepping-stone to a" yes". Just say, " Thank you for your time," and go on to your next sale.

7. People feel best doing something they want to do, not something they're forced to do. This is true for customers as well as salespeople. Relax, be friendly, feel good about what you're doing.

8. Rehearse your sales technique with others. Switch roles back and forth as buyer and seller. In each role visualize a successful conclusion. When you're out selling, choose to be successful.

9. Imagine you are the buyer. How do you feel and respond to the items offered and the sales pitch used? Also ask friends and relatives for their opinions about sale items and sales pitches.

10.. What are your personal goals for this fundraising event? Write out your goals and your sales pitch on a single sheet of paper. If you don't have any set goals or a defined sales approach, write one or two of your best ideas. There are no wrong answers.

11. While you create your own reality, if you focus on things going wrong, they probably will. Instead, focus on all the things that can go right. See your reality as positive, dynamic and upbeat.

12. If you feel uncomfortable, do a few easy sales first . Start with relatives and friends. With a few of these sales under your belt, your sales pitch will be polished and your confidence up. Now go out and sell to the world.

13. Ask people who successfully sell similar items in fundraisers for their sales suggestions and tips. Find out what they did right, what they did wrong and how they would do it differently today.

TELEMARKETING

Telemarketing techniques can be used with various fundraisers or to generate outright donations. There are several approaches used by professional marketers, but we'll just outline a few ideas that generally work well for groups.

To make telemarketing really effective for your group, limit calls to your members' immediate neighborhoods. Now you'll be able to identify yourself as a local group active in community life. This marketing strategy makes your community standing a powerful sales tool.

Let's begin to create a selective phone list. Use a local map to identify all the street names in the area you'll contact. Then use a Polk Directory (your public library has one) to look up and photocopy all the names, addresses and phone numbers of people living in the area you've chosen.

Next, assign each member of your group a list of people to call (use the Polk photocopies here), preferably in their own neighborhood. The idea is to make your phone calls more personal. People generally dislike telemarketing, but are often open to a call from someone living in the area and

working on a fundraising project for a local group.

A sample neighborhood telemarketing call may go like this, "Hi, I'm Sally, I'm a member of the XYZ High School Band. We're selling concert tickets to raise money so the band can play in our state finals. Will you help us by buying some tickets?"

You can focus your selling efforts on members, neighbors, friends and relatives. Others to contact are local PTA/PTOs or families with children in the school system. Always emphasize they'll be supporting a group in their community.

Have callers use the *Telemarketing Sheets* on pages 84 and 85 to keep a log of all calls made and their responses. Ask your volunteers to print legibly.

> *To make telemarketing really effective for your group, limit calls to your members' immediate neighborhoods. Now you'll be able to identify yourself as a local group active in community life.*

If you can't read their information, it's hard to collect it all.

SOME TELEMARKETING COURTESY "DOS" AND "DON'TS":

- *Do all your calling during reasonable hours.*
- *Do keep your message short and to the point.*
- *Don't ever try to pressure anyone into buying.*
- *Do identify yourself as well as your group.*
- *Do be courteous and polite at all times.*
- *Do verify the spelling of their name and address if they donate.*
- *Do sound upbeat and cheerful.*
- *Don't be cutesie or fake.*
- *Do speak slowly, carefully and clearly.*
- *Do rehearse your message several times before you make your first call; use written notes to assist you.*

Before you make that first phone call, have a rehearsed script ready. Begin each call by identifying both yourself and your group, then state your purpose. Be specific about what you're selling or the kind of donation you seek.

If they're going to buy or donate, be sure you verify their name, address and phone number. Always make specific arrangements to get their money as well as deliver their goods to them. Be sure to thank them for their help.

MASTER TELEMARKETING SHEET

Project _____   Date _____

Group Leader _____   Telephone _____

Use this Master Telemarketing Sheet to record totals from individual member's telemarketing sheets

MEMBER'S NAME	PHONE	TOTAL UNITS	TOTAL $ AMOUNT	TOTAL $ PAID

MAKE AS MANY COPIES OF THIS PAGE AS NEEDED

TELEMARKETING SHEET

Project _____

Date _____

Person In Charge _____

Telephone _____

Member's Name _____

Use this sheet for tracking your fundraising phone calls. Be polite, courteous and verify their address. If you get a recording or no answer, simply hang up and try again later.

NAME, ADDRESS & PHONE	NO ANSWER	NO	YES	ADDRESS VERIFIED	AMOUNT

MAKE AS MANY COPIES OF THIS PAGE AS NEEDED

TELEMARKETING SHEET

Project _____   Member's Name _____

NAME, ADDRESS & PHONE	NO ANSWER	NO	YES	ADDRESS VERIFIED	AMOUNT

MAKE AS MANY COPIES OF THIS PAGE AS NEEDED

Advertising is a dynamic force in our economic life as well as a big business. It can also be a growing source of funds for your group. Advertising can be sold for nearly all printed pieces, from a pancake break-fast flyer to a deluxe business directory. Advertising sales can generate additional funds from every fundraising event.

There are many approaches to advertising sales, ranging from fairly simple to huge and complicated undertakings. Let's look at a few:

PUBLICATIONS

When schools sell yearbooks, they make money from the sale of the book as well as the ad-vertisements that are sold to local businesses. If your group is producing a cookbook or a theme book as a fundraiser, why not sell some ads?

Advertising is generally sold by the ⅛ page, ¼ page, ½ page, or whole page. Ads can also be sold by the line or by column inch. Talk to your printer before you set up your advertising rates. Be sure to charge enough to cover your cost of printing the advertising as well as to make a profit.

Before selling ads, have some samples ready to show businesses that don't already have ads. Business cards and old ads can be cut and pasted to make new ads. Again, check with your printer for sugges-tions and cost guidelines.

DIRECTORIES

There are many kinds of direc-tories your group can create and market. You could sell a membership directory with ad space. This type of directory would be sold only to your members. If you want to produce a business directory on a larger scale, you can approach it as a school- church- or neighbor-hood-wide project with listings for businesses, services and hobby clubs.

Use your target market as a guideline to help you approxi-mate the size, paper and cover stock of your finished product. For instance, a membership di-rectory will be smaller and often printed on less expensive paper than a neighborhood or city directory filled with ads.

Get a quote from your printer to determine the cost of having the directory printed and bound. From there you'll be able to decide what to charge for listings and ads to cover your costs and make a profit.

This information also tells you how many listings and ads you must sell to generate a profit. You may want to have several price ranges for listings: one for businesses and profes-sionals and a lesser rate for youths offering babysitting or household work.

Your printer can also assist you in working out a time frame for the project. He can advise you as to how long it will take to produce the direc-tory once you have given him all of the infor-mation. Set a specific deadline when all listings and ads must be submitted and paid for.

Make sure all members selling listings have the latest detailed information regarding ad prices, listing prices, art requirements, dead-lines, etc. You will also need a form to collect information for the directory. See *Ad Sales Worksheet* on page 87.

To make your directory really successful, be sure you contact everyone in your target

> *Advertising can be sold for nearly all printed pieces, from a pancake breakfast flyer to a deluxe business directory. Advertising sales can generate additional funds from every fundraising event.*

continued on page 88

AD SALES WORKSHEET

Group's Name

Ad To Be Placed In: Number of Copies:

Sales person   Date:

Name of Business: Address:

Contact Person   Phone

Nature of Business/service   Hours:

SIZE OF AD	PRICE	SIZE OF AD	PRICE
Business Card	$	1/2 Page (_____"X_____")	$
1/8 Page (_____"X_____")	$	Full Page (_____"X_____")	$
1/4 Page (_____"X_____")	$		

FEE $

AMOUNT PAID $

SIGNED: BUSINESS CONTACT   BALANCE DUE $

SIGNED: SALESPERSON

Please pay balance due within 30 days. Make checks payable to: _____

Copy for ad: attach sheets, examples, business cards, etc., as needed

MAKE AS MANY COPIES OF THIS PAGE AS NEEDED

market. This includes every member of your church, school or neighborhood. Contact them by mail, phone or in person.

As you gather listings and ads, you'll need to separate them into directory sections (businesses, services, hobbies, etc). Then put the listings in alphabetical order within their categories. If you're unsure about which category a listing goes in, call the person buying the listing for their suggestion.

You can charge a fee for the directories or give them to all participants free, depending upon your profit margin.

PROGRAMS

Another opportunity to sell advertising is in the program for an event you're doing. This can be a show, a concert, parents' night or another fundraiser. You don't need a big program to sell ads. A simple one- or two-page program with ads or coupons on the back would suffice. These ads can help offset the cost of printing and, if you sell enough, also generate some extra funds. To get your sales force going, see the *Ad Sales Worksheet* form on page 87.

Programs can be as plain or fancy as your needs and budget allow. For a small event, a program can be carefully laid out using a computer or typewriter and printed on a photocopying machine.

For a larger event, you may go to a printer for his assistance in creating a more professional-looking program. Cost information from the printer will help determine the ad prices you'll need to charge.

GENERAL NOTES ON SOLICITING

When you contact small businesses about placing an ad, remember to look at the cost from their viewpoint. In marketing, advertising is viewed on a per-person-reached cost basis and percentage of responses.

Be courteous and upbeat, no matter what kind of response you get. If they buy an ad, be sure to send a copy of their ad in the finished program along with a note thanking them for their support of your project.

Encourage your members and supporters to patronize businesses who buy your ads. Treat your supporters well and they're likely to look kindly upon your cause the next time.

CHAPTER 4
FESTIVE EVENTS

CHAPTER NOTES:

ATHONS

Billy played his guitar on Saturday night and helped his group rock in over $90. Susie jumped rope for 45 minutes and raised $45 for her group. Fred bowled a 150 and made $30 for his group. "Athons" are fun, popular fundraisers with a limitless number of variations.

In an Athon, each participant signs up his or her sponsors to pledge a set fee per minute, mile, basket, bowling pin, or whatever it is they are doing during their event.

For example, in a bowl-a-thon, sponsors pledge a monetary amount for each pin bowlers knock down in a specific game. After the event, each participant contacts all of his or her sponsors and collects their pledges. Make sure your participants are aware that they are responsible for collecting all their pledges after the event. Be sure to give them a very specific but realistic deadline for turning in their pledges.

To begin your own athon project, first choose the type of event you wish to hold (bowl-, skate-, walk-, rock-athon). Then decide where to host the event, keeping in mind:

• *Is it an indoor or an outdoor event?*

• *How much space do you need?*

• *What kind of equipment is needed?*

• *Will participants bring their own equipment (skates, rocking chairs, basketballs)?*

• *Are there any local health and safety regulations for this kind of event?*

Next, set a date and time. List a rain date or alternate location if it's an outdoor event. Avoid scheduling your event during another popular event, unless it's coordinated to work with the other activity.

Always schedule your event to be convenient for the majority of your anticipated participants. Determine how many players you can handle and, if needed, limit the number.

Get sponsors to donate refreshments or buy them at cost.

SUPPLIES & EQUIPMENT

Provide all necessary equipment for participants or be sure they understand they are to provide their own.

Hand out pledge forms well in advance of the event, so your participants will have time to sign up plenty of sponsors. (see *Pledge Sheet* page 92). If participants are under-age, their parents may need to sign a release form.

Have water and/or other refreshments available. The type of refreshments should be dictated by the nature of the event (i.e. water or Gatorade for walk-a-thons).

Have all kitchen supplies on hand to serve refreshments and make sure your trash cans are readily available.

Set up tables for food/drinks. Be sure to have ice or some form of refrigeration if you're serving cold drinks. Always have first-aid supplies on hand.

MANPOWER

You'll need lots of participants with sponsors. Scorekeepers and "check" people are also needed to verify scores, times, etc. First-aid personnel should be on hand in case of an emergency and you'll need even more people to work in the refreshment areas. Your group will have lots of fun raising funds with your own *Athons!*

> *"Athons" are fun, popular fundraisers with a limitless number of variations. ...In an Athon, each participant signs up his or her sponsors to pledge a set fee per minute, mile, basket, bowling pin, or whatever it is they are doing during their event.*

PLEDGE SHEET

Event Name _____   Member's Name _____

Group _____   Address _____

     Telephone _____

A NOTE TO OUR SPONSORS:

Thank you for contributing to our group's fundraiser. The pledge you make is on a per unit basis times the total units accomplished (miles, time, number, etc.). You can make a lump sum donation if you wish, instead of a per-unit pledge. Please don't use fractions of cents.

NAME	ADDRESS (STREET, CITY, ZIP)	PHONE	PLEDGE PER UNIT	TOTAL UNITS	TOTAL PLEDGE	TOTAL DONATED	TOTAL PAID

MAKE AS MANY COPIES OF THIS PAGE AS NEEDED

PLEDGE SHEET

Event Name _____   Member's Name _____

NAME	ADDRESS (STREET, CITY, ZIP)	PHONE	PLEDGE UNIT	TOTAL UNITS	TOTAL PLEDGE	TOTAL DONATED	TOTAL PAID

MAKE AS MANY COPIES OF THIS PAGE AS NEEDED

MASTER PLEDGE SHEET

Event Name _____   Date _____

Group Leader _____   Telephone _____

Use this Master Pledge Sheet to record totals from individual member's pledge sheets.

MEMBER'S NAME	PHONE	TOTAL/PLEDGE PER UNIT	TOTAL UNITS	TOTAL PLEDGED	TOTAL DONATED	TOTAL PAID

MAKE AS MANY COPIES OF THIS PAGE AS NEEDED

BIG BUS SPORTS TRIP

It's the last minute of the big game, everyone in the crowded stadium is on their toes. The pass is good, the touchdown scored, the crowd goes wild. And your group is there in the midst of all the excitement! This kind of event is a lot of fun for sports fans in your area. It does require some careful advanced planning, but it can be a very good source of income.

First you'll need to decide what sports event your group would like to attend. Contact the home team's box office and get game dates, ticket availability and cost. Buy your tickets in a block to enhance the group's feelings of togetherness.

Depending upon the length of the trip and the time of day you'll be leaving, you may want to serve coffee, juice, sodas, doughnuts and/or other sorts of snack foods to your sports fans.

Next, call several local charter bus companies and get their costs for a bus and driver to take your group to and from the event. If you're serving any food or drink, make sure your bus has a restroom.

Once you have your game, bus and refreshment costs figured, be sure to add a mark-

> *This kind of event is a lot of fun for sports fans in your area. It does require some careful advanced planning, but it can be a very good source of income.*

up (your profits) to go to your group for organizing the trip.

Find out when you must confirm both game and bus tickets and the deposits they need. Give your group as much selling time as possible *before* the deadline when your deposit will no longer be refunded. All tickets must be prepaid, since you'll need to prepay both game and bus tickets.

Advance publicity is a *must* for this project. Put up posters and make announcements at local high schools, colleges, grocery stores, etc. Have group members spread the word with friends and relatives. Include in all publicity: date of event, cost, time and place of departure (usually a centrally-located

mall lot), game time and place/time of return. Be sure to mention other perks (like free breakfast) included.

SUPPLIES

After the event tickets and a bus to get your crowd there, the only other supplies you'll need are snack foods and equipment to hold/heat/refrigerate all this. If it's a long bus trip, schedule a stop so everyone can get off the bus and buy their own meal.

The bus company will handle the rest of the details: driver, parking, etc.

MANPOWER

You'll need a committee to contact game ticket vendors and bus companies. Price shop, ask if any discounts are available. This committee is responsible for paying the game ticket vendor and bus company from monies collected.

More than anything, you need volunteers to sell tickets. Get everyone in the group to participate. The project chair should keep a list of all who've reserved tickets and payments made. On event day, this person should bring the list and check off everyone as they arrive. Be specific about your departure time. Advise everyone to be there at least 15 minutes early to guarantee a prompt exit. Enjoy the game!

"**B**ingo!" The shout echoes across the crowded room. A disappointed sigh rises from those only a number away. But that's okay too, the next game always looms just ahead.

Before your group decides to sponsor a bingo event, be sure to check its legal status in local and state ordinances. Bingo is a popular fundraiser in many areas, but illegal in others. Also see how your group's charter deals with bingo. For instance, Scouts don't consider bingo an acceptable fundraising activity.

If bingo is both legal and acceptable for your group, it can also be a fun and effective way to generate money. To begin, set a date and time for your bingo. Depending on the number of games you'll have, your bingo session can run for several hours or more.

Next, decide if you'll give money or prizes to winners. If you're giving prizes, get as many donated as possible. Gear your prizes toward the age group of anticipated players. Baked goods, seasonal ornaments and wreaths, toys, games, table decorations, all are good bingo prizes.

If you plan to award cash prizes, calculate how much to give each game winner. For instance, if you have 100 bingo

> *Before your group decides to sponsor a bingo event, be sure to check its legal status in local and state ordinances. Also see how your group's charter deals with bingo.*

players paying $1.00 for five cards, you'll have a gross income of $500.00. If you plan to keep 50% of the income your group keeps $250.00 and has $250.00 available for cash prizes.

If you have ten games, you can give each winner $25.00. Or, give winners of the first nine games $20.00, then give the final winner the remaining $70.00 in a "cover-all" game.

Make it clear to all players at the beginning what is and is not a winning card (four corners, diagonal, straight, picture frame, little picture frame, etc.) Also, set a standard procedure to deal with a tie (split the winnings, or give both a special prize).

You can have "special games" at various intervals. Specials can be the letter "X", a double bingo, the number "7," etc. A typical bingo has twenty regular games with special games at every fifth game.

SUPPLIES & EQUIPMENT

If your group doesn't have a bingo kit, you can borrow, rent, or buy one from a party supply or novelty store. If you plan regularly-scheduled bingos, consider buying your own. If it's a one-time or once-a-year event, it may be more cost-effective to borrow or rent a kit.

You'll need a hall, gym or cafeteria with tables and chairs to hold your bingo. A school or church facility for a nominal fee or rent-free is your best option. If you are having concessions, you'll need a kitchen to handle the food and drinks you're providing.

Keep it simple: Sell soda pop, coffee and some snacks: pretzels, chips, or cookies. These items take minimal preparation and equipment. You will need an institutional-size coffee pot, cups, sugar, creamers, stirrers, and coffee. Soda pop can be bought in cans and kept on ice in coolers.

You could provide separate recycling bins for cans. Buy snacks in bulk and bag them in small plastic bags to be sold. Don't forget the napkins.

Keep your concessions simple and they'll provide easy additional income from your event. Have a change box with lots of change for the concession stand. Make a poster listing all your offerings along

continued on next page

ARTS & CRAFTS FAIR

You're walking through a room filled with people. At one table, a vendor shows her hand-crafted jewelry. Further down the aisle, you see packages of freshly-baked cookies and breads. At the next table, an artist displays oil paintings. Welcome to the *Blueberry Hill Arts & Crafts Fair!*

Producing your own arts & craft fair can be a profitable, fun way to raise funds. And, done with a certain sense of style, it could become an anticipated annual event in your community. Contact artists and craftspeople from your church, local schools and universities, and the community at large to participate. Rent booth spaces for a reasonable fee. If you are providing the tables and their coverings, include this cost in the booth rental charge.

You can divide the show into different areas: plants, home-baked goodies, clothes, paintings, ceramics, jewelry, etc. Keep in mind when selecting a site that you'll need plenty of room for displays as well as enough parking for the anticipated crowd.

Advertise, advertise, advertise! Use every available media for PSAs, buy as many ads as you can afford, create brochures and posters to hand out

> *Producing your own arts & craft fair can be a profitable, fun way to raise funds. And, done with a certain sense of style, it could become an anticipated annual event in your community.*

at local businesses. If your group does low-cost direct mail (see *Non-Profit Mailing* on page 29), mail to your list of supporters. Borrow or rent lists from other organizations and mail to them also.

Your group can charge an entrance fee, perhaps $1, but entrance fees can limit the number of people who attend. A refreshment stand run by your group would be a welcome addition to the fair and will generate some extra cash for your group. Remember to have your own information/ membership booth at the event.

This is another event that can generate ever larger amounts of income for your group year after year.

---

continued from preceding page
with their prices.

If you're giving prizes instead of cash, you'll need to make, purchase or have them donated. Get prizes that appeal to your targeted market (for example: toys, games and candy for kid bingo games; hand-made craft items, decorations, baked goods for adults).

If you're giving cash prizes, have plenty of $1.00 bills and coins on hand so you can pay winners in exact change.

Target your publicity to your specific market. Create flyers and posters, then saturate your market. Announce your bingo at as many meetings and other events as possible.

MANPOWER

You'll need volunteers to set up, tear down and clean up the room where your bingo is held.

You'll also need several cashiers at the door, selling bingo cards for a set price.

Appoint your caller. Make sure this person has a good strong voice that carries well in a crowded room.

Use "runners" to deliver the prizes to game winners. You can have winners come up to collect their prizes but that slows things down.

If you're having non-cash prizes, you'll need a committee to get prizes donated or bought at wholesale prices. If there is the time and energy, hand-made items are nice prizes, too.

OK, let the games begin!

CARNIVALS

Remember those long ago days when your school was magically transformed into a fantasy setting for its annual carnival? Your group can help create these kinds of exciting memories for a whole new generation and raise some funds by holding a carnival.

A well-planned and produced carnival will attract large crowds of people of all ages. Get your volunteers together, put on your brainstorming caps and create a great carnival!

First you need a catchy carnival theme. The theme should tie in with your group's mission, some aspect of your city, a holiday or season such as *Saint Joseph School's Spring Strawberry Fest*. Keep your food, attractions and activities consistent with your theme. This makes the carnival more interesting and memorable.

Plan special events or attractions to bring your theme to life. Book as much live entertainment as your budget allows. Musicians, magicians, puppeteers, artists, storytellers and chefs all generate a greater public interest. Arts and crafts areas and/or food contests are also strong attractions.

> *The theme should tie in with your group's mission, some aspect your city, a holiday or season such as Saint Joseph School's Spring Strawberry Fest. Keep your food, attractions and activities consistent with your theme.*

In our area we have an annual *Johnny Appleseed Festival*. All festival folks dress in early 19th century garb and speak period language. You can buy apple pies, apple slices, apple butter, caramel apples, apple dumplings, apple nearly everything. You get the idea!

A well thought-out theme can multiply the effectiveness of your promotional efforts.

Once your theme is defined it's time to decide when and where to hold the carnival. As with all fundraising events, avoid conflicts with holidays, area festivals, sports, or other popular activities in your area.

With a firm date set, scout around for the best possible location. A church or school is an excellent carnival location. And each of these institutions has a built-in audience.

Be sure you have adequate parking. If your event is outdoors, lay out your carnival so there is absolutely no confusion about where to park and where the carnival is being held.

Arrange for tents, an indoor location or alternate date in case of rain. When looking for a location, remember a paved parking lot is easier to work and walk on than a muddy field if the weather turns foul.

Let your budget and available manpower help you decide what activities, attractions, rides, games and food to have at your carnival. Rides generally increase dollar volume but they also increase liabilities.

After you have all the major details of your carnival locked in place, it is time to plan your marketing strategy. A strong mix of free and paid publicity is vital in drawing a large crowd. For more detailed information about this entire process, see *Marketing* on page 44.

If you decide to have amusement rides, contact several vendors for quotes. Check out their business credentials and ask for references. Call all references and see how they feel about the ride vendor.

Ask if the company's rides were clean and safe with a well-maintained appearance. Find out about the fee or percentage the ride vendor keeps. This can help you decide if the rides fit your carnival budget.

Games are always popular.

You can create, borrow or buy games. Local party & equipment rental companies rent wall tents, dunk tanks, moon walks and similar equipment.

Find a local coin-operated equipment dealer who will equip a game tent with pinballs, video games and will split the profits 50/50. A well equipped game tent can generate several hundred dollars a day in profits.

Other carnival attractions to consider could include:

- *Bingo (page 96)*
- *Food Stands (page 127)*
- *Cake Walk (page 100)*
- *Dunk Tank (page 106)*
- *Money Tree (page 115)*
- *Barbecues (page 119)*
- *Arts & Crafts (page 97)*
- *Fishing Pond (page 107)*
- *Pocket Lady (page 107)*

MAZES: Young children love 'em. First design your maze on paper. Following this layout, set bales of straw 5 to 6 foot high. Clearly mark the entrance and exit and let the kids enjoy!

Mazes generally have a small fee or are free. Try to borrow straw bales from a local farmer. Return all undamaged bales and purchase the balance.

TUG OF WAR: This event is most fun when the opposing teams tug over a small body of water or a muddy area. A grassy field can be fun, too.

The first thing you need is a strong rope long enough to cross the area in question. Next mark the "safe" area on each side with chalk or paint so everyone knows exactly where it ends. Charge a small entry fee and give simple prizes (extra tickets, small gifts or certificates) to the winning team.

> *Invite other groups to rent space and set up their own events at your carnival. ... Each additional group will make your carnival a bigger event, spread out responsibilities and boost attendance.*

An alternate twist to your basic tug-o-war is a fire hose competition. You'll need the support of a local fire department to provide a firetruck with pumps, water, hoses and rainsuits. You provide the location.

A paved area is best, as this competition gets very, *very* soggy. A heavy-duty clothesline is set up approximately 10 feet above the ground. A large rubber ball with a loop (like a tetherball) is hung on the line. Each team uses water from its hose to push the ball to their opponents' end of the line. This is good, clean, wet fun for all!

GRAB BAGS: These perennial favorites always surprise. When choosing your grab bag price, make sure it's reasonable for your crowd or you won't have many buyers.

Buy grab bag supplies in bulk. When assembling the grab bags keep the average dollar value 20% to 40% lower than your price. Have some extra-nice items in a few grab bags so some of your customers get really great prizes.

Gear the grab bag contents to your projected audience. For a children's carnival, fill the grab bags with small toys, candy, gum, snacks, pencils, stickers, erasers, etc. For an adult crowd, try small kitchen items, stationery, foods, snacks, carwash tickets, coupons, etc.

FOOD: Foods are always popular carnival feature. Your culinary offerings should reflect the overall theme and can be as simple as hot dogs and soda or more specialized like apple dumplings and strawberry shortcake. Specialty foods like hot pretzels, cotton candy, elephant ears, caramel apples, ka-bobs and pizza-by-the slice usually sell well. Bake sales are popular, too. Be sure to have lots of iced tea, coffee, lemonade and soft drinks.

OTHER GROUPS: Invite other groups to rent space for their own events at your carnival. If it's a church carnival, make sure other church groups and clubs have a chance to sponsor a booth or event. Approach the church choir, scouting and youth groups, women's and men's clubs. Get all other non-profit church groups involved.

Each additional group will make your carnival a bigger event, spread out responsibilities and boost attendance. Get as many like-minded groups together as possible and you'll have a memorable carnival!

On the big day try your hand at ring toss, eat an elephant ear and have a great time!

CAKE WALK

A John Phillips Sousa march is storming away. Suddenly it stops and everyone in the circle scrambles for a chair. They all look at the delicious cakes and wonder who will get to pick the cake of their choice this time. It's cake walk time!

A cake walk is an exciting, festive way to sell cakes and other baked goods. This project is especially popular with the younger set. It's great for pre-schoolers or grade school students at fairs and carnivals.

Set up a circle of 10 to 20 chairs, depending upon the size of your crowd. Number each chair on the back and front with paper tags, one number per chair. Next number tickets to correspond with the chairs. Sell just enough tickets to fill all the chairs. You're now ready for your first "walk".

Begin the music (a portable tape player works great for this event). As the music plays, all of the participants walk around inside the circle of chairs. After a short period of time stop the music. Then each "cake walker" jumps into the nearest chair while you draw the winning number out of the bowl or hat.

Next, call out the winning number. The person in the chair with that number wins the cake of his or her choice.

> *A cake walk is an exciting, festive way to sell cakes and other baked goods. This project is especially popular with the younger set. It's great for pre-schoolers or grade school students at fairs and carnivals.*

SUPPLIES & EQUIPMENT

You'll need lots and lots of cakes and/or other baked goodies. Ask all group members to bring one or more cakes, have even more donated by family members, friends and sponsors. With all the prizes donated, this is a very low cost event to produce.

You'll need 10 to 20 chairs, depending upon size of crowd, along with enough tables to display all the cakes until they're won. Small boxes or plain wrapping paper can help keep the newly-won cakes in fine condition for the trip home.

Use a "boom box" and tapes for music. Use festive, upbeat music that is fun to dance and move to. You'll also need paper, scissors, scotch tape, a big marker and pens to make chair numbers as well as slips with numbers to be drawn.

Tickets are needed for the participants. If the cakewalk is being held in conjunction with a carnival or festival, check with the organizers and see if tickets are already available there. If not, buy a roll of tickets and charge each "cake walker" a set fee to enter.

MANPOWER

You'll need one or two people to sell and collect tickets, another to play the boom box. This person can also draw numbers from the hat.

You'll need someone to monitor the cake display table. One or two people are needed to set up and take down the tables and chairs before and after the event. It's a fun, musical way for kids of all ages to win cakes and other goodies!

NOTES: *This project can be handled easily by two or three people overlapping the duties.*

Another way to generate more interest is to make your event a specialty theme walk. You could have a "Cookie Walk," a "Brownie Walk," a "Candy Walk," or even an "Ice Creme Cone Walk."

Whatever theme you choose, be sure it suits the specific tastes of your target audience.

CONTESTS, GAMES & MATCHES

The room is stone silent. All eyes are on the defending champion who is as still as an ancient sphinx. A slight smile breaks across his face, his hand gently nudges his Queen into her final position. His opponent slumps forward, his carefully constructed defense shattered beyond repair. Checkmate!

Everyone likes a good game so why not capitalize on this and sponsor a contest for your next fundraiser?

Contests can be either professional or amateur. A professional contest will have celebrity or superstar participants and your customers will pay to watch the pros play. Prizes are usually large sums of cash. In amateur contests, entrants often pay a registration fee to compete for smaller cash prizes and their moment in the limelight.

Sponsoring a professional contest is a large undertaking. It may be smarter for your group to begin with an amateur event.

You have many options for contests. You could have a sports event: golf, volleyball, tennis, bowling or frisbee. Or, maybe a board game like: Monopoly, Scrabble, chess, checkers or backgammon. Card games like bridge or euchre are also popular. Decide what kind of contest you want to sponsor, then begin planning.

Start by setting a date for your contest. It can run for one day, a weekend or series of consecutive weekends or even an entire week, depending upon the type of competition and number of contestants.

Make sure you have an official set of written rules for the game to eliminate any misunderstanding. Also provide in writing how winner(s) will be determined: by category, elimination, etc.

Encourage a good cross-section of participants. With enough participants, you can have winners in various categories like: age, group, team or gender. Challenge other groups to compete in your games.

On the day of your contest have each contestant fill out a *Contest Registration Form* (see page 105). Use the *Master Contest Worksheet* (see page 103) to keep track of all contestants, their categories and who they compete against. *The Contest Elimination Form* (see page 104) helps you to track winners in each division.

Publicity is important. You need as much interest in your competition as possible. Distribute flyers and posters, put announcements in church and school bulletins. Contact all local media for possible coverage.

When sponsoring a contest, there are several ways your group can raise funds: by ticket sales (so spectators can watch the competition) and/or with a registration fee paid by competitors, by concession stand sales and by selling advertising in your program book. Refer to *Food Stand* (page 127) and *Selling Advertising* (page 86) for more information. Keep your entry fees low to draw a wide range of contestants.

Ask local businesses to help underwrite your contest expenses by donating money, services or goods. Another way businesses can support your contest is by sponsoring a team or contestant. Local restaurants

> *When sponsoring a contest, there are several ways your group can raise funds: by ticket sales (so spectators can watch the competition) and/or with a registration fee paid by competitors, by concession stand sales and by selling advertising in your program book.*

continued on next page

STRAWBERRY FESTIVAL

Summer is just beginning and the strawberries are now bursting with flavor! It's time to celebrate the arrival of sunny days with a strawberry festival. This fun and tasty event is run much like the old favorite, an ice cream social.

You'll want to schedule your strawberry festival to coincide with the peak growing period for local strawberries (check with some knowledge-able garde-ners in your area). Use a scaled-down version of the

> *You'll want to schedule your strawberry festival to coincide with the peak growing period for local strawberries (check with some knowledgeable gardeners in your area).*

Dinner Social on page 125 for practical guidelines in setting up your festival. Hang attention-grabbing posters in high traffic areas and get all the free publicity you can.

Encourage members to sell as many advance tickets as possible, so you'll have a better idea about the number of short-cakes to prepare. Of course, always prepare some extra so you don't run out early.

For the festival itself, use local strawberries if possible and serve them with shortcakes and whipped cream made especially for this event by your group. To bring out the spirit of the occasion, dress your volunteers in red (red with white polka dots is great).

And on festival day, remember to take the time to stop and enjoy the shortcake!

---

continued from preceeding page

may donate snacks for the participants. You can also buy food at wholesale prices and sell for retail at a concession stand you operate.

Enlist the support of local sports, game or hobby stores to generate interest in your contest by posting flyers in their stores. Also approach them to donate games or sports equipment as prizes for your contests.

Get as many prizes as possible donated. Cash prizes, gift certificates and dining or entertainment passes are always welcome.

SUPPLIES & EQUIPMENT

You will need a place to hold the event. If it's indoors, get a hall or gym large enough to hold all contestants, spectators and a concession stand.

Sports or game equipment will be needed: Ask contestants to bring their own or borrow and/or rent what you need.

If you have some local sports/game equipment vendors as sponsors, they may have equipment you can borrow.

If your contest is based upon a card or board game, you'll need enough tables and chairs for all participants.

If you have a concession stand, you will need the necessary foods and equipment. For more information, refer to *Food Stands* on page 127.

Tickets may be necessary for the participants or spectators. These can be bought in rolls at a novelty store.

MANPOWER

All members are needed to publicize this event. Encourage them to stir up interest among family and friends, sell tickets, get the competition going! You'll also need a publicity committee to create and circulate flyers and posters, and to contact all the local media to encourage their coverage.

A crew will be needed to set up, clean up and tear down. Several people will be needed to run the concession stand if you have one.

Referees or judges are needed to settle any questions about the fairness of play. Local celebrities, as judges or referees, can really boost attendance. Ready, set, go!

MASTER CONTEST WORKSHEET

Organization's Name: _____ **Date:** _____

Event: _____ **Categories:** 1. _____ 2. _____

Person in charge: _____ **Telephone:** _____ 3. _____ 4. _____

CONTESTANT'S NAME	AGE	CATEGORY	COMPETING AGAINST

MAKE AS MANY COPIES OF THIS PAGE AS NEEDED

CONTEST ELIMINATION FORM

GRAND CHAMPION

CONTEST REGISTRATION FORM

Event
_____

Date
_____

Name
_____

Address
_____

Telephone
_____

Age
_____

Category
_____

Return form by
_____

Sponsored by
_____

CONTEST REGISTRATION FORM

Event
_____

Date
_____

Name
_____

Address
_____

Telephone
_____

Age
_____

Category
_____

Return form by
_____

Sponsored by
_____

CONTEST REGISTRATION FORM

Event
_____

Date
_____

Name
_____

Address
_____

Telephone
_____

Age
_____

Category
_____

Return form by
_____

Sponsored by
_____

CONTEST REGISTRATION FORM

Event
_____

Date
_____

Name
_____

Address
_____

Telephone
_____

Age
_____

Category
_____

Return form by
_____

Sponsored by
_____

MAKE AS MANY COPIES OF THIS PAGE AS NEEDED – CUT ON DOTTED LINES

DUNK TANK

"Your Mama wears combat boots!" Bam, chunk, splash you're in the tank now.

"You couldn't hit this even if it was the broad side of a barn!" Bam, chunk, splash again.

"Hey you, yeah, I'm talking to you, go on, show the lady you can throw a ball overhand!" Bam, chunk, splash yet again.

Putting some of your rowdier volunteer workers in a dunk tank will splash up new funds for your group. Dunk tanks are great at any event where you have crowds of people walking by. Many people like to try to dunk someone. It's fun fundraising on a hot summer day and works best with a larger festival or carnival.

> It's best to have outgoing, fun-loving types do this job. Some good-natured crowd heckling by the person in the tank generates interest and boosts ticket sales because people just naturally want to dunk the heckler.

Most dunk tanks dump their occupant into the water when a lever is hit by a ball thrown by a participant. Tickets for the watery event are generally two or three chances for a dollar. Keep your prices close to those for other nearby booths.

SUPPLIES & EQUIPMENT

You need a dunk tank for this project. You'll find them at local party supply or equipment rental places. If possible, do some comparison shopping to get the best rates on the best-looking tank available.

Check with event organizers to find the best way to fill your tank. You may need to bring hoses. Water should be at the site. If they're not provided by the dunk tank owner, you'll need to supply the baseballs or softballs to throw at the dunk tank's lever.

Tickets for this event can be be sold in one of two ways: a fixed price per toss or two or three tosses per ticket. You can get tickets at a party/costume/novelty store or, maybe, through event organizers.

Or you could use a simple cash method of three tosses for a dollar, no tickets needed!

MANPOWER

Volunteers first need to find a dunk tank supplier, then make arrangements to pick-up, operate and return the tank. Be sure to find out if hoses and balls come with the tank. If not, your group will need to provide them.

The most important people in this event are the brave and selfless volunteers who'll sit in the tank, waiting to be dunked! It's best to have outgoing, fun-loving types do this job. Some good-natured crowd heckling by the person in the tank generates interest and boosts ticket sales because people just naturally want to dunk the heckler.

Make working shifts in the tank about an hour long, especially if the weather is not very nice. Tell volunteers to bring plenty of towels and a change of dry clothes to wear after their shift is over.

You'll also need people to work as cashiers. Use other volunteers to act as promoters on the day of the dunk tank. Their job is to create interest in the passing crowd and sell tickets.

Another creative approach to wooing the crowd is to make a few sandwich board signs advertising your dunk tank. Have volunteers walk throughout the crowd with them. Use a catchy slogan like, "Spend a buck to dunk Chuck!" on it. This works especially well at larger events.

On the day of the event, get ready to make some soggy but fun bucks for your group!

FISHING POND

The fishing pond is a perennial favorite, especially with the little people, at carnivals and fairs. For a fee, each "fisherman" catches a fish. Each fish has a number hidden on its underside that goes with a prize, such as a small toy or several pieces of wrapped candy or other snack items.

> *A small children's swimming pool or nice wash tub with some bright, colorful designs painted on the outside makes a great tank.*

To do your own fishing pond fundraiser, start by getting rental prices from local party/ rental stores for a tank and numbered plastic fish. Or if you have some handy people in your group, you could design and build your own fish tank. A small children's swimming pool or nice wash tub with some bright, colorful designs painted on the outside makes a great tank. Buy small plastic fish from a toy or craft store and paint a number on the bottom of each.

You can solicit donations of prizes or find suppliers who will sell to your group at wholesale prices. Group prizes by number, so when someone chooses fish # 6, you give them a prize from the # 6 section of prizes. This game is particularly popular with the wee folk, since everyone gets a prize!

POCKET LADY

She's in the center of a group of happy, bouncing children who, after giving her a ticket, gleefully pull a prize from one of dozens of colorful pockets on her skirt. This pocket lady idea is an unusual variation of the old favorite fishing pond.

You'll need a special skirt or apron with many colorful and interesting pockets sewn into it. Keep in mind several volunteers will be wearing the skirt, so make it a style that easily fits different figures. Each pocket of the skirt contains a prize such as a small toy, wrapped candies or other snack items.

For a set fee or ticket, each person gets the prize from a pocket they choose. This project works great at school carnivals and fairs.

How about reaching into a pocket lion's mouth for a prize? Or lifting a bird's wing to find the pocket beneath it. Let the sky be your limit as you design the skirt. Be sure to make the pockets attractive to the little people. Animals, clouds, balloons, flowers or fruit shapes are all simple, interesting shapes for pockets. Use bright colors and make all bows and buttons big enough for little hands to easily work.

> *You'll need a special skirt or apron with many colorful and interesting pockets sewn into it. ... Each pocket of the skirt contains a prize such as a small toy, wrapped candies or other snack items.*

Try to get prizes donated. If that's not possible, see if you can buy them from a party/ novelty store and/ or distributor at wholesale prices. See *Appendix A* for suppliers.

HAUNTED HOUSE

The tour guide disappears into a dark room. You try to follow him, but can't see where he went. You walk forward cautiously, brushing cobwebs away from your face and arms. Something scurries across your feet. The girl behind you screams. Welcome to *Bimini Youth Group's Haunted House!*

A haunted house is a fun, creative way to raise money on a seasonal basis. It can range in size from one room (a haunted basement, choir loft, classroom, or barn) to a full-scale haunted building (a church, house, fire or train station). The bigger the building, the more elaborate your hauntings can be. If you're planning to haunt an entire building, be sure it has two doorways to create easy entry and exit paths without backing up your flow of "tourists".

SUPPLIES & EQUIPMENT

The first matter to be resolved is to find a location to haunt. Check with your church, school and among your members for places you can "borrow" for the haunting season. The location should be scary-looking or have frightening potential, but must be structurally sound. You may need to get a permit or on-site inspection from your local fire department to certify the building's safety level. You don't want any of your guests getting hurt at your haunted place. Next, decide how long you'll offer your haunted tour. If it's just one night, Halloween is the natural choice. You could run it the weekend before or even the several weeks leading up to Halloween. Haunted houses can also work well in conjunction with a church or school festival that has nothing to do with Halloween. If it's out of the Halloween season you could build your haunted event around an interesting local legend.

Once you have a location and the times scheduled, the real fun begins. Set up a traffic

> **The location should be scary-looking or have frightening potential, but must be structurally sound. You may need to get a permit or on-site inspection from your local fire department to certify the building's safety level.**

pattern through the room or house to be scary, yet safe. Use all of your guests' senses to frighten them: scary sights, sounds, smells and feelings. Strategic lighting and recorded sounds can do much to create a creepy mood.

You'll need to design your hauntings and decide exactly how they'll work. Then you'll need to collect all the necessary props. Get your creative juices flowing: go to thrift and goodwill stores, yard and garage sales, craft and costume shops. Have members rummage through their basements and attics for props. See what you can get donated or at cost for your haunted house.

Decorate each room or area of the building with a different theme: a werewolf's den, Count Dracula's coffin, a witch's kitchen, etc.

Depending upon how elaborate your house is and how long the tour is, you can charge anywhere from fifty cents to four dollars for admission. Make your rates close to other haunted places near you.

You can purchase a roll of tickets from a party store to sell for entrance tickets or you can

continued on next page

BALLOON BUST BONANZA

The crowd mills around your tables full of attractive prizes at your next big carnival. Before long some of the more curious crowd members are buying your balloons, popping them and finding the number hidden inside. This number corresponds to the prize they'll take home. By the end of the day your now-empty tables are littered with popped balloons and your group's coffers are a bit fuller. Everyone's happy.

To get this fundraiser underway, have group members gather as many donated prizes as possible. In the process, aim for a wide array of inexpensive but nice quality items.

Houseplants, craft items, sports equipment, baked goods, fresh fruit and vegetables all make good prizes. Throw in a couple of bigger ticket prizes like theater tickets, dinner gift certificates, money, a radio, television or small stereo. After all the prizes are gathered, assign a number to each prize.

Set up tables to display your 100 prizes at the carnival then make 100 small helium-filled balloons with a corresponding prize number folded inside. Be sure the number is not readable from the outside. Set up a sign that explains how this event works. Charge a dollar or two for each balloon. The customer selects a balloon, pops it and then gets the prize that corresponds with the number found inside their balloon.

After you've filled enough balloons, use the remaining helium to fill some large balloons. These balloons can then be sold for a dollar or so and provide some additional fundraising income from the event!

> **Before long some of the more curious crowd members are buying your balloons, popping them and finding the number hidden inside. This number corresponds to the prize they'll take home.**

---

continued from preceding page

use an ink pad and stamp to mark your guests' hands after they have paid their entry fee. A glow-in-the-dark ink works well here.

MANPOWER

You'll need guides. They may lead your guests throughout the entire tour or in the case of a small, one-room haunting they may simply greet the guests at the door and point them in the right direction. If they're in contact with your guests, they should be in costume.

If you're haunting a large building, you'll need plenty of volunteers to be live monsters, witches, vampires, werewolves and corpses throughout the building. Help your volunteer creatures create their own costumes and short dialogue or action for the "tourists".

You will also need a creative committee to be in charge of the design and construction of all the props. This group should also map out the proposed tour (be sure to throw in a couple of scary detours for the not-so-faint of heart).

NOTE 1: *You should have some sort of liability insurance for an event of this sort. Check with an insurance agent or a lawyer to be sure you have appropriate coverage. Perhaps you can get a sponsor to underwrite the cost of the insurance for your group.*

NOTE 2: *Haunted houses work well in conjunction with carnivals or festivals. For example, the tour could end at a bake sale, refreshment stand, or craft sale. Maybe you'll scare them into buying some of your goodies!*

LIVE SHOWS

Bring out the clowns, magicians, jugglers, musicians and performers of all stripes in your group and let 'em give the public a live show they'll long remember. Lights, curtain, action: Let the fun begin!

You have many options when thinking about a live show for a fundraiser. You could have an amateur's night, put on a play, have a sing-along or even a cooking demonstration. Fashion and theme shows (like vacation and bridal) are also popular. Anything either entertaining or educational can be considered for a live show.

If you don't want to produce your own live show, the next best thing is to buy a block of tickets to a live show at a discount, then resell them at retail. If your group is big enough, you could buy all the tickets for one specific performance, then resell them. If you like this idea but aren't big enough to handle it all by yourself, you can co-sponsor the event with another group and split the workload which is primarily selling tickets.

Another live show opportunity is to hire a professional entertainer for one performance and charge admission. Locally known magicians, musicians,

> *You could have an amateur's night, put on a play, have a sing-along or even a cooking demonstration. ... Anything either entertaining or educational can be considered for a live show.*

storytellers and/or dancers are all potential performers.

SUPPLIES & EQUIPMENT

Unless you are buying ticket blocks to a show someone else is producing, you'll need some sort of theater for your show. A school gym or a similar facility is best, especially if it has a stage. If it doesn't have one, you can rent stage materials from a rental store or build your own simple stage. A partition or curtain is nice, but not absolutely necessary. You will also need chairs for the audience. If you're using a school or church facility, these should be available.

To sponsor a fashion show, contact a local clothing merchant to help you bring the clothes and models together. The models will need a private room for dressing and storing clothes. Your clothing supplier can help you figure out the number of outfits, sizes and models you'll need.

If you are sponsoring a theme show with vendors and booths, you'll need enough space for their displays. They'll each be responsible for their own booths, of course, but some may need access to electricity for their displays, videos, etc. Charge each vendor a rental fee for their space.

If you are hosting a show with an entertainer, check with him or her to see if you'll need to furnish any special props, stage effects, assistants, etc.

You can make your own tickets or buy them from a party/novelty store. Keep track of who's selling tickets and how many each has. See *Ticket Sales Sheet* on page 112.

Consider adding simple concessions to this project. Selling refreshments can help generate additional funds in these kinds of projects. Refer to *Food Stand* on page 127.

MANPOWER

The manpower you need varies with the type of show you're having. No matter what type of show you do, you'll want all members selling tickets.

If it's a fashion show, you'll need volunteer models. For a

continued on next page

CHILDREN'S ART FAIR

Imagine buying a work of art by a young Piccasso, Van Gogh or Monet. If you have some really talented children in your group, this project can make that all possible. A *Children's Art Fair* is a good project for youth groups, especially those that draw members from a wide cross-section of the community. This event also works well as part of a larger festival or carnival.

To get your children's art fair underway first set a realistic show deadline. It could take from several weeks to months for all the art to be finished. You'll also want to plan show publicity at this time.

Have one or more brain-storming sessions with adult leaders and other helpers, and the kids themselves. At the end of these sessions each artist should have some ideas and a

feeling of where they're heading. The goal is to facilitate the process so each child in your group creates one or more works of art for the sale.

> *The goal is to facilitate the process so each child in your group creates one of more works of art for the sale. ... The wider the variety of art work in the sale, the better.*

SUPPLIES & EQUIPMENT

Next gather as many art, framing and matting supplies as you can. Seek donations from local businesses, parents, supporters and the artists themselves.

Art works can be in any medium the artist chooses and you have supplies for. Some examples are: charcoal drawings, watercolor or acrylic paintings, silk screen prints, papier mâché or wood sculptures, etc. The wider the variety of art work in the sale, the better.

MANPOWER

When the art work is all finished, enlist enough adult leaders and/or parents to help the young artists mount, mat and frame the artwork. Assign a number to each piece of art.

When it's time for the show, set up a gallery-like display for the artwork and run the sale like a *Silent Auction* (see page 160). In this style of auction, bidders write their bids on a piece of paper posted next to each item. The highest bidder then buys it.

OK, get your young artists ready to create, then get set for an exciting, great-looking fundraiser!

---

continued from preceding page
demonstration, you might need assistants to help.

Theme show committees need to contact vendors, service suppliers and others who'll set up display booths to sell their wares or explain their services.

Advance publicity is crucial with this event. Carefully select your market. Then appoint a committee to create and circulate flyers, mailers and posters.

Announce the event in church newsletters and school bulletins. Put flyers and posters on as many public bulletin boards as possible. Emphasize advance ticket sales so you'll have an idea of the crowd to expect. You could offer a discount price on advance tickets then sell tickets at the door at a higher price.

Volunteers are needed to collect tickets or money at the

event, others are needed to staff the concession stand, if you have one, and to set up, tear down and clean up after the show. If you need more help than is available, offer free show admission to volunteers who'll help during the event.

This fundraiser will not only earn your group some money, it'll also give you a night of exciting entertainment. Lights, curtains, action!

TICKET SALES SHEET

Show Name: _____

Date of Show _____

Chairman: Name & Telephone _____

Money Due Date: _____

MEMBER'S NAME & PHONE	TICKETS TAKEN	TICKETS SOLD	TICKETS RETURNED	AMOUNT DUE	AMOUNT PAID
TOTAL					

MAKE AS MANY COPIES OF THIS PAGE AS NEEDED

RAFFLES

Let's take a chance on it! Almost everyone dreams of winning a boat, a car or even dinner for two at a nice local restaurant. And, when your group is selling raffle tickets at a buck or two a pop, it's a fairly popular and affordable chance many folks are willing to take.

Raffles, like bingo, are popular in some areas and illegal in others. So before you decide to hold a raffle, check its legality against local ordinances. Also check with your chartering organization's rules about raffles. For instance, the Boy Scouts do not allow their members to hold raffles.

After you've checked the legal and ethical status and decided your group wants to do a raffle, go for it! Raffles can be as large or as small as you'd like. An in-house raffle can be just selling tickets inside your group and giving the winner part of the proceeds or a prize.

To put together a large-scale raffle, see what kind of donations your sponsors will give. Don't even let the sky be your limit! Some good raffle prizes: gift certificates, dinners, entertainment passes, tickets to sporting events, toys, bicycles, autos, boats, appliances, week-

> *Almost everyone dreams of winning a boat, a car or even dinner for two at a nice local restaurant. And, when your group is selling raffle tickets at a buck or two a pop, it's a fairly popular and affordable chance many folks are willing to take.*

end get-away certificates; the list goes on and on.

Depending upon the scale of your raffle, publicity can range from simple meeting announcements to a complex multi-media effort with free and paid ads.

Now get out there and make your contacts. Once you've got your donations lined up, it's time for the troops to start selling raffle tickets!

SUPPLIES & EQUIPMENT

The only supplies you need for this project are tickets and, of course, the raffle prizes. In an in-house raffle, just devise your own tickets. See *Standard Raffle Ticket Form* page 116.

Make as many sheets of tickets as you'll need, with each number listed on both ticket halves. The purchaser gets one ticket and the other ticket (with the same number) goes into the drawing.

If you're raffling off something of moderate value (dinners, movie passes, etc.), buy rolls of tickets at novelty stores or other suppliers. They are printed in doubles so they can be used in drawings like raffles.

If you're raffling off a large dollar value item, get your tickets professionally printed. On these two-part perforated tickets, lines are provided for the buyer to write his name, address and phone number. You keep this ticket half. The other ticket half goes with the purchaser. His half should have the following information: date of drawing, items to be awarded and his ticket number. Most printers are familiar with ticket printing and can give you helpful advice in this area.

The prizes you'll have to raffle off will depend upon the generosity of your sponsors and the ingenuity of your members who request donations!

MANPOWER

You need volunteers to solicit donations. Then your entire group should be part of selling raffle tickets. To get the sales campaign off to a good start, be sure you buy the first ticket!

MOO-DOO LOTTERY

Excitement ripples through the crowd as they wait to see which square the cow will mark as the Moo-Doo Lottery winner! This is an old-timey favorite at rural festivals, county fairs and similar events.

The event is simple enough. Start with a fenced off area, a football field works very well. Mark the fenced area into 10 x 10 grid for 100 squares total. Use something non-toxic, like white flour, to mark squares. Provide water and scatter a little hay on the field for the cow to munch.

Next, lead a cow onto the field and wait for nature to take it's course. The section where the "moo" drops it's first "doo" is the winner.

Sell chances for five or ten dollars a square. The prize can be a percentage of the project's income, or, preferably, a donated gift. To create greater interest, offer prizes for 1st, 2nd and 3rd place finishes.

Moo-Doo Lottery (or Bingo) works best with other events. Effectively promoted, this can generate a lot of money.

One area high school homecoming sells its 100 Moo Doo Lottery squares for $100 apiece to raise $10,000 every year. The winner gets $1,000 and the rest of this income covers the annual band, cheerleaders and football budgets over and above ticket and concession sales.

This is a large school and their lottery is an ongoing annual event. Your lottery will probably start small then, over the years, can grow into something this size.

Moo-Doo Bingo works in a similar way. Mark the field into a Bingo grid and use several cows. Have a manned Bingo tote board set up and sell Bingo cards. As people walk around the festival or fair, they can check back to see their progress. The first one to Bingo wins. See *Bingo* on page 96. Add straight Bingos, Figure X, four corners and other varieties in combination so you'll have several winners.

Put on your cowboy hat, kick the doo off your boots and bring on the cows!

> The event is simple enough. Start with a fenced off area, a football field works very well ... Next, lead a cow onto the field and wait for nature to take it's course.

COW CHIP TOSS

In the mood for some real rural fun? A cow-chip toss always raises laughs and piles of cash. It's a fun extra for a festival or fair. To begin, get a supply of dry cow chips from a local farmer. This works best in late summer, when hot, dry weather makes chips more manageable.

On the day of the toss, each player selects their chip and pays a fee of one or two dollars. The object is to see who can toss their chip the farthest. Give prizes for first, second and third places. With enough players, divide prizes into categories: men, women, teenagers, etc. Instead of distance, have 'em toss for accuracy. For example, paint a *Bulls Eye* on the ground and see who gets closest to the center.

Always provide plastic gloves for the contestants and a place to wash their hands. Let the chips fall where they may!

> It's a fun extra for a festival or fair. ... This works best in late summer, when hot, dry weather makes chips more manageable.

MONEY TREE

"If only money grew on trees!" You can make this dream a reality for one lucky winner when you sell chances to guess the amount of cash on your *Money Tree!*

This project is essentially a raffle with a different twist. The winner is the one who guesses the amount of cash you have on your *Money Tree*. If you have two or more winners this can be handled in one of two ways: First, the multiple winners could split the cash or, two: the winners have another drawing among themselves and the winner takes all.

In either case, decide what method your group will use beforehand to eliminate any possibility of hurt feelings later. See *Raffles* on page 113 for general raffle guidelines.

> *This project is essentially a raffle with a different twist. The winner is the one who guesses the amount of cash you have on your Money Tree. ... Whatever design theme you choose for your tree be sure to appeal to the majority of people you plan to reach.*

This can be "members only" or a church- or school-wide event. It works especially well in conjunction with a festival, carnival or similar event.

SUPPLIES & EQUIPMENT

To make your money tree, put a tree branch in a heavy pot filled with sand so it's free-standing. Next, spray paint it. Gold and silver are catchy colors. Or your tree can reflect a theme or holiday. For example, decorate an orange and black money tree with pumpkins and bats for Halloween. A Christmas money tree can be hung with pretty cash "ornaments". An Easter tree with pastel "money eggs" can be used.

If a holiday theme doesn't work, use your imagination. For the younger set, create a tree with dinosaurs, space aliens, cartoon characters and/ or animals. An adult audience can appreciate a sophisticated Victorian tree made with yards of period lace, buttons and bows. Whatever design theme you choose for your tree, be sure to appeal to the majority of people you plan to reach.

After you've decorated your tree decide how many raffle tickets your group can reasonably expect to sell. Multiply this by the ticket price to get your budgeted income for the project. Now decide the total money value you're going to put on the tree. Keep it at about 50% of your anticipated income figure to ensure the project's profitability.

Next, purchase the right amount of dollar bills in various denominations, fold them accordian-style and tuck the ends inside so viewers can't see the value of each bill. Tie these money "leaves" to the tree with metallic or colorful ribbons.

MANPOWER

Now get your volunteer troops out selling chances to win the tree. Use pre-printed tickets or create your own tickets. Have the drawing at a well-publicized time. The winner takes the tree and all the cash on it.

So even though money doesn't normally grow on trees, this money tree could put some valuable green leaves in your group's coffers!

NOTE: *A money tree can also be made with coins tied on individually or in small bags to tree branches. Use lush materials (velvet, gold, or silver bags are best) to catch the eye and the interest of passers-by.*

STANDARD RAFFLE TICKET FORM

Ticket # _____

Name _____

Address _____

Telephone _____

Ticket # _____

Sponsored by _____

Prizes _____

Ticket # _____

Name _____

Address _____

Telephone _____

Ticket # _____

Sponsored by _____

Prizes _____

Ticket # _____

Name _____

Address _____

Telephone _____

Ticket # _____

Sponsored by _____

Prizes _____

Ticket # _____

Name _____

Address _____

Telephone _____

Ticket # _____

Sponsored by _____

Prizes _____

MAKE AS MANY COPIES OF THIS PAGE AS NEEDED

CHAPTER 5
FUNDING WITH FOOD

CHAPTER NOTES:

BARBECUES

The mouth-watering aroma of barbecue sauce wafts through the air. Hungry crowds begin to gather, attracted by the fragrance. It's the annual *River City Booster Club BBQ* and people are lining up for a great meal.

Sponsoring a barbecue can be an easy and surprisingly effective money-maker. To really streamline this project, hire a professional caterer to do the cooking. They'll generally provide the meats of your choice, along with side dishes, serving containers, etc.

Your group's job then is to publicize and sell tickets to the event.

> **Sponsoring a barbecue can be an easy and surprisingly effective money-maker. To really streamline this project, hire a professional caterer to do the cooking.**

Start with the *Ticket Sales Sheet* on page 112, modify if needed, to handle members' ticket consignments.

Advance sales are very important so you can give the cooks as accurate a head-count as possible. This helps your group avoid excessive waste and non-profitable leftovers.

Barbecues are generally held outdoors during nice weather. You may decide to hold your event in a park, on church or school grounds, a mall's parking lot or wherever space is available. You should be able to reserve any of these areas for a nominal fee or even rent-free.

This project requires a lot of advance publicity. A publicity committee should get the word out to all local papers, TV and radio stations. Use every possible media to get your PSAs in front of the public.

All members should actively sell tickets. The more advance sales you generate, the better your odds are for a profitable event. Advance ticket sales enable you to judge more accurately how much food to prepare, how many tables and chairs to set up and so on.

You'll need a detailed plan for setting up your cafeteria tables and chairs. Make sure to clearly designate the food serving tables and keep them widely separated from the food preparation areas.

On barbecue day, ice down beverages in tubs or coolers or serve iced tea and lemonade from large pitchers. Coffee can be served to your patrons from institutional-sized coffee urns.

Before you set your ticket price you'll need to pin down all your raw costs as accurately as possible. A little extra time spent here can avoid some large headaches later on. The major costs for this project include: food, food prep, place settings, beverages and hall rental (if any).

Check with your local Board of Health and see if any sort of food handling permit is needed for this project. Use the *Product Sales Projected Budget* on page 21 and check all your assumptions at least twice.

SUPPLIES & EQUIPMENT

You'll need a place big enough to hold your barbecue's expected turnout. In addition, you'll need an adequate number of tables, chairs, place-settings, serving dishes and utensils. Be sure to have enough beverages and garbage cans with plastic liners available.

If you hire a cook, they'll handle their own grills, the meats and most other cooking supplies. Find out exactly what is included in their fees. Then you'll know just what your group will be responsible for.

If you're doing the cooking, you will need to borrow or rent large grills to cook on. You'll

BARBECUE TAKE-OUT

In a small park, not far from a busy road one man tends a grill, keeping a practiced eye on the slowly smoking pieces of chicken. As soon as each piece is cooked to perfection, he picks it up with tongs and puts it in a large cooler to keep it piping hot for its soon-to-arrive customer.

Two more volunteers are working nearby. One takes the money from customers who've stopped to buy some carry-out barbecued chicken. The other volunteer, wearing rubber gloves, bags up the hot, steaming chicken for each order.

They have created a U-shaped drive-through in the parking lot and all three communicate by walkie-talkies so they are able to deliver their hot food very fast.

The real beauty of this project is that it is relatively quick and easy, and works great with just a handful of people.

It can also make your group some big bucks fast. With a minimum of publicity (ads and PSAs in local papers, posters in public places), one local school group always sells out within hours. They've done this project for several years running and readily vouch for it's continuing success.

This project is perfect for a highly targeted, local telemarketing campaign, see *Telemarketing* on page 82 for more details.

> *The real beauty of this project is that it is relatively quick and easy, and works great with just a handful of people. … With a minimum of publicity (ads and PSAs in local papers, posters in public places), one local school group always sells out within hours.*

SUPPLIES & EQUIPMENT

Ultimately it is the excellence of your food that will determine the success of this project. Some groups prefer to hire an experienced, professional cook for the project. In these cases, the cook brings his own barbecue rig, all the chicken and his own special barbecue sauce. The cook will also obtain any necessary food handling permits, which further simplifies your operation.

He'll cook a specific amount of chicken for a set price and then it's sold by the half-chicken only. Check with local commercial food suppliers for the best packaging materials to use to keep your barbecued chicken fresh and warm. Your group will mark up the chicken 100% and provide the take-out bags and coolers to keep the chicken hot until sold.

MANPOWER

You will need a minimum of three people: a cook, a cashier and a food server to adequately staff your barbecue take-out stand. Be sure to have a well-stocked change box on hand so you can easily make change for your customers.

With some additional planning and a few more volunteers, you could also offer to deliver the chicken. This adds some complexity to the project but can definitely increase your sales (refer to *Donut Delivery Express* on page 126 for details about setting up this kind of delivery service).

Another option is to offer your barbecued chicken at a bake sale. This way customers can get an entire meal at once.

This fundraiser is good to schedule on a regular basis because, if your food is good, you'll develop a loyal following. Get your own special barbecue sauce ready!

BLOCK-LONG BANANA SPLIT BONANZA

Imagine a row of banana splits long enough to span the length of a city block. Think about how many people it would take to eat such a sweet extravaganza.

Now, to sweeten the vision, imagine how much money your group could make selling tickets to enough people to eat the entire block-long row of banana splits. If your taste buds are turned on and the dollar signs are flashing in your head, this fundraiser is just the event for you!

The number of participants you hope to have will dictate the size of serving area you'll need to create and serve your banana splits. If you expect a small crowd, set up a cafeteria table or two. If you are going for a larger crowd, get permission to rope off a block or two of a city street for this event. A city park is also a good location for your sweet creations.

Your publicity efforts should mainly use free PSAs in local newspapers and on local radio and TV stations. Also post lots of eye-catching posters in high traffic public places. If this is an outdoor event, be sure you have a well-publicized rain date!

> *Imagine how much money your group could make selling tickets to enough people to eat the entire block-long row of banana splits.*

SUPPLIES & EQUIPMENT

First and foremost, you'll need plenty of ice cream, bananas, toppings, bowls, spoons and napkins! Find local vendors who will donate or give your group wholesale prices on supplies for this incredible, edible fundraiser.

If possible, contract a soft-serve truck to fill your ice cream order. To estimate the quantity of ice cream you'll need, figure each ticket sold equals one serving or about four ounces of ice cream.

You'll also need enough tables, chairs, serving dishes and flatware for your customers to use in eating their banana splits.

Buy a roll of numbered tickets at a party store. Numbers are important so you can have an accurate idea of how many banana split eaters to expect. Modify the *Ticket Sales Sheet* on page 112 to handle all your ticket consignments.

MANPOWER

This project needs a lot of volunteers. You'll need one committee to handle all your publicity efforts, another to gather all the supplies (ice cream, toppings, containers, etc.) Volunteers are also needed to set up, create and clean up after this banana split festival.

If it's a warm day, you'll need lots of hands to make the banana splits as fast as possible. Ticket holders are usually more than willing to help your volunteers. As the banana splits are finished, each participant is given one along with a fresh spoon and told to dig in.

Be sure to have a good supply of garbage bags, so after

continued on next page

BARBECUES
continued from page 119

also need to prepare side dishes in large enough quantities for the expected crowd. Use serving dishes designed to keep each dish either hot or cold, as necessary.

Keep your offerings simple yet tasty. Make sure your side dishes are those that can readily be made in bulk. Salads, breads, potatoes or rice dishes can all easily be prepared in large quantities.

Last, but certainly not least, have a good supply of plates, utensils, cups and napkins on hand. For additional information about sit-down meals, refer to *Dinner Social* on page 125.

MANPOWER

If you hire out the food preparation, your group's manpower needs are cut drastically. If you're cooking your own food, first you'll need to line up volunteer chefs. Make sure they can really cook: the success of this project is hanging in the balance! It's a good idea to schedule a Saturday afternoon practice run before the event.

The side dishes can be prepared a day in advance by a special committee. Food for large groups is most efficiently prepared in a school, church or other institutional kitchen.

On the day of the barbecue, servers will need to first set up the dining tables with place-settings, side dishes and drinks. When the grilled food is ready, they'll need to get it to your patrons as quickly as possible.

Okay, now plan your menu, line up your chefs and servers and get those grills going. Ah, the sweet smell of a successful barbecue!

JAMAICAN "JERK" BARBECUE SAUCE

This Carribean favorite can be used as a general purpose marinade/barbecue sauce for vegetables, pork, chicken, shrimp; the choice is yours! This recipe can be halved or doubled depending upon the size of your crowd.

- 15 green onions, chopped
- 3 Jalapeno peppers, cleaned and chopped (more or less to taste)
- 2 medium onions, chopped
- 1 cup red wine vinegar
- 1 ½ cups soy sauce
- ½ cup vegetable oil
- ⅔ cup brown sugar
- 2 Tbs. dried thyme
- 1 tsp. ground cloves
- 1 tsp. ground nutmeg
- 1 tsp. ground allspice or cinnamon

Combine all ingredients into a food processor or blender. Run on high speed for 15 seconds. Use as a marinade and/or as a cooking sauce.

SOUTHERN BARBECUE SAUCE

This tangy barbecue sauce, a traditional southern favorite, is especially tasty with chicken. This recipe can be halved or doubled as necessary.

- ½ cup flour
- 1 cup prepared mustard
- 2 lbs. onions
- 2 cups salad oil
- 2 ½ Tbs. salt
- 2 tsp. pepper
- ¾ cup brown sugar
- 1 quart vinegar
- 1 quart chicken broth
- 28-32 oz. ketchup
- 28-32 oz. tomato purée
- 1 cup Worcestershire sauce

Chop onions and sauté in oil. Combine mustard, flour, salt, pepper and brown sugar with sautéed onions. Add remaining ingredients and bring to a boil, stirring constantly. Simmer 15 minutes, then refrigerate until ready to barbecue.

---

continued from preceding page

everyone's eaten their fill, all garbage can be quickly and neatly carried away. This leaves only the tables and chairs left to take down.

When planning this project, decide how many tickets you'd like to sell and line up material donations accordingly. With enough supplies donated, you should be able to sell tickets in the two to three dollar per person range. The more tickets you sell, the more banana splits you'll make and the larger your profit should be. If ticket sales turn out far different than your plans, you may have to contact more vendors for additional donations. Then get ready for a real fundraising treat.

"On your mark, get set, eat!"
NOTE: *This project could be done with a sandwich theme: a block-long submarine sandwich or hot dog. In planning this event remember that health codes do not permit more than one person to eat from a serving dish. So if you're planning to build an extremely long banana split or sandwich or other food item, remember you'll still have to serve each person's portion in a separate dish.*

COOKING CONTEST

All eyes are on the judge as he takes a cautious taste of Joe's Five-Pepper Chili. Will he like it? Will he pass out? Who will win the coveted *Chili Cook-Off Antacid Award?*

The variations you can do with this project boggles the mind! You can have chili or burger or rib cook-offs, pizza or pie or bread bake-offs, or whatever fires your imagination and culinary skills. After you've brainstormed and determined the cooking category for your contest, decide how big you want to make it. Should it be church-wide, school-wide, city-wide?

Define your parameters, then get busy publicizing the event. For big events you'll want to do a more extensive campaign with both free and paid advertising.

Usually, there are no age limits in contests like this. To generate interest, encourage competition. A fun way to do this is by posting challenges in bulletins, flyers, etc. (i.e. Mary Smith challenges John Doe to a chili cook-off). The sense of competition will increase interest in your event.

Line up area chefs, members of your board of directors, sponsors and local "celebrities"

> *The variations you can do with this project boggles the mind! You can have chili or burger or rib cook-offs, pizza or pie or bread bake-offs, or whatever fires your imagination and culinary skills.*

to act as judges. Have all contestants fill out a registration form so you can identify their entries. Number the registration forms and the entries correspondingly.

Let the participants know their culinary creations are the property of your group once they're entered in the contest. Schedule the judging to begin at a set time and after winners are announced, you can auction or sell the contest entries as a whole or in individual portions.

For added fun, give gag gifts to the winners (i.e. antacid tablets for the chili cook-off winner, a pie server to the pie bake-off winner, etc.).

SUPPLIES & EQUIPMENT

To host this event, you will need enough tables for the contestants to display their dishes. You should also have a separate table with chairs for the judges. Depending upon the food, you may need equipment to keep it either warm or cold. You'll also need serving utensils and plates or bowls for the judges.

Contest participants will provide the main food items, but you may want to provide some condiments and beverages, too.

If you're selling or auctioning off the entries to take home, you'll need some kind of food wrap to cover the items. Or, if you plan to sell the contest entries to be eaten at the event, you'll need plates, utensils and napkins.

MANPOWER

You will need enough manpower to set up, then later tear down and clean up the contest area. If you're selling food to eat during the event, you'll need servers. You will need a panel of judges and, if you are auctioning off the contest entries, an auctioneer.

In any case, you'll need a cashier to take payment for all purchases. All in all, this event is a tasty way to raise some cash for your group.

NOTE: *With the winners' OK, your group could also publish a cookbook of the winning recipes. (Refer to* Cookbooks *on page 170).*

DINNER BY THE DIP

The table is heavy with mouth-watering dishes. Casseroles, breads, vegetables, desserts, salads and main dishes all clamor for your attention. Decisions, decisions! How many should I try? How much can I fit on my plate? How much can I possibly eat?! Warm up your flatware and bring a large plate for this delightfully different dinner fundraiser!

Essentially, this is a cafeteria-style dinner with a charge for the number of scoops of food each diner takes. This can be a fun, low-cost fundraiser for the whole family.

Line up the dishes on cafeteria tables and let your hungry customers go through the line, choosing their food by the dip. The price of their dinner depends upon the number of dips of food they have on their plate.

Have a cashier ready at the end of the line, to count the number of dips on each plate. Make the charge per dip a round number, so it will be easy to calculate the price for each dinner.

SUPPLIES & EQUIPMENT

First, decide how big you want the dinner to be. Are you going to serve your entire group, neighborhood, school or church? Gear publicity efforts according to the number of people you want to attract.

Use flyers, posters and other announcements to get the word out. Promote it as a fun, family-oriented fundraiser. To keep supply costs and clean-up to a minimum, ask people to bring their own place settings to dinner. Have some available for those who forget;

> **Essentially, this is a cafeteria-style dinner with a charge for the number of scoops of food each diner takes. ... Promote it as a fun, family-oriented fundraiser.**

you don't want anyone left out! Estimate how many people you expect to attend. Have all of your members bring enough covered dishes of their favorite home-made foods to serve your anticipated crowd. Make sure there are serving spoons for each dish. Solicit donations of back-up staples like rolls and butter, beverages, napkins and condiments or arrange to buy at wholesale.

MANPOWER

You'll need volunteers to cook special dishes and bring them to the event. You'll also need people to set up tables, chairs and table settings before dinner. During the meal you'll need one or more cashiers and a couple of general helpers to take care of last minute details. After the event you'll need a clean-up crew and people to return everything to its proper place. See *Dinner Social* on page 125 for more details about supplies, manpower and set-up.

Grab your plate and your appetite and enjoy this fundraiser!

SIMPLE & TASTY CHERRY CRISP

Fruit Mixture:
- 1 tsp. butter
- 1 ¼ cup sugar
- 1 qt. cherries
- ½ t. vanilla
- ½ t. cinnamon
- 2 ½ T. Cornstarch

Simmer all ingredients together. Cook until thick. This mixture can be prepared early and frozen until needed.

Cake Mixture:
- 9 oz. white or yellow box cake mix
- ½ c butter
- ½ c chopped nuts

Preheat oven to 350⁰. Spread fruit mixture evenly in pan. Sprinkle boxed cake mix over mixture. Melt butter and drizzle over the top of the cake mix. Sprinkle chopped nuts on top. Bake @ 350⁰ for 45 minutes.

DINNER SOCIAL

The large room is full of people talking, laughing and eating. It's an evening of fun, relaxation and the breaking of bread together. Your group is the host, providing the meal, the waitresses and the busboys. And when it's done sucessfully, your group's treasury will be pleasantly full again.

The first step is to decide what type of meal you want to have (pancake breakfast, chili supper, spaghetti dinner, salad bar, baked potato bar, deli-style sandwich bar, specialty soups, or even a dessert or sundae bar). Next, find a place to have the meal, keeping in mind: rental cost, kitchen facilities needed and room for the diners.

Set a date and time that is convenient for the people you're targeting as well as for your volunteers. Avoid conflicts with other popular local events or coordinate with them if possible. Determine how many people you can realistically serve and how many you can expect to attend. Advance ticket sales are a great help on this score.

Aim all publicity efforts to reach your target market. Use low or no-cost announcements in church bulletins, school, neighborhood and volunteer newsletters. Put posters up on high traffic community bulletin

> *It's an evening of fun, relaxation and the breaking of bread together. ... And when it's done sucessfully, your group's treasury will be pleasantly full again.*

boards in your target market.

SUPPLIES & EQUIPMENT

After you've decided on a menu, request donations of food and supplies (plates, napkins, cups, etc.). If donations don't provide enough, try to buy all additional items at cost or purchase them through wholesalers.

Estimate the number and types of serving dishes and utensils that you'll need. Check with the facility where you're holding the event. They may have these items available.

Figure out what condiments, beverages or other extras are needed (sugar, cream, spices, butter, syrup, grated cheese, crackers). Arrange for the donation or purchase of these items, as well as any other needed dispensing/serving containers for the meal.

You should serve coffee, tea and ice water at the very minimum. You can add soft drinks and, if alcohol is acceptable, you could offer a variety of dinner wines. Hiring a caterer to serve alcoholic berverages makes all this easy and inexpensive. And the caterer will provide the liquor license.

MANPOWER

You will need people to set up, cook, serve, bus and do general clean-up. Depending upon the size of the crowd you anticipate, you may want a chairperson to coordinate volunteers in each of these areas.

Make arrangements to send leftovers to a local soup kitchen or home with volunteer workers. Don't forget to collect and dispose of all trash. It's a great way to feed your supporters and put some cash in your treasury too!

NOTE 1: *For variety, you may want to hold a* Health-Conscious Dinner. *Prepare a menu that is vegetarian, low-fat, low-cholesterol, low salt, or a combination of these. If possible, combine the meal with a presentation and /or health screening by a qualified health professional.*

NOTE 2: *You could combine a "silent auction" with your meal for added fundraising. (see* Silent Auction *on page 160).*

DOUGHNUT DELIVERY EXPRESS

What's better than fresh doughnuts on a Saturday morning? Having them delivered right to your home, that's what! It's a great treat for those receiving doughnuts and it's a great fundraiser for your group.

A good time to do a doughnut delivery is an early spring or fall weekend when many people tend to be outdoors doing yardwork and are not as likely to be gone on vacations. Winter weekends can be tougher because of the weather. To begin this project, contact local bakers or doughnut shops. Explain you'll be ordering a large number of doughnuts on an upcoming Saturday morning and ask what kind of discount they'll give on your order. After you've selected a baker, get his input on what kinds of doughnuts to offer and how much to charge for them. Be sure to include delivery costs in your price structure.

To get the ball rolling, take advance orders (with one dozen minimum) for doughnuts to be delivered in a specific area (your neighborhood, members' families and friends' neighborhoods, etc.) on a specific Saturday morning.

This is a good time to use a

> *A good time to do a doughnut delivery is an early spring or fall weekend when many people tend to be outdoors doing yard work and are not as likely to be gone on vacations. Winter weekends can be tougher because of the weather.*

highly focused telemarketing campaign. Divide your target market and have each member call a specific number of potential customers. See *Telemarketing* on page 82 for more details.

Use a simplified version of the *Product Order Form* on page 179. Let your customers know when you'll deliver the goods, for example from 8 a.m. to 10 a.m. Make duplicate copies of orders: one for your records, the other to attach to the bag of doughnuts to help the delivery people. Make advance arrangements with your baker so he'll be prepared for your order.

Compile your orders and give them to your baker as soon as possible. Ask your baker for food handling advice. It may be more appropriate to have the individual doughnut orders pre-bagged by the doughnut shop instead of your volunteers because of local health codes.

If not, have one person pick up the doughnuts and enough bags so you can bag all the orders on delivery morning. Take them to a central location where the individual orders will be bagged and given to the volunteers for delivery.

In either case make sure your delivery people have plenty of change with them. Also let them know that tips are graciously accepted. Pick up payment for the doughnuts when delivered.

SUPPLIES & EQUIPMENT

Your supplies are doughnuts, which you'll purchase from a bakery. The only equipment you'll need is vehicles to pick up and deliver the doughnuts.

MANPOWER

Volunteers will be needed first to take orders and then to deliver the doughnuts. Make sure all your drivers have good maps along with names and phone numbers of all customers to expedite delivery. The project chairman will need to contact bakers and get quantity prices. After a baker is selected, enlist his help to decide what kinds of doughnuts to sell.

Happy delivering!

FOOD STANDS

Selling food, snacks and beverages at public gatherings can be a one-time event or an ongoing, year-round income producing project. A well thought-out food stand is a good fundraiser when held in conjunction with school or church functions such as plays, carnivals, sports events and festivals. It can also work well with auctions and flea markets.

To take your food stand to an event, you'll first need to contact the event's sponsoring organization and seek their permission. Find out if they're charging booth fees and what utilities are available.

Your group will be responsible for set up, supplies and clean up of the concessions. Keep your offerings basic and simple. Coffee, doughnuts, cookies, chips, lemonade, soda pop and hot dogs are all easy foods and drinks to supply.

SUPPLIES & EQUIPMENT

You will need a table or stand to sell the food and drinks from. Hang a colorful banner behind your table. Make sure it includes your group's name, logo and some graphics to tell your customers who you are and how their purchases will benefit your group. Be sure to have your products and their prices clearly listed on one or more signs.

> *Hang a colorful banner behind your table. Make sure it includes your group's name, logo and some graphics to tell your customers who you are and how their purchases will benefit your group.*

The type of coolers or containers you'll need will depend on the foods and beverages you're selling. You'll also need serving containers and utensils for every type of food and drink you sell. Some condiments such as sugar, cream, salt, pepper, mustard, catsup, etc., may be necessary. If appropriate, provide napkins and plates of some type.

If you're providing hot dogs, either preheat and wrap them to keep them warm or purchase, rent or borrow a hot dog warmer or portable microwave. Remember you'll need to have electricity available at the site to run this equipment.

To serve coffee, you'll need an institutional-sized coffee pot and cups. Hot water and tea bags are always a good idea. In addition, a cooler filled with ice can hold several brands of canned sodas. Provide enough garbage cans for the expected crowd and be sure your group recycles as much as possible.

MANPOWER

You will need several people to set up the stand, cook and serve the food, make change and keep everything moving smoothly. You'll also need a crew to clean up after the event. Supplies can be purchased in advance and if this becomes an ongoing fundraiser, you'll want to buy your staples in bulk for a better price.

You could also purchase cases of individually-packaged chips, nuts and other snack foods from wholesale suppliers. These pre-packaged goodies will keep for an extended period until you've sold them and will not require any special food handling techniques or equipment. Store all supplies until needed.

NOTE: *Contact people organizing events in your area for additional leads. Always check with those in charge to see if there are any food and beverage regulations or restrictions.*

GREAT DINNERS TO GO

In dining rooms all over the city, the finer china is out and the wines gently breathing as hundreds of people prepare for a great dining experience. It's your 7th annual *Great Lasagna To Go* and hungry crowds are coming your way.

This fundraising event is a simplified meal fundraiser. It's simplified because you send the meal home with your customers. And that means you won't have the usual tables, dishes and flatware worries.

First, decide what type meal to have. Pick a proven big crowd-pleaser like casseroles, soups or pasta dishes. Or do a "brown bag" lunch with deli sandwiches.

Next, choose the time and date for your dinner to go. Some popular times for carry-outs are just before major sporting events, after church services on Sunday and right after work during the week.

Get your publicity out several weeks before the event. Send news releases to your local papers, put posters up in churches, local stores, high schools and colleges. If you're coordinating with another event, publicize your dinner in the same geographic areas the other event is publi-cized. Maybe you can buy your own ad space in their newspaper ad.

> *Some popular times for carry-outs are just before major sporting events, after church services on Sunday and right after work during the week.*

Sell as many advance tickets as possible so you can more accurately gauge how much food you'll need.

Check with your local Board of Health to find out what, if any, food-han-dling permits are needed.

On the day of the carryout, package leftovers and sell them as freezable dinners.

SUPPLIES & EQUIPMENT

Solicit donations and/or find suppliers who'll give wholesale prices on meal ingredients as well as carry-out containers, napkins and utensils. You'll need a place big enough to prepare, package, and store all meal items.

Carefully calculate your ingredients, prep, cooking and packaging time so your meals will be ready and waiting (but not too long) when your first customers arrive. Depending upon your menu, you'll need to keep your entrees warm or cold until they are picked up.

MANPOWER

All members should sell tickets before the event. Appoint a chairman to handle publicity. Target your market (i.e. school-wide, church-wide, city-wide) and publicize accordingly.

You'll need volunteers to solicit donations of food and supplies and pick them up at the proper times. Whatever is not donated, purchase in bulk.

The day before the event and the day of the event, you'll need people to prepare the meals. When producing large quantities of food, an "assembly line" often makes it all easier. Assign a specific

BULK ITEMS & TYPICAL NUMBER OF SERVINGS

• 1 lb. coffee	50 cups
• 1 gal. pancake syrup	50 servings
• 1 lb. butter	50-60 pats
• 1 lb. Parmesan cheese	32 servings
• 1 gal. ice cream	14 people

As a general rule, be generous in your estimations. You should be able to sell all leftovers or send them home with your volunteers. Or, to really be generous, take your leftovers to a local mission or soup kitchen.

A REAL ITALIAN FEAST

CASA DA BURO SALAD
A local Italian favorite

DRESSING
- 6 anchovies
- 8 oz. wine vinegar
- ¾ t oregano
- 1 ½ t pepper
- 1 T salt
- 1 ¼ oz. sugar
- 1 ½ t garlic salt
- ¼ cup corn starch
- 1 pint (16 oz.) oil

Blend first eight ingredients in a blender. Pour in oil in a stream.

This makes more than you'll need. It keeps about two weeks refrigerated.

SALAD
- 1 head Iceberg lettuce, torn
- 1 bunch Romaine lettuce, torn
- 1 red pepper, chopped
- 6 green onions chopped
- 2 oz. Parmesan cheese, grated
- 2 oz. Romano cheese, grated
- 2 oz. Provolone cheese, grated
- 2 oz. Mozzarella cheese, grated
- croutons (recipe below)
- 2 strips Bacon pieces

Toss everything but croutons and bacon. Add dressing 15 minutes before serving. Add croutons and bacon when served.

CROUTONS
- 6 English muffins, cubed
- ½ cup Casa da buro dressing
- ¼ cup Parmesan cheese, grated

Toss all ingredients together. bake at 350⁰ on a cookie sheet, stirring every five minutes. They're done when lightly browned.

ITALIAN TOMATO SAUCE

Leftover sauce is good over poached eggs or added to soup or gravy.

- 4 T olive oil
- 3 to 4 onions, sliced thin
- 2 cloves garlic, split
- 1 to 2 pounds ground beef
- 2 cans tomato paste
- 2 lg. cans of tomatoes (4 to 5 cups)
- 2 T sugar
- Salt, black pepper, cayenne, oregano and basil to taste.

Put olive oil, onions and garlic in a large skillet or saucepan. Cook until the onion is golden. Next add ground beef, cook and stir five minutes. Now add tomato paste, canned tomatoes, sugar and spices.

Simmer at least one hour. Add water as needed but remember the sauce should be thick and smooth. For the finest blending of flavors, let the sauce "mellow" for a day before serving it. Serves approximately 10 people.

SPAGHETTI
- ½ pound (serves 4)

Have ready a deep kettle of rapidly boiling water (salt optional). Take care not to break spaghetti. Take handful of spaghetti and dip one end into the boiling water until the ends begin to soften. As they do, coil the spaghetti into the boiling water. Cook until just tender, about seven minutes.

Drain in a colander. Arrange spaghetti in layers in heated serving dish, spreading a generous layer of sauce on each layer. Serve with extra sauce and plenty of grated Parmesan or Romano cheese.

NOTE: For cooking large quantities, the following guidelines may be helpful.

EQUIVALENT WEIGHTS & MEASURES

DRY

3 t	=	1 T
6 t	=	2 T
12 t	=	4 T
18 t	=	6 T
24 t	=	8T
36 t	=	12T
48 t	=	16T

LIQUID

1/8 C	=	1 fl . oz.
1/4 C	=	2 fl. oz.
1/3 C + 2t	=	3 fl. oz.
1/2 C	=	4 fl. oz.
3/4 C	=	6 fl. oz.
1 C	=	8 fl. oz.

WEIGHT

1/4 lb.	=	4 oz.
1/2 lb.	=	8 oz.
3/4 lb.	=	12 oz.
1 lb.	=	16 oz.

PORTIONS PER PERSON

Meat (main)	=	2 ½ to 3 ½ oz.
Fish (main)	=	4 oz.
Sandwich meat	=	⅛ to ¼ lb.
Sausage (links)	=	3
Sausage patties	=	2
Hot dogs	=	1 or 2
Bacon strips	=	3
Vegetables (side)	=	4 oz. (½ cup)
Pie	=	⅙ or ⅛ of pie
Chili/soup (main)	=	8 oz. (1 cup)
Fruit (frozen/canned)	=	4 oz.(½ cup)
Bread (with a meal)	=	1 ½ pieces
Lettuce (for salad)	=	⅙ to ⅛ head
Salad dressing	=	1 T
Sandwich filling	=	⅓ cup
Spaghetti	=	4 oz.
Spaghetti sauce	=	4 oz
Pizza	=	1 or 2 slices
Pancakes	=	3
Waffles	=	1 or 2
Beverages	=	8 oz.

---

job to each volunteer (i.e. Jill chops the carrots for the salad). When the meals are ready, you need volunteers to package and get it ready to go. Again, use the assembly line approach.

You'll also need cashiers to sell the carry-out packages the day of the event. Done well, this kind of event can raise both money and your group's standing in the community!

You've been under the spell of highway hypnosis for the past few numbing hours. A rest area looms on the horizon. What a welcome sight it is! As you park your car you see they're serving free coffee, lemonade and cookies. The clouds part and it's a beautiful day!

A holiday rest area food stand is such a popular fundraiser it may be hard to break into since many of the good spots are already taken. The idea is to set up a refreshment stand at an interstate rest area during holiday peak travelling hours and give free refreshments to weary travellers.

Of course, you do accept donations and that's why these are such popular and effective fundraisers. Once you have a location, choose a specific time slot or, with enough help, man the stand for an entire 24-hour period. If it's a three-day holiday weekend, like Memorial Day, cover all three days. If your group can't cover the entire stretch, team up with another group.

Keep your refreshments simple: coffee, lemonade, and cookies are welcomed by the road-weary traveller. Give everyone the refreshments free of charge, but, at the same time, make it clear that donations are gratefully accepted.

> **The idea is to set up a refreshment stand at an interstate rest area during holiday peak travelling hours and give free refreshments to weary travellers.**
> **Of course, you do accept donations...**

A nicely-decorated, well-placed donations cannister will let the folks know you'd like a donation.

Most people will be generous and probably give more than if you had regular prices. Set a limit of one or two "free" drinks or cookies per person. Of course, if someone wants to buy five cookies for

five dollars, don't turn them away! Tell them, "No problem—we'll even do 12 for $10 if you want!"

The project chairman will need to contact the State Highway Department and find out about any regulations for this type of event. Go for a rest area within 50 miles of home, but be ready to take what's available. This project can generate large sums of money.

SUPPLIES & EQUIPMENT

You'll need a concession trailer with an awning or a tent and cafeteria-style tables or both. Borrow these items if you can; if not, try to negotiate a discount price with a rental company. Cups for coffee and drinks are needed, as well as sugar and creamers. Contact local restaurants, wholesalers, and grocers for donations and/or wholesale purchases of food and supplies. Cookies can be donated or purchased at a bulk rates from local bakeries.

Wearing plastic food handling gloves, wrap cookies individually in plastic wrap. Place some in a large bowl so travelers can help themselves.

For the lemonade, use bulk cans and mix five gallons at a time in large coolers. You'll need several 50-cup coffee makers to keep a constant supply of hot coffee. Offer both decaf and regular coffee

HOT WEATHER CONCESSION ITEMS:
• Lemonade
• Iced tea
• Coffee (smaller amounts)
• Cookies
• Fresh fruit

COLD WEATHER CONCESSION ITEMS:
• Coffee (lots of it!)
• Hot chocolate
• Hot tea (smaller amounts)
• Cookies
• Donuts

continued on next page

JUMBO PRETZELS

It's twenty minutes before the varsity game's kick-off and your hot jumbo pretzels just sold out. By game time the stand is closed up and the "Thank you for your support" sign is out. You're in the stands, ready to see the game.

Selling jumbo pretzels is a great fundraiser when held in conjunction with other events. Perhaps you can set up a stand at upcoming school sports, musical and theater events.

You can make the pretzels early and freeze them. If you're selling outdoors, you'll need to heat them and keep them warm (wrapping them in

foil while hot and layering in a cooler works for short periods). Inside, keep 'em warm in an oven until they served. Wrap in foil so they don't dry out.

Cooked to perfection and served with their traditional condiments, mustard (the spicier the better) and grated cheeses (or sauces), jumbo pretzels really please a crowd.

JUMBO PRETZELS

- 4 cups flour
- 1 ½ cups warm water
- 1 package yeast
- 1 egg, well beaten
- 1 tsp. sugar
- coarse salt

Mix yeast with ½ cup warm water in large bowl. Add sugar and flour, and mix in the remaining water slowly. Knead dough thoroughly. Cover bowl with moist towel and let raise for 20 to 30 minutes. Separate into 12 pieces and roll each piece into a ball. Roll each ball out into long rope then twist it into a pretzel shape. Arrange the raw pretzels on a greased cookie sheet then baste each one with the beaten egg. Sprinkle with coarse salt. Bake in pre-heated 425 degree oven for 20 to 25 minutes until golden brown Makes 12 pretzels. Serve warm. Freeze in plastic bags if needed.

continued from preceding page

to keep all your donors happy. In cold weather also have a pot of hot water and both tea bags and hot chocolate mix packets.

Use outdoor extension cords. Contact the State Highway Department for access to their power supply. Keep lots of ice on hand for lemonade.

It's difficult to predict how many customers you'll have, but figure about 100 people per hour during peak times. Based on that figure, plan on giving away 50 cups of coffee, 50 cups of lemonade and 100 cookies per hour. These numbers will vary, of course, depending upon the weather. Try to have enough to accommodate 2000 people.

After the first few hours, you'll be able to estimate your

average outlay of goodies per hour. Multiply your per-hour averages by the number of hours you'll be open to approximate your total holiday customer count. If you think you'll run short, send one of your members on a grocery run.

Have a banner, posters and/or other signs, identifying you and your sponsors. Make a big sign that indicates the refreshments are free, but donations are gladly accepted. A nicely-decorated coffee can with a slot cut in the lid is a great donations catcher. Next check the State Highway Department's guidelines, then put a sign on the highway, near rest area exit signs, telling travelers when free refreshments are available.

MANPOWER

You will need people to coordinate the project with the State Highway Department. Volunteers are also needed to set up and tear down the stand, and handle all other equipment rental, pick-up and delivery.

Another committee is needed to find donations of food and supplies and coordinate the pick-up of these items. Plan on having two or three people per shift to operate the stand. If possible, have a back-up person available in case of illness or a shortage of supplies. If you have three people per shift, working six- or eight-hour shifts, you'll need from 9 to 12 people per day for this project. Let's get brewing!

LEMONADE STAND

The mid-July sun beats down mercilessly upon the crowd. Parched throats cry out for relief, then one crowd member sees your lemonade stand. Many of them fall in line and before long, you've sold all your ice-cold lemonade. It's a simple but effective fundraiser.

First, you need a large public event. Memorial Day, Fourth of July and Labor Day parades are good times to sponsor lemonade stands. Don't forget other local festivals or carnivals either. Consult with event organizers to see if there are any fees or restrictions on booths.

Check with your local Board of Health to see if you need food handling permits. They can also tell you about any other regulations.

> **Make your booth attractive and eye-catching. ... Don't forget to have your group's name clearly visible on your booth. That way people will know who benefits from their purchase.**

Make your booth attractive and eye-catching. Use a theme that fits with the parade or festival yet reflects your own group as well. Have prices and specialties (i.e., fresh-squeezed Florida lemons, etc.) clearly posted. Don't forget to have your group's name clearly visible on the booth. Then people will know who benefits from their purchase.

SUPPLIES & EQUIPMENT

You'll need materials to make both your booth and banners.

Check with parade/festival officials to see if they have any booth construction regulations.

For the lemonade, you'll need a good recipe, lemons, sugar, water, a juicer, cups and plenty of ice. You'll probably need a sharp knife and cutting board for the lemons. Food handling gloves

LEMONADE

If frozen lemonade from concentrate is too sweet, improve it by adding fresh squeezed lemon juice to taste.

Each serving:
- 2 T lemon juice
- 2 T sugar
- 1 cup ice water, crushed or cubed ice
- Maraschino cherry or fresh mint sprig

In a suitable glass, mix the lemon juice and sugar. Stir thoroughly to dissolve sugar. Add water and ice. Stir well and decorate with a Maraschino cherry or sprig of fresh mint.

are also a good idea (and may be required by local laws). Have a change box with plenty of change.

You'll also need a cooler to keep your ice cold. Have plenty of supplies on hand. If possible, have back-up volunteers ready to run to the store should supplies run out.

MANPOWER

Probably the hardest part of this project is building the booth. But a few volunteers with minimal carpentry skills and a little imagination can have a lot of fun! Make sure your booth is both attractive and functional. Make it big enough for two people to move comfortably in. Also allow space to store your supplies in the booth.

If your group has few construction skills or supplies, you can always use a card table or cafeteria table for your booth. Get some inexpensive skirting (from party supply stores) to put around the table. You may also want to use a large umbrella to protect both your workers and your ice cold lemonade from the sun.

All in all, this is not a demanding project. All you need is someone to make and serve lemonade and someone to make change. It's a great idea to have a back-up crew to give those working the stand an occasional break. Keep it sweet and fun!

MIX 'N' MATCH COOKIE SALE

"**I** want one of those cookies," you think to yourself. "I want one of those, too, and one of those and one of those," your mind races on. You start to get dizzy, but no need for that because you can have 'em all. That's the beautiful part of this mix 'n' match cookie sale.

This is a popular rendition of the time-tested cookie sale. To get yours rolling, have each member agree to furnish a specified number of cookies (1 to 3 dozen works well). On sale day the cookies are displayed and sold mix 'n match style by the dozen for one set price. Use coffee cans or gallon-size plastic bags to package the cookies.

> *A mix 'n' match cookie sale can be a real money maker when held with a festival or carnival. ... This is the time for everyone to get out grandma's best cookie recipes and make double batches!*

Add festive touches with wrapping paper or plain paper and stickers or graphics.

This event works well on either a small- or large- scale. It can be as simple as a "members only" exchange or you can open it to the general public. If it's "members only," simply advertise it in your newsletter and through anouncements at all meetings.

A mix 'n match cookie sale can be a real money maker when held with a festival or carnival. If you plan to do this project as a public event, use all available channels. Put posters on high-traffic bulletin boards, hand out as many flyers as possible, mail a news release to local papers, radio and TV stations.

On the day of the event add more posters in the sale area and mark your sale booth with a bold, eye-catching banner with all necessary information. Remember to check with your local Board of Health for any food-handling permits that may be needed.

SUPPLIES & EQUIPMENT

Cookies should be donated either by members or local vendors. This is the time for everyone to get out grandma's best cookie recipes and make double batches!

Tables and trays or boxes lined with wax paper are needed to display the cookies on sale day. Everyone handling cookies should wear plastic food-handling gloves.

You will need containers for your customers. You can use coffee cans, tins, boxes, baggies or something really unique (put on your thinking cap!).

MANPOWER

Volunteers are needed to bake or pick up cookies. Have each member responsible for a specific number of cookies (2 dozen works well). If they can bring more or get other people to bake also, that will increase both your variety and sales!

Several people are needed to staff the table and handle the cookies. Make sure they have a neat, clean, appearance and wear food-handling gloves. Have a cashier who does not handle any cookies. This will make a more sanitary operation and save a lot of gloves!

NO BAKE COOKIES

- 2 cups sugar
- 3 T cocoa
- ½ cup milk
- ¼ lb. butter (1 stick)
- ½ cup peanut butter
- 3 cups quick oatmeal
- 1 t vanilla

Mix the sugar, cocoa, milk and butter together and boil for one minute. Then add the peanut butter, quick oatmeal and vanilla. Drop cookies on a greased cookie sheet and chill until firm.

Once properly chilled these cookies will stay in great shape for quite a while unless your cookie sale is outdoors on a hot, sunny day. Then you may need to keep these in a cooler.

Makes about three dozen cookies.

PRODUCE STAND

The fresh scents of cantaloupe, onions and tomatoes waft through the crowd. People are busy filling their baskets and carts. The long hours everyone toiled in the garden is paying off now!

A well-stocked and managed produce stand can be a major income-generating project for your group. It works best with about 40 to 50 people involved.

A good location for your produce stand is absolutely crucial. It should be in an area with a lot of public traffic. Once the site is selected you'll need to design the stand itself. A small wall tent with wooden tables works well. Set it up to have good ventilation during the hot summer months.

Plan to keep your stand open at regular hours, perhaps Monday through Friday 2 - 8 p.m., Saturdays: 8-5 p.m., Sundays: 12-5 p.m. (right after church services). With 40 to 50 members working on the above schedule, each member only needs to donate one or two half days (4 to 8 hours) a month to work at the stand.

Excellent quality produce is another essential key to a really successful produce stand. With a reputation for fresh, top-notch

TODAY'S FEATURES
Fresh Strawberries!
Great Sweet Corn!
Vine-ripened Tomatoes!

> **With a reputation for fresh, top-notch produce, you'll develop a faithful following. … a good produce stand could generate thousands of dollars a year for your coffers.**

produce, you'll develop a faithful following. With enough members participating, a good produce stand could generate thousands of dollars a year for your coffers. And everyone will get involved in gardening on some level or another. As part of your research, check out other local produce stands to see how they're set up and how they market their produce.

After you've decided what range of produce to offer, you can start your preparations the winter before by buying vegetable seeds in bulk and dividing them between members who've agreed to grow for the produce stand. Encourage all your members to either plant a small garden specifically for the group effort or devote a section of

their family garden to this purpose. If your group has access to a suitable garden site, you could set up your own "group garden" for members to tend.

If any members have fruit trees, ask them to donate some of their Grade A fruit to your stand. You could also approach an area fruit farm and ask if they'd consider an exchange of fruit for labor donated by members of your group.

Make sure your produce stand is ready for business when the vegetables and fruits start to ripen. Have everybody donate their Grade A produce to sell at the stand and price it competitively for your area. Encourage all members, their families and friends, to buy their fresh produce from your stand. Develop and implement a low-cost marketing plan to reach the general public, too.

Create a large roadside sign to use at the stand to announce each day's featured produce: fresh strawberries, great sweet corn, new green beans, vine-ripened tomatoes, etc.

Be sure to rotate your stock and reduce prices on older produce. You can give away excess to homeless shelters, a local mission or soup kitchen, food bank or women's shelter. Don't throw away any produce unless it's absolutely necessary.

You may want to offer or-

continued on next page

APPLE DUMPLINGS

What could be better than Mom's apple pie? Mom's apple dumplings, of course! Get your mother's best apple dumpling recipe, fire up the groups' ovens and prepare for one sweet-tasting and profitable fundraising event!

One church circle in our part of the country makes 3000 dumplings twice a year. They sell them for two dollars apiece at the church's spring and fall festi- vals and they sell out every time. They mass- produce their dump- lings in the church kitchen the week before each festival. All of the ingredi- ents are purchased in bulk.

It is a lot of work, but these large home-made apple cinnamon dumplings are excellent. They're sold in a styrofoam box so customers can freeze them if they want. Many folks place large advance orders every year so they'll get their share of dumplings. This project can be an Apple Festival, carry-out by itself or with an art/craft fair or seasonal festival. Take advance orders for as many as possible then sell the rest first come, first serve. And don't forget to get an apple dumpling for yourself!

> *One church circle in our part of the country makes 3000 dumplings twice a year. They sell them for two dollars apiece at the church's spring and fall festivals and they sell out every time.*

continued from preceeding page

ganically-grown produce. If you advertise a product as being organic, be certain it is. Check with local and state laws and see how they define organic. You can market your produce as "pesticide-free" or "chemical-free" if you've grown it without the use of pesticides or chemicals. Check local ordinances and your state's agricultural department for regulations that apply to produce stands and the kinds of marketing terms allowed.

As an added benefit to your customers, include recipes and directions for preparing or freezing the produce you sell. As you generate a loyal following, you'll want to consider making your produce stand an annual event that runs from early June until the first frost.

GOOD VEGGIES, FRUITS & HERBS TO GROW!

These popular vegetables, fruits and herbs range from easy to moderate to raise and market. Some, like pumpkins and corn, require larger spaces and don't work well in small garden plots.

Herbs, however, are growing in popularity with the more adventurous cooks and they require very little garden space. Plan your crops in accordance with the space you have available.

VEGETABLES
- Green Beans
- Beets
- Broccoli
- Carrots
- Sweet Corn
- Cucumbers
- Eggplant
- Lettuce
- Onions
- Snap Peas
- Sweet Peppers
- Hot Peppers
- Potatoes
- Pumpkins
- Radishes
- Summer Squash
- Winter Squash
- Tomatoes

FRUITS
- Apples
- Grapes
- Pears
- Strawberries
- Blueberries
- Raspberries
- Peaches
- Plums
- Cantaloupe
- Watermelon

HERBS
- Basil
- Rosemary
- Sage
- Thyme
- Mustard
- Parsley
- Mint
- Garlic
- Chives
- Lemon Balm
- Cilantro
- Oregano

You could extend your selling season if you offer pumpkins for sale until Halloween. If the stand really works for your group, consider selling Christmas trees or wreaths, oranges, grapefruit and other seasonal items. A produce stand can be as big or small as you want.

Get your garden plots ready, your stand set up and get those seeds planted!

PICNIC BASKET SURPRISE

It's a Sunday afternoon in the park. People are out strolling, enjoying the fresh air and sunshine. Amidst the trees and flowers, a crowd comes together around dozens of beautiful picnic baskets on display. A nearby sign tells one and all that these baskets will be auctioned at 2:00 p.m. and all proceeds will benefit the *Little Shepherd Youth Group.*

For this different kind of auction, picnic baskets are filled with goodies and put on display for the participants to view from the outside only! No one knows what kinds of "surprise" goodies are carefully packed inside each basket.

Suggestions for basket themes can include:

- *Homemade breads*
- *Gourmet crackers*
- *Specialty pastas*
- *Gourmet cheeses*
- *Home-style jams/jellies*
- *Packaged specialty teas*
- *Gourmet coffee*
- *Dried soup mixtures*
- *Fancy napkins*
- *Sparkling beverages*
- *Canned meats/fish*
- *Gourmet mustards*
- *Home-baked cookies/cakes*
- *Fancy nut mixes*
- *Assorted dried fruits*

Each individual basket's decorations give just a hint of

> **For this different kind of auction, picnic baskets are filled with goodies and put on display for the participants to view from the outside only!**

what's inside. For example: doilies and gingham could decorate a picnic basket featuring home-made breads and jams, Italian lace for bread and cheese, fresh sprigs of greens for a basket of health-food, etc.

SUPPLIES & EQUIPMENT

Your supplies for this project consist of the baskets, their decorations and contents. Get as many baskets and contents donated to your group as possible. Buy the remaining items you need at cost from various vendors and grocers.

Use members of your group to fill and decorate baskets in an attractive manner. Avoid using refrigerated food items in your baskets to prevent any possible spoilage.

At a pre-arranged time the bidding begins, with each basket going to the highest bidder. Depending upon your investment in the baskets and their contents, you may want to stipulate minimum bids on some or all of them.

MANPOWER

Prior to the event, you'll need volunteers to collect the baskets and their contents and put them all together. On the day of the event, you'll need people to set up, do the auction, collect the money, make sure the merchandise is on the way and clean up. Refer to *General Auction* on page 155 for more details.

Since this auction has all the elements of a social event, you may want to provide cheese and crackers, punch and cookies or some other light snacks for auctiongoers to munch on as they browse through your decorated baskets.

Be sure to mention these free snacks in your publicity. This will help draw a larger group of participants. Bill the event as a Sunday social outing in the park, as well as a fundraiser for your worthy cause.

Refer to *General Auction* on page 155 for the specific details about how to conduct a successful auction.

On auction day be sure to bring a blanket, buy your favorite basket and find a sunny spot to enjoy a great picnic!

CHAPTER 6
HELPING OTHERS

CHAPTER NOTES:

BABYSITTING

It's a familiar scene: Mom or dad trying to shop while three kids try to escape (so far unsuccessfully) three different ways. About now most parents would gratefully welcome a handy, reliable babysitting service. Here's where your group, with a little creativity and planning, can set up and operate a fun money-maker.

First, decide when to offer babysitting services. You could offer them year-round (after school and on week ends), seasonally (during holiday seasons, especially Christmas) or just on selected dates.

Next, decide if your babysitting services will be one-on-one, where the individual goes to the parents' house to sit for their children, or be organized as a service offered at your group's meeting place, church basement, etc.

Another variation is a "babysitting pool." Use one phone number for interested parents to call. This person is then in charge of scheduling the members to sit at specified dates and times. This person will need a frequently updated list of available members to work from.

No matter which version of babysitting services you finally decide to offer, you'll want to advertise it widely. A strong

> ... most parents would gratefully welcome a handy, reliable babysitting service. Here's where your group, with a little creativity and planning, can set up and operate a fun money-maker.

basic advertising campaign would likely include posters in churches, schools, grocery stores, department stores and other high traffic public places. You can often find a cooperative grocery or department store that will stuff your posters or flyers into their customer's bags, sometimes there is a nominal fee involved for these "bag stuffers," see *Marketing* on page 44.

Large one-day babysitting events will benefit from strong PSA-based marketing. As with all marketing efforts, the goal is to reach those most likely to want your services.

If you are planning on babysitting for a large number of

children at one time (i.e., an all-day babysitting service on a Saturday just before Christmas), you'll want a large facility with kitchen, play area, and restrooms. Church or school recreation areas are usually good places. For an "all-day" babysitting service, you could include the following activities:

- *Simple crafts to make*
- *Easy, do-it-yourself type finger foods for snacks*
- *Easy-to-fix lunches*
- *Story-telling time*
- *Mime, puppets, or other entertainment*
- *Games for various ages*
- *Creative projects (cover a table with white butcher's paper and make a mural)*

Before you offer babysitting services, hold a "babysitting class" covering the basics. This class should cover:

- *What to do in an emergency (medical, fire, etc.)*
- *Strategies for entertaining children of various ages (including games, crafts, stories and songs)*
- *Strategies for handling challenging children*
- *What information to get from the guardian (phone numbers to reach them, medical or dietary restrictions, time when they'll return).*

Once you have covered the basics with your group, set a price schedule for babysitting. Start by asking babysitters in

continued on next page

CAR WASH

"**A** clean car runs better," so the old phrase goes. Most people like to drive a clean car. And because of this your group can bring in some cash with fundraising's soggy classic, the car wash. You'll need a lot of helping hands to do it.

This event works best on a Saturday or Sunday. Advertise the car wash one to two weeks in advance. Put posters and announcements in local church bulletins, newspapers, grocery stores, laundromats and other high visibility places.

On car wash day, put signs by the road close to the car wash site. Give clear directions and list prices.

Assign volunteers to groups with specific jobs: washers, rinsers, polishers and window washers. Interior cleaning and vacuuming can be extra charge services. Have each group bring their own cleaning equipment and supplies.

> "A clean car runs better," so the old phrase goes. ... And because of this your group can bring in some cash with fundraising's soggy classic, the car wash.

SUPPLIES & EQUIPMENT

Buckets, rags, soap, window cleaners, hoses, lots of water and elbow grease are needed to run a car wash. Find a site with a plentiful water supply so you can use several hoses. If you're offering interior cleaning service, make sure you have enough power to run all the vacuums you'll need.

MANPOWER

You need volunteers for each segment of the car wash: washers, rinsers, dryers/polishers, window cleaners and vacuumers. Make sure you have plenty of people in each group. Remember, the faster you wash each car, the more cars you'll be able to wash and the more money you'll make.

NOTE: *For a different car wash twist, offer it to a company (one with a lot of vehicles such as a utility company, cab company, a delivery company, etc.) or have a carwash on a week day and catch the working people.*

---

continued from preceeding page
your area what the going rates are, then set a standard rate schedule for babysitting. You may want to give "group rates" to mothers who bring more than one child.

The money earned from babysitting can be handled several ways: The sitter can donate a predesignated portion of their earnings (say 50%) to the group and keep the rest. Or, if the babysitting is totally a group effort, the entire earnings can go into your group's coffers.

SUPPLIES & EQUIPMENT

Supplies for this service depend on if you are working at your location or someone's home.

If it's your location, have as many of the following items on hand as possible: games, toys, craft supplies, snack foods, beverages, first-aid kit, paper, crayons, tissues, and paper towels. If you are providing a meal, have as much of the food pre-made as possible. Keep cooking to a minimum while the children are present. Get as many items donated as possible (including food supplies as well as the games, craft items, etc.)

MANPOWER

The amount of volunteers you'll need will depend upon the number of children you want to sit for. As a rule of thumb, figure at least one sitter for every two or three children. Check local ordinances to see if youths are required to have an adult present if they're offering a babysitting service at a church or school.

CHRISTMAS GIFT WRAPPING

Your feet hurt, your legs are tired and your head is still buzzing but your Christmas shopping is done! What would really make this shopping trip complete is to come home with all your gifts wrapped. Not surprising, a gift wrapping service is a popular Christmas-time fundraiser.

Start by approaching local discount/variety stores or the mall and see if you can set up a package-wrapping booth in their facility. Ask them well in advance (September is a good time) and set specific dates to offer your wrapping services.

Publicize the event as widely as possible. Use posters in high traffic public areas, hand out flyers and get as many PSAs in newspapers and on radio and television stations as you can. Some nearby stores may even include your wrapping services in their newspaper ads. Also have members ask their family and friends to use your gift-wrapping booth.

SUPPLIES & EQUIPMENT

You'll need a wrapping booth of some sort; a card table or two with chairs will suffice in most cases. If possible, get a table with a tough, non-scratchable surface. If you can't find a table that durable, be sure to cover the table so it won't be damaged by all the cutting and taping going on. Make a large, attractive sign telling of the service you're providing, the prices and who benefits from the service.

> *Not surprising, a gift wrapping service is a popular Christmas-time fundraiser. ... you could wrap gifts on a "donations only" basis. Most people are quite generous during the holiday season.*

Line up plenty of wrapping paper of various types and quality, tape, scissors, tags, bows and ribbons. Contact paper/party supply stores seeking donations of wrapping materials or the ability to purchase needed supplies at wholesale prices.

If most of your group is not very adept at making bows, you can buy instant bows that pop open with the flick of the wrist.

You can also use small ornaments or stickers for an extra touch of holiday glamour.

Make sure you have plenty of gift boxes in all popular sizes on hand. If the store where you have your booth sells these items, ask the manager if he'd like to donate supplies or if you can purchase them from him at wholesale. Set up your fees according to the size of the gift wrapped. Two or three price ranges is sufficient. Charge extra for any gift boxes used. Set your gift wrapping fees at several times your raw costs.

Or, you could wrap gifts on a "donations only" basis. Most people are quite generous during the holiday season.

MANPOWER

You'll need lots of volunteers skilled in gift wrapping, particularly if you offer this service on a day close to Christmas! Make sure you have adequate back-up personnel ready in case of a last-minute scheduling conflict or illness.

Before the event, schedule a gift wrapping practice session, with your "expert" wrappers offering time-tested pointers to the rest. With a few tips and a little practice, almost everyone can learn to wrap attractive gift packages.

Once shoppers see the quality of your wrapping service, they'll be standing in line to have their presents wrapped, too!

CARE PACKAGE

It's finals week at college. Tension is high, nerves taut. What could be more welcome than a Care Package filled with home-baked goodies? This project is a different sales twist. Essentially, it's marketing a care package of "goodies" to a group through their supporters.

First, define your market. Who are the most likely recipients of "care packages"? College students in finals week are one hot prospect. Nursing home residents or enlisted folks during the holiday season are two more likely groups.

After determining your target market, get the word out! If you choose college students, get a student home address mailing list from the registrar's office.

To work with a nursing home, first contact the administration office and see if they have a mailing list of residents' family members to approach about a care package.

To provide the care packages to our armed forces, you'll need to reach their families, your target market, through regular media channels. The armed forces do not give out names and addresses of enlisted people or their families.

Before you start selling care packages, check with the post office for specific mailing guidelines or restrictions. If you're sending foodstuffs overseas, there are stricter mail guidelines.

> *This project is a different sales twist. Essentially, it's marketing a care package of "goodies" to a group through their supporters.*
> *... College students in finals week are one hot prospect.*

After choosing your market, look for ways to reach those who will be sending the care packages to students, elders or enlisted people. Send them a letter explaining what your care packages include and how much they cost. Have them send a check with their order. See *Sample Letter* on page 143. Give a firm order date to ensure delivery at the proper time.

SUPPLIES & EQUIPMENT

The supplies needed for this project depend on your market. For college students during exam week, fill the care package (a box or grocery sack) with lots of edible goodies: cookies, granola bars, fresh fruit (that doesn't need refrigeration), crackers, etc.

For nursing home residents, a care package with stationery, toiletries, easy to open and eat snacks, candies, mints or small decorations are appropiate. The contents of your package should fit your market's needs.

You may find a local supermarket to donate some foods as well as the grocery sacks or, at least, only charge wholesale for them. Contact department stores or pharmacies for donations of toiletries, books, magazines or small gifts.

Know your out-of-pocket costs in detail before you set the package prices.

MANPOWER

You'll need people to sell packages using letters, flyers, announcements, whatever suits your market best.

Volunteers are needed to help shop, bake, and prepare all goodies for your care packages.

Get a volunteer "assembly line" together a day or two before delivery to assemble the packages. Tape a copy of each order to its bag. This makes life easier for the delivery people.

Deliveries need to take place on the designated day and are more easily done in pairs. It's great to see the surprised smile on a recipient's face when you give them their care package!

SAMPLE LETTER/ORDER FORM

DEAR_____:

As you are probably aware, final exams are coming up at _____college. This is a tense time for students; they could certainly use a little tender loving care from home. We have just the thing for you! Imagine the look on your favorite student's face when he or she receives a care package filled with home-baked goodies, crackers, fresh fruit, and bottled water!

We will be delivering these packages ($_____ each) on _____at _____college. If you would like to send one to a student, please fill out the enclosed form and return to us with your check or money order by_____. We know your thoughtfulness will be appreciated!

NAME_____

Address_____

Phone_____

Please send _____(#) CARE PACKAGES TO:

STUDENT(S) NAME(S)_____

Room/ Hall_____

Phone_____

I am enclosing a check/money order for:_____

NAME/MESSAGE ON CARD_____

_____

RETURN THIS FORM BY_____**TO:**_____

_____

_____

THANK YOU FOR YOUR ORDER AND YOUR SUPPORT!
(ENTER THE NAME OF YOUR GROUP HERE)

NOTE: *Make duplicate copies of the orders: Keep one for your records and attach one to the package for the delivery person.*

MAKE AS MANY COPIES OF THIS PAGE AS NEEDED

COMMUNITY CALENDAR

Wouldn't it be nice to have a calendar hanging in your kitchen that featured all your group's meetings, events and every member's birthday? Or how about a community-wide calendar listing all local events, special historical anniversaries, town meetings, celebrations and other special days?

Or how about a band calendar that shows all your competitions, practices and school events? If you have a specialized calendar idea in mind, this could be the fundraiser for you!

Community Calendars have been successfully produced for non-profit organizations by the Gordon Bernard Company, Inc. since 1949. The idea is popular and the company has a copyrighted version it franchises to individual groups.

Basically, it's a calendar custom-made for your group and your locale. It can feature members' birthdays and anniversaries, or any activities or events of interest to your group.

A calendar can focus on school activities or have a business, astrological or scriptural orientation. It can list prayers or local historical events of note. You can get calendars that feature general

> **There are three ways to make money with the Community Calendar: by selling ads; by selling special events listings, birthday and anniversary listings; and finally, by selling the calendar itself.**

trivia, music, sports or arts-oriented calendars. All calendars are designed to meet your group's unique needs.

Some potential markets for specialized calendars include: churches, scout troops, local schools, colleges and their organizations, communities and their many groups, local sports leagues like Little League softball, tennis or bowling.

There are three ways to make money with the Community Calendar: by selling ads; by selling special events listings, birthday and anniversary listings; and finally, by selling the calendar itself.

MANPOWER

Your manpower needs for this project will vary depending upon how you choose to market your calendar. Your main needs will be for skilled, enthusiastic sales people. To get everyone up to speed, see *General Selling Tips* on page 81.

To help boost members' enthusiasm and intensify sales efforts, you can sponsor a sales contest within your group. Give prizes to the top two or three ad, special event and calendar salespeople.

The company has all of the forms, price-listings, ad and event information forms you need to design a profitable calendar. They can show how much profit you'll make on whatever volume of calendars, listings and ads you sell.

They have several different sales approaches: You can sell the calendar on a small scale (to your group for example) or you could sell it on a larger scale that is school-, church-, or even city-wide.

SUPPLIES

The Gordon Bernard Company will walk you through every step of this project from selling the advertising, to gathering all the listings and things to look for in the group photograph you'll feature on your calendar.

For more complete information, contact:

The Gordon Bernard Company, Inc.
5601 Ridge Ave.
Cincinnati, OH 45213
(513)531-1484

LEAN & MEAN CLEANING MACHINE

Imagine a lean, mean "cleaning machine" of 8 to 10 youths and 2 to 3 adult leaders doing house and yard cleaning for your group's soon-to-be-satisfied customers. Everyone has a specific job: raking, cleaning gutters, washing down walls or trimming hedges. And they come fully equipped with tools and cleaning supplies.

Think about how much work a team like this can do in just a few hours. Think about how much work three teams can do. What you have are the makings of a great fundraiser!

Target specific neighborhoods with your marketing efforts. Both newspaper and grocery bag stuffers (see *Marketing* page 44) work well because they let you focus on reaching your target markets in specific neighborhoods. A local telemarketing effort can add big sales, see *Telemarketing* on page 82.

Set specific dates when you'll provide yard and house cleaning services. Organize your volunteers into groups specializing in specific areas:

• *Yardwork: raking, trimming dead limbs from bushes and trees, mowing, edging driveways and other areas*

• *Home Exterior: cleaning gutters, washing exterior walls with power washers, washing windows and screens*

• *Home Interior: vacuuming, washing walls or woodwork, polishing and/or cleaning and moving furniture*

• *Cars: exterior washing, interior vacuuming, waxing.*

> **You'll need many hard-working volunteers for this project. ... With large teams, you'll get a lot done and make some great cash.**

After you've decided what services to provide, set a fee schedule either by the hour or the job. If you're unsure how long a job will take or what to charge, do a trial run at a group member's house and accurately time each service. This gives you a pricing guideline.

For example, if it takes two volunteers one hour to clean the gutters on a one-story house, multiply your hourly rate times two to set a price for this job.

Next divide volunteers into teams and fill out a *Cleaning Teams* form, on page 147, for each. When you schedule work for a customer, leave them with a completed *Cleaning Services Worksheet* on page 146. Be sure they know about how long it will take to complete services and that you'll collect payment when the work is finished.

Publicize your services with flyers and posters. Put it in your church bulletin and school or neighborhood newsletter. List a phone number people can call for more information. As you schedule work for your teams, allow time for travel and lunch.

Finally, create a master schedule sheet indicating approximately when your team will be at each house, what specific services will be done and the fees to be collected.

SUPPLIES & EQUIPMENT

You will need the proper tools, equipment and cleaning supplies for services you'll provide. These can range from lawn mowers and hedge trimmers to brooms and vacuum cleaners. You'll also need rags, soap and gloves. Make sure all equipment is in good working order. Bigger equipment, like a power washer, can be rented.

MANPOWER

You'll need many hard-working volunteers for this project. Encourage all members to participate. With large teams, you'll get a lot done and make some great cash. Even if someone can't work all day, sign them up for part of the day!

CLEANING SERVICES WORKSHEET

Customer Name _____   **Work Date** _____

Address _____   **Starting Time** _____

Telephone _____

SERVICES

YARDWORK

❑ Raking	Fees	
❑ Trimming Bushes	Fees	
❑ Tree Trimming	Fees	
❑ Yard Mowing	Fees	
❑ Edging Driveway	Fees	
❑ Edging Sidewalks	Fees	
❑ Other	Fees	
❑ Other	Fees	

HOME EXTERIOR

❑ Cleaning Gutters	Fees	
❑ Exterior Power Wash	Fees	
❑ Window & Screen Washing	Fees	
❑ Trim Touch-up Painting	Fees	
❑ Patio & Deck Cleaning	Fees	
❑ Other	Fees	
❑ Other	Fees	
❑ Other	Fees	

CARS

❑ Washing	Fees	
❑ Waxing	Fees	
❑ Interior Cleaning	Fees	
❑ Other	Fees	
❑ Other	Fees	
❑ Other	Fees	
❑ Other	Fees	
❑ Other	Fees	

HOME INTERIOR

❑ Vacuuming	Fees	
❑ Washing Walls	Fees	
❑ Washing Woodwork	Fees	
❑ Polishing Furniture	Fees	
❑ Dusting Pictures/Knick-knacks	Fees	
❑ Other	Fees	
❑ Other	Fees	
❑ Other	Fees	

TEAM LEADER: _____

CUSTOMER APPROVAL: _____

Total Due

Total Collected

NOTE: Use carbon paper and make two copies for each customer. One copy will be their receipt.

MAKE AS MANY COPIES OF THIS PAGE AS NEEDED

CLEANING TEAMS

Organization Name _____ **Date** _____

Person in Charge _____ **Date/s of Event:** _____

Telephone _____

TEAM # _____

Leaders _____ Telephone _____

Team Members _____

_____

_____

_____

TEAM # _____

Leaders _____ Telephone _____

Team Members _____

_____

_____

_____

TEAM # _____

Leaders _____ Telephone _____

Team Members _____

_____

_____

_____

MAKE AS MANY COPIES OF THIS PAGE AS NEEDED

MONEY BAGS OF POTENTIAL

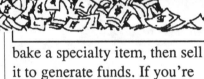

It's been one suprise after another all day long. Then your club treasurer gives you a small bag with ten silver dollars in it and tells you to make it grow. What do you do?

That's just the first surprise with this project. Instead of asking each participant to give money, you're giving it to them!

Everyone participating in the project, usually members only, is given a small velvet bag with five or ten silver dollars in it. The bags should be of a high quality; you can buy them at a variety store or make your own drawstring bag out of a velvet-like material with a hem at the top for the drawstring.

> *Everyone is to use their money to make more money for your "cause" ... There are no limits to the ways participants can make their money grow.*

Everyone then is to take their money and use it to create more money for your "cause," whatever that may be (i.e. raising funds for camp, a local shelter, etc.). Be sure you set a specific date, usually at a meeting, when the fruits of everyone's money bag are due.

There are no limits to the ways participants can make their money grow. One could use his cash to buy materials to make a craft item, then sell the item and donate the money earned. Or, they could use the money to buy ingredients to bake a specialty item, then sell it to generate funds. If you're skilled at woodworking, you could buy some premium grade wood and make high quality picture frames in standard sizes to sell.

Five or ten dollars spent at a paint store could get you started in re-lettering or re-numbering mailboxes in your neighborhood for a fee. Or you could spend the money at a wholesale supplier and re-sell the items at retail prices (this usually works well with candy).

You could use your money to buy gourmet popcorn, then resell it by the bag. Or buy everything you need to make one-of-a-kind pairs of earrings, necklaces or bracelets to re-sell. You could even spend the money for cleaning supplies, then offer your cleaning services for hire. The list of fundraising activities is limited only by the limits of your group's imagination!

When everyone gets their money bag, set a date by which they must return the money they've made. A spirited brainstorming session is a great addition to this meeting.

This project lends itself well to awards: for the most creative, unusual, funniest and most lucrative ways to make money with your money.

If you let people know there will be awards in various categories, it may help jumpstart them with their brainstorming for this project. An awards dinner is a great finish for this event.

Keep a list of the "best" ideas. They may be used as another fundraiser at a later date!
NOTE: *Our church has had great success with this fundraiser. Our minister asked all participants to use their money to purchase supplies to create something. All these creations were then brought to the church on a designated date. All the items were displayed, then auctioned off at a nice profit for the church. You could use the same auction idea to sell your creations at a PTA, school or membership meeting. See* General Auction *on page 155 for more about holding your own auction.*

NURSING HOME BAZAAR

It often takes so little to brighten someone's day—a smile, a small gift, a hand-made decoration. These kinds of things are especially appreciated by people who live in nursing homes. Why not provide a real service and a good fundraiser for your group by sponsoring a shopping bazaar for folks in a nursing home?

Choose a day in December to set up your bazaar. Check with the nursing home administrator to see if they have any special guidelines for the gifts you'll be offering. Ask all members to help make small craft items, gather donations, and purchase inexpensive ornaments and goodies (wholesale if possible).

Publicize your bazaar several weeks in advance so residents and their relatives will know about your event and can plan to participate. Put posters on all the home's bulletin boards and, if they have one, put an ad in their newsletter.

If the nursing home sends mailings to the resident's caretakers, ask if you could include one of your flyers in a mailing close to the date of your event.

On the day of the bazaar, decorate your tables in a festive fashion. Make sure prices are

clearly marked on all items. Then open your bazaar for business. When the sale is over, a Christmas carolling session with your volunteers and the residents would be a great finish!

> *Why not provide a real service and a good fundraiser for your group by sponsoring a shopping bazaar for folks in a nursing home?*

SUPPLIES & EQUIPMENT

Get as many items donated as possible, so you can keep your prices low for your customers.

Jewelry, cards, ornaments, craft items, games, books, packages of cookies or candies, perfumes/colognes, handkerchiefs are all great gift items.

Make some attractive, inexpensive craft items, too. Check with nursing home staff members and residents for other possible gift suggestions.

The nursing home will quite possibly have tables you can use to display your wares.

Price your items very reasonably and make the tags large enough to be easily read.

It's a nice festive touch to serve everyone punch and cookies during the event.

MANPOWER

You'll need people to gather and make sale items. At the event, you'll need people to set-up, sell, and clean up. This is a great group project and all can participate by visiting with the residents and carolling after the sale. Your group will reap large rewards in the happy smiles of the residents.

BASIC BUTTER COOKIES

- 1 cup soft butter
- 1 ½ cups confectioners sugar, sifted
- 1 egg
- t vanilla
- 2 ½ cups flour
- 1 t baking soda
- 1 t cream of tartar
- ¼ t salt

Cream butter, add sugar slowly until mixture is fluffy. Add egg and vanilla, beat well. Blend in sifted ingredients and chill in refrigerator.

To make cut-out cookies—Roll chilled dough out on floured board to ⅛" thickness, then cut-out cookie shapes. Bake for 6 minutes at 375⁰. After cookies cool, decorate with icing. Makes about four dozen cookies.

For Cinnamon Balls—Roll dough into 1" balls. Roll in mixture (4 T sugar and 2 t cinnamon) until well coated. Bake 8 to 10 minutes at 400⁰.

QUICK & EASY PUNCH

- Sherbet (flavor of your choice)
- Lemon-lime soft drink

Put a scoop of sherbet in each cup, then fill with a lemon-lime drink. Enjoy!

PAINTING STREET NUMBERS

You're driving slowly through an unfamiliar neighborhood, looking for your new friend's home. Most of the street numbers are incomprehensible and your frustration grows.

Again your eyes scan the neighborhood, this time they're stopped by a painted white box on the curb. In the box are street numbers. Seconds later you find your friend's home.

Street numbers on the curb in front of each house are both a great finishing touch to a neighborhood and a fundraising project with lasting impact.

> *Street numbers on the curb in front of each house are both a great finishing touch to a neighborhood and a fundraising project with lasting impact.*

This is a low-budget, minimal manpower project with good earning power. First check local ordinances for any restrictions on painting street numbers on curbs.

Begin your sales efforts by contacting neighborhood associations. See if they'd like a discounted group rate for having a lot of neighborhood house numbers painted.

Or maybe their members will pay full price and, for the association's help with sales, they earn 10% to 20% of your proceeds. This kind of project works best with lots of street numbers in a concentrated area.

Your group can also sell directly to homeowners. Create a poster, brochure or a postcard to explain that your group will paint house numbers on front curbs for a fee, for example, of five dollars a house.

Be sure to list a phone number or a form to fill in and mail back. Also divide your prospect list so each member can call their share of potential customers.

Use your posters as stuffers in neighborhood newsletters, selected newspaper routes and in local grocery store bags. See *Marketing* on page 44.

Make sure all publicity gives the date the painting will be done, a rain date, price and payment terms. Customers can pre-pay or pay on painting day. Double-check each name, address and telephone number.

Make three copies of each work order. One copy for your records, the next is for the work crew and the last copy is the customer's invoice.

Double-check each address before painting. If a customer is not home when you paint, leave their invoice and a self-addressed envelope in their door.

SUPPLIES & EQUIPMENT

You'll need stencils, a ruler, white paint, black spray paint, brushes, paint remover and rags. Paper stencils do not work well. Brass interlocking stencils are best, as they both change numbers and clean up easily.

Practice on members' curbs to perfect your equipment and methods. A good outdoor latex paint works well for the white background. It can be bristle-brushed on the curb and is less expensive than spray paint.

When the background is dry, spray paint black stenciled numbers in the white frame. Depending upon manpower and workload, you may want to get several sets of supplies so your members can work in teams.

MANPOWER

As few as two people can do this fundraiser. Teams of two to four people work best. Several teams can work in tandem, the first team paints white frames and team two follows, after the paint is dry, with stenciled numbers. This can be done in one day, weather and paint permitting or as a two-day project.

Grab your paint and brushes and get to work!

NOTE: *An idea that goes well in rural areas is painting mailbox flags. You'll need red paint and brushes—skip the stencils. It's an equally fast service.*

TEACHING CLASSES

Most people have a hobby, skill or area of special expertise. Offering classes for a fee is an often-overlooked means of raising funds. Check with your members, parents, friends, and group sponsors to see what skills and talents they're willing to share in a class. The following list is a sample of classes your group could offer:

• *Conversational languages (Spanish, French)*

• *Crafts (macrame, basket-weaving, shirt-painting)*

• *Building trades (carpentry, drywalling, plumbing)*

• *Arts (drawing, painting, photography)*

• *Cooking (French, Italian, Indian or Chinese cuisine)*

• *Dance (square, jazz, interpretive)*

• *Sports (table tennis, volleyball, badminton)*

Perhaps your group is very good at a certain service or skill. If other people can benefit from your expertise, you could sponsor a seminar to explain how you succeeded at civic action, making crafts, or whatever it is you are successful at.

If you can't find any willing teachers in your membership or their contacts, don't despair. You can hire a professional to teach a class for you.

Some kinds of people who could teach classes:

> *Offering classes for a fee is an often-overlooked means of raising funds. Check with your members, parents, friends, and group sponsors to see what skills and talents they're willing to share in a class.*

• *Medical personnel (basic first aid, health awareness)*

• *Dietician (nutrition, healthy cooking)*

• *Law enforcement personnel (self-defense)*

• *Accountants (basic personal and family finance, tax preparation, estate planning)*

• *Physical education teacher (aerobics, body-building).*

Before setting fees, find out from your teachers what they charge for teaching. If they know your class is a fundraiser, they may reduce or waive their charges. Your fee schedule should range from $10 to $20 for a one-night seminar, to $40 to $50 for a four to six week class. To keep your prices competitive, compare with fees for similar classes in your area.

Advance publicity with a specific sign-up deadline for classes is a must. You'll need a minimum number of students to hold a class. And you may need to set an upper limit on class size. With pre-registration, you'll know how many people to expect in each class.

SUPPLIES & EQUIPMENT

You'll need a place for your classes to meet. The location you need will be determined by the nature of the class.

For example, you'll need a large kitchen for a cooking class or a big area with an appropriate floor (wood or tile) for a dance or exercise class. If students need to bring equipment or supplies, be sure it's clearly stated in all publicity.

MANPOWER

First and foremost, you need a teacher. After you find someone to teach a class, then you must publicize it. Put up posters and hand out flyers at school, church and other public places. Attach a registration form to the flyers or list a phone number for more information.

Your registration form can be a 3 x 5 card listing class name, meeting times, dates and cost. Leave spaces so participants can fill in their name, address and phone number. Print your mailing address on the form and be sure to indicate to whom they should write their checks for class fees.

TRASH INTO CASH

Poof! What once were piles of old newspapers, twisted pieces of metal, tin cans, aluminum and glass instantly becomes cold, hard cash for your group's treasury.

With this project your group will not only raise funds, you'll also perform a valuable community service! You'll help beautify neighborhoods as you give people an easy way to get rid of their recyclable items. Their trash becomes your treasure when you sell your "junk" to scrap dealers and recyclers in exchange for cash.

Begin by contacting local recyclers and scrap dealers to find out what items they'll buy, and how much they'll pay for them. You will also need to know if there are any stipulations (i.e, should the newspapers be bundled with string? Should tin cans have their labels removed?) The dealer can provide you with all pertinent information. Ask specific questions about all the materials you'll collect like: glass, tin, aluminum, metals, styrofoam, plastic, newspaper, etc.

You may want to focus your efforts on a few of the more lucrative materials. But to make your project be a real commu-

> **With this project your group will not only raise funds, you'll also perform a valuable community service! You'll help beautify neighborhoods as you give people an easy way to get rid of their recyclable items.**

nity service, accept all recyclable items, even though the money you'll earn on some of them is minimal.

The idea is to make recycling as easy as possible. Set a "clean-up day" (or days) and publicize at least two weeks before the event.

Create posters and flyers that advertise your recycling. Put notices in church, school and neighborhood bulletins and newsletters. Next, distribute flyers in schools, churches and grocery stores (as bag stuffers if possible) in your area.

Since this is a community service project, contact local media to make PSAs about your project (see *Marketing* on page 44 for more details).

SUPPLIES & EQUIPMENT

You'll need a location to sort your scrap and recyclables. A church or school parking lot works fine. Try to have one truck at the drop-off point for each material (i.e. one truck for newspapers, one for plastics, etc.). You'll need vehicles and drivers to take all collected materials to the recyclers or scrap dealers.

Keep in mind you may get some heavy scrap metal items that require special handling. In fact, some clean industrial scrap, called "Grade A" materials in the recycling business, are real moneymakers.

MANPOWER

A publicity committee is needed to get this project off to a great start. First decide if you want to go school-, church-, neighborhood- or city-wide.

If you decide to open the project up to the entire city, be ready for mountains of recyclables. Have lots of volunteers ready to sort and transport the materials gathered.

If you keep your project smaller (say school-wide or church-wide), you might offer a pick-up service. Provide a phone number for people to call for pick-up of their items. Since you won't be sure of the exact pick-up time, ask them to leave the items in a specific spot. Keep a master list of all scheduled pick-ups, with donor names, addresses, phone numbers and items to be picked up. Have fun and earn some environmentally sound cash!

CHAPTER 7
SENSATIONAL SALES

CHAPTER NOTES:

GENERAL AUCTION

Who can resist the lure of an auction? With lots of lost treasures waiting to be discovered and bought, an auction can be a competitive bargain-hunters' paradise as well as a great fundraiser for your group. There are many varied twists you can apply to an auction. Some of our favorites are explained later in this chapter. To start, let's simply review the procedures for a standard auction.

First you need a date as well as location to hold your auction. You'll need a large area, especially if you're going to have large items. School gyms or church all-purpose rooms are great for auctions.

Remember, this is not a garage sale, so you'll want to stay away from garage sale type merchandise. Some of the more popular donated items are: dinner certificates, theater tickets, paintings, collectibles, antiques and kitchenware. Also get new or used appliances, sports equipment and clothes. Free video rentals, musical instruments, tapes or CDs, canned goods, baseball cards and baked goods are all potential money-makers. Quality items generate interest and draw a good crowd.

Use the *General Donation Form* on page 156 to keep track of all the donations received. You'll need a place to store, sort and catalogue donations until auction day. Sort items by categories and/or size. If you have many of a specific item (such as clothing), you may want to sort it according to size and box it up. Then you can sell these items by the box (i.e., four pair of size 32 jeans).

Publicize your auction throughout your neighborhood, school and church. Put your posters in grocery stores and other high traffic areas. Mention interesting items in all your publicity.

Prior to the event, set up display tables for your items. Leave plenty of room for people to walk around the tables to browse and inspect. Give your buyers an hour or so to check out your wares before you start the auction. Be sure to number all auction items and post minimum bid amounts where applicable.

SUPPLIES & EQUIPMENT

You will need a place big enough to hold the auction, along with enough display tables for all items. If possible, provide folding chairs for your buyers (they'll appreciate it).

Solicit donations from group members, family, friends, neighbors, relatives, school, church, etc. Approach local businesses for gift certificates, dinner passes, appliances, books, kitchenware and specialty items. Buy a receipt book and give receipts to all donors who want them.

To make the bidding process easier, you may want to provide numbered paddles or tags of some sort for each bidder. This also makes keeping track of successful bids a little easier. At the end of the auction, successful bidders can pay the cashier for their purchases and collect them.

> **Remember, this is not a garage sale, so you'll want to stay away from garage sale type merchandise. ... Quality items generate interest and draw a good crowd.**

MANPOWER

This project requires a lot of "behind the scenes" work. A major part of your manpower needs will occur before the event. You'll need volunteers to solicit, pick up, categorize and store all donated items.

On the day of the event (or the day before) crews will be needed to set up tables and arrange the auction items on

continued on page 164

GENERAL DONATION FORM

Event Name: _____   Date of Event _____

Leader: Name & Telephone _____

Form filled out by: _____   *(Use for garage sale and/or auction donations)*

DONATED BY; NAME, ADDRESS, TELEPHONE	ITEM DESCRIPTION	APPROX. VALUE	RECEIPT ISSUED
	APPROXIMATE TOTAL VALUE	$	

MAKE AS MANY COPIES OF THIS PAGE AS NEEDED

MASTER AUCTION BID FORM

Auction Name:

Date of Auction

Leader: Name & Telephone

Form filled out by:

BIDDER'S NAME OR #	ITEM #, LOT # OR DESCRIPTION	FINAL BID ($ AMT)	PAID FOR ( )	PICKED UP ( )
TOTAL				

MAKE AS MANY COPIES OF THIS PAGE AS NEEDED

SPECIALTY AUCTIONS

Joe bids five dollars, Anne bids ten and Molly tosses in a fifteen dollar bid. The excitement grows, the auctioneer pulls the winning bid from the basket and Joe's five dollar bid wins. What? The lowest bid wins? That's just how it is at times with some of these wackier kinds of auctions.

CHINESE AUCTION

The reason, if any ever existed, why this is called a Chinese auction is lost in the mists of time. It is however a different twist on your average auction. To begin, all participants receive a packet of tickets. Then they write their bid, name, address and phone number on the ticket and place it in the basket in front of the item they want. Auction-goers can use as many tickets as they want and put them in every basket they want.

At a pre-assigned time, the auction is over. The *auctioneer* now goes from item to item, drawing one random ticket from the basket in front of each auction item. The person whose ticket is drawn has the winning *bid* on that item and can now pay for it and take it home.

You may want to specify minimum bids on most items to maintain fairness in the bidding. Minimum bids guarantee

your group more funds, since it is the luck of the draw that dictates the successful bid, not the highest bid.

> *These* specialty *auctions are lots of fun. Since they are not your standard, typical auctions, be sure to explain the rules carefully to all participants to eliminate any confusion.*

Refer to the *Silent Auction* on page 160 for details about auction set-up, manpower and equipment needs.

CUMULATIVE AUCTION

Another unusual slant is a "cumulative" auction. The auctioneer has a timer and sets a specific time for each bid (generally between one and three minutes). Each bidder is assigned a numbered paddle. Bidders raise their paddles when they want to make a bid. The auctioneer calls on each bidder by number.

Bidders now call out their bids. When the timer sounds,

the last person to bid gets the item for the total of *all* of the bids made on that specific item.

The bids do not have to go in ascending order. For instance, the bidding on an item could go like this: Mary bids $1.50, John bids $2.00, Joe bids $1.00, then the timer goes off. Joe buys the item for $1.50 + $2.00 + $1.00, or $4.50.

You'll want to keep this auction as simple as possible, using a short time span for bidding so bidders can remember the total bids made. You also need a secretary to write down all bids so there's no question about bids made and total due.

These *specialty* auctions are lots of fun. Since they are not your standard, typical auctions, be sure to explain the rules carefully to all participants to eliminate any confusion. With either type of auction, refer to *General Auction* on page 155 for more specific ideas about publicity efforts, manpower, equipment and supplies you'll need for a successful event.

As with any auction, seek donations of items from every possible source: friends, relatives, school or church members, businesses, restaurants, theatres, etc. Use the *General Donation Form* on page 156 to keep track of items donated. Be sure to buy a receipt book (available at office supply stores and most drugstores) so you can provide receipts for all donated items. Have fun!

FATHER & SON CAKE BAKE & AUCTION

"I'll bid $5 for the *Double Fudge Brontasauras Brownies*."

"I'll bid $5.75!"

"Going once, Going twice—Sold to the $5.75 bidder!"

This event is a lot of fun. It can be run as mother/son, father/daughter, or whatever combination you choose. The idea is to get the kids to bake with help from the parent with the least cooking ability. It may sound illogical at first but this approach gives you a much more interesting event.

Set up prizes and/or awards in different categories. Use your imagination to create awards unique to your event, like: biggest, best theme, homeliest, tallest, most artistic, best design, most unusual, funniest and on and on. Set up a ballot so the participants can vote on cakes in the different categories.

If your group is big enough, you can approach this project as a members, family and friends only event. In this case the project becomes a more family-oriented social event.

Auction off the cakes to the highest bidder. Try to find a professional auctioneer who will donate their time or recruit a local personality for the auctioneer's job.

This auction needs someone

> **The idea is to get the kids to bake with help from the parent with the least cooking ability. It may sound illogical at first but this approach gives you a much more interesting event.**

who can heckle the crowd. It should be fast and fun: You could consider a clown as an auctioneer. In any case, keep the actual auction to about an hour to hold everyone's attention. Payment is cash and carry. This event works best for groups with 20 to 100 entrees. Since it's a fundraiser, let the kids bake more than one cake if they wish. You should earn about five to ten dollars per cake.

Get everyone involved in your publicity efforts. Send invitations to friends, relatives, and neighbors. If you are reaching for a more public audience, hang posters in high traffic public areas. Put notices on area church, school and neighborhood bulletin boards. Notices in local organization newsletters and PSAs in the larger media would round out a strong publicity campaign.

SUPPLIES & EQUIPMENT

You will need a school or church room big enough for the expected crowd. Serving something to drink is a nice idea, along with a few cakes cut and served as refreshments. You'll also need napkins, plates, flatware, cups and tables to display the cakes, and chairs for the people.

A podium with a microphone is a must. Voting slips and awards need to be prepared along with a cash box with enough change. It's also nice to have participant ribbons made for the kids involved. Have a lot of various-sized boxes on hand so people can re-pack the cakes if they wish.

MANPOWER

The auctioneer is most important, so be particular about who you choose to fill this position. In addition to all the kids and parents who'll bake the cakes to sell, you'll also need people to set-up, serve, make change and clean up after this event.

NOTE: *This event works well for Brownies, Cub Scouts and groups with kids in the 6- to 12-year old range. It is also a good social event/outing for your group. Keep it light and fast!*

SILENT AUCTION

Jenny watches Steve closely examine the antique rocking chair in the bidding area. He finishes looking at the chair, picks up a pen and writes his bid on the form in front. As he leaves, Jenny walks to the chair and writes a slightly higher bid. This quiet competition is getting hotter by the minute. Who'll finally get Grandma's old rocker?

A silent auction can be a "members only" fundraiser, it can be school- or church-wide or it can be open to the public. A private high school in our area has held an annual silent auction & dinner event for over ten years now. It is their largest fundraising event each and every year.

> *A private high school in our area has held an annual silent auction & dinner event for over ten years now. It has been their largest fundraising event each and every year.*

This project can be as large or small as you want. Much of that is determined by how many volunteers and donations you can attract to your cause. Unless your auction is geared towards youngsters with a lot of small dollar items, you may want to have a minimum age restriction for bidders.

You'll need a room or a hall large enough to hold all display tables for the items to be auctioned. Set up the tables with plenty of room so people can walk around them. Allow enough space between items so bidders can write down their names, phone numbers and bids on a lined bid form placed by each item. See *Silent Auction Bid Sheet* on page 161.

All items should carry a brief written description, who donated it (unless they wish to remain anonymous), and its approximate retail value.

If the item is too big to put on the table, a photograph, drawing or very specific written description is necessary. Items like cruises, vacation/travel packages, yachts, cars and RVs all fall in this category.

Advise all volunteers and participants of the auction rules beforehand. In addition, post auction rules in prominent places throughout the area where the items are on display.

Establish specific time limits for the bidding. The highest bid on each item buys the item when the allotted time has elapsed. At a set time, the bidding begins. Bidders write down their name or number, phone number and bid on the bid sheet for each item they want. Auction-goers can bid as often and on as many items as they wish. Each successive bid on an item must be higher than the previous bid.

You may want to have minimum bid raises of one dollar, five or ten, depending upon the item's value. If there is minimum bid on an item (use 50% of the retail value as a rule of thumb), it should be written prominently on the bid sheet for that particular item.

At the designated stopping time, close the bidding and collect the bid sheets. Assemble all participants in one area and begin reading off the list of each item and the highest bidder's name and bid.

After all bids are read, have several people ready to serve as treasurers and accept payments for each item before they are removed from the tables. If you have enough manpower, it's nice to hand-deliver these items to their respective buyers.

SUPPLIES & EQUIPMENT

You'll need a room or hall large enough to host the event. Make enough bid sheets for each item. See *Silent Auction Bid Sheet* form on page 161. Put out a pencil, pen or marker at each bid sheet. Have cash box(es) and change ready.

Your main supplies will be the donated items to auction

continued on page 164

SILENT AUCTION BID SHEET

Item #: _____   Date of Auction _____

Description _____

Donated by: _____   Approximate $ Value _____

Minimum Bid Amount _____

BIDDER'S NAME OR NUMBER	TELEPHONE #	AMOUNT BID

MAKE AS MANY COPIES OF THIS PAGE AS NEEDED

SERVANT AUCTION

You've put off cleaning the chimney and even the gutters for what seems like forever. And, (surprise, surprise!) they still aren't done. So it comes down to this: It's time to go to the servant auction and hire someone to do it for you!

A servant auction works like this: You sell a number of hours of service to be done by your group's members to the highest bidders. All the services need to be done by a specific date. Payment can be made at the auction, or half down and half upon completion of the work, or all at once when service is rendered.

Fill out the *Servant Auction Worksheet* on page 163 with volunteers' names, phone numbers, preferred services to deliver and number of hours they're willing to work. Sometimes a group will set a minimum block of hours for everyone selling their services.

These services can include: babysitting, housework, yardwork, painting, car cleaning and so on. Match services offered to an individual member's abilities. As an added bonus you can let your members keep a percentage of what they earn. You might point out that if they do a very good job they could end up with some part-time work for themselves.

> *A servant auction works like this: You sell a number of hours of service to be done by your group's members to the highest bidders. The services need to be done by a specific date.*

Publicity can include sending invitations to members' friends, relatives and neighbors. On the invitation, list the members' first names, services offered and hours available. Make it look old-fashioned. Get ideas from auction posters or handbills to use in your invitations and posters.

Try to get a professional auctioneer to donate or at least discount their fee. If you can't get an auctioneer, get a well-known local personality to do the auctioning. The trick is to pump the crowd for as much as you can. Keep the auction fast and fun. Serve refreshments.

SUPPLIES & EQUIPMENT

You'll need a room and parking area big enough for the expected crowd. Refreshments and serviceware are also needed. Set up chairs and prepare a cash box with adequate change. Nicely printed invitations/handbills should be sent early and posters hung in prime locations. Have several calendars available the day of the auction so bidders and members can arrange dates for completing their services.

MANPOWER

It cannot be stressed enough that auctions are made or broken on the strength of the auctioneer. This is the first and foremost of your manpower needs. Even if you hire one, the auctioneer should bring in more than their fee.

In addition to members to be auctioned off as servants, you'll need people to set up, serve refreshments, run the event and clean up. You need people in charge of invitations, publicity and follow up. Now you have no excuse for clogged gutters!

NOTES: *Follow-up and follow-through are very important for the success of a servant auction. Have your group members try to firm up a date at the time of the bid and do their best to fulfill their service as agreed. If they can't complete their service, get someone else to do it. Set a deadline of 30-45 days to get all work done and money collected. Make follow-up phone calls and/or send postcards to group members and bidders as needed.*

SERVANT AUCTION WORKSHEET

Use this worksheet to sign up members, the number of hours they wish to donate and their job preferences, if any. Then record the highest bidders' name, phone number and dollar amount bid per hour. Make sure the bidder knows how much will be due upon completion of the work and the terms for payment. Follow-through is important for the financial success of this event.

MEMBER & PHONE	HOURS DONATED/ JOB PREFERENCE	BIDDER & PHONE	$ PER HOUR	TOTAL PLEDGE

MAKE AS MANY COPIES OF THIS PAGE AS NEEDED

GENERAL AUCTION
continued from page 155

them. You'll also need to set up chairs if you have them. Another group will be needed to take down and store tables and chairs after the auction.

One of the most important people for this project is the auctioneer. Either hire a professional or get a talented, outgoing volunteer to handle the job. It is *very* important that the auctioneer be familiar with standard auction etiquette. Post a list of general auction rules and have the auctioneer announce them as well before he begins the bidding process. The auctioneer must keep the auction going at a fast pace to keep buyers interested.

A "secretary" is needed to write down the number of the successful bidder and the final amount bid for each item. (See *Master Auction Bid Form* on page 157.) You'll need to have several cashiers, each with an assistant or two, on hand to help customers pay for and pick up their items. As each item is paid for and picked up, it should be marked accordingly on the master list.

NOTE: *With any auction, check with your local and state ordinances for laws regarding sales and taxing.*

SILENT AUCTION
continued from page 160

off—these can be hand-made craft items, baked goodies, groceries, electronic equipment, clothing, vacations, dinners, movie passes, entertainment, toys, dolls, gift certificates for anything from hair salon appointments to chiropractic adjustments, catering services, lessons, babysitting services, furniture, cars, vans. This project can be as large or as small as you want to make it!

MANPOWER

Your first manpower need is for an energetic committee to solicit and then collect, catalog and store all of the donated auction items. On the day of the event you'll need people to set up tables, wares and bid sheets. Each item to be auctioned should be numbered and the bid sheet for that item should be numbered correspondingly. Volunteers will be needed to collect the bid sheets at the auction's close.

Pick one of your more outgoing people to read off the names of the highest bids and bidders at the close of bidding. Have people around to help bidders collect their items.

Cashiers will be needed to collect the money from the highest bidder on each item.

Check your local and state ordinances for any laws regarding sales taxes, etc.

If you sell tickets, each participant can use their ticket number instead of their name for bidding purposes . It's a relatively quiet way to raise some substantial cash!

NOTE 1: *If the successful bidder is not present at the close of the auction, be sure to call them right away and make arrangements for pick up or delivery of their item and collection of their donation.*

NOTE 2: *This type of auction is best if limited in some fashion: either as a "members only" function, members and guest, or a select group of interested participants, possibly even another local group or club. If you decide to open it to the* general public, selling admission tickets will help you control the number of bidders.

OPTION: *To make your silent auction even bigger, you can hold it with a fancy dinner. Pre-sell tickets for an accurate head-count. Each ticket, priced in the $50 to $100 range, gets its owner an elegant dinner as well as an opportunity to bid during the auction. The funds made from the dinner are more monies for your coffers. Refer to* Dinner Social *on page 125 for dinner ideas and concerns.*

This combined dinner and auction can be a huge money-maker, but it demands a lot of work, many volunteers and careful planning. You'll also need lots of community support for donations and ticket sales.

Schedule the evening along these lines: Three p.m. to 5 p.m. preview of auction items and social hour. Five p.m. to 6 p.m. dinner. Six p.m. to 8 p.m. auction hours. Eight p.m. on is for reading the winning bids, collecting the money and distributing the items sold.

BIG BALLOON GIVEAWAY DAYS

Look! In the sky! It's a bunch of birds or planes or, yes, even better, it's balloons! Balloons are fun to play with, they make you and those around you smile and they're very, very affordable. Balloons are at the center of this zany and profitable fundraiser.

Simply take a lot of helium-filled balloons, find a busy streetcorner and tell your volunteers, "Give 'em away!" At the same time let the public know, with nearby posters and road signs, that donations are gratefully accepted! You'll raise peoples' spirits as well as new funds for your cause.

To create a greater public awareness before the giveaway, get as many PSAs as possible.

If you can get some prizes donated, you could stuff your balloons with coupons to heighten the public's interest. Lots of small prizes and one or two bigger ones works best.

SUPPLIES & EQUIPMENT

This project takes more volunteers than supplies. You'll first want to contact a party supply store to get their best prices for a helium tank, balloons and string.

Find out how much it would cost to have your group's logo

and/or slogan printed on the balloons. If it fits your budget, printed balloons can help get your group's name and slogan out before a wider public (always a good idea).

> *Simply take a lot of helium-filled balloons, find a busy streetcorner and tell your volunteers, "Give 'em away!" At the same time let the public know, with nearby posters and road signs, that donations are gratefully accepted!*

Plan the big balloon giveaway so your volunteers are at busy street corners during peak traffic times to give them out. This project works best if you man the corners during selected hours for an entire weekend. Check with your local law enforcement agencies for tips and suggestions about where and when to schedule your giveaway. This will keep your project fun, safe and legal.

MANPOWER

For this project you'll need volunteers, volunteers and, probably, a few more volunteers. Modify the *Cleaning Teams* form on page 147 to use as an organizing tool for your balloon giveaway teams.

Before sending the troops out, review the fundamentals of safety and courtesy regarding street "sales." All volunteers should wear bright-colored clothing for easy visibility and safety. Advise them to be aware of the traffic patterns, street lights, etc. Make sure they understand how not to interfere with the flow of traffic.

Prepare a quick speech for volunteers to give each recipient of a free balloon, such as, "Hi, I'm Julie, with the XYZ group. Would you like a balloon? There's no charge for the balloon, but we gladly accept donations!"

All volunteers should wear pins, name tags, vests or sandwich boards that clearly state your group's name and who the funds will benefit. Use plastic fish bowls to collect donations. Start with a few dollar bills in each to serve as "seed money." This encourages your happy balloon recipients to give bills instead of coins.

Make sure everyone wears a bright smile, is courteous and gives away all your balloons. Then watch those donations bounce and tumble in!

BOOK SALE

When do you think you'll really re-read *Gone With The Wind,* or *Tom Sawyer* or even the unabridged *War And Peace?* Everyone has books they've read, lying around the house when they could be with some other family and, probably, read by more people.

You can clear some deadwood from your library and help your group generate some cash with a used book sale! This can be fun and turn up some interesting books along the way. Begin planning by targeting a date to hold your book sale (Saturdays are generally good). If possible plan to hold your book sale with another event. Then start to gather books to sell.

> *You can clear some deadwood from your library and help your group generate some cash with a used book sale! This can be fun and turn up some interesting books along the way.*

You'll want to get plenty of local publicity for your sale. Get your poster and flyers out to schools, churches, grocery stores and post them on as many bulletin boards as you can. PSAs on local radio and television stations can be quite effective. Your publicity efforts should intensify in the last 14 days before the book sale.

SUPPLIES & EQUIPMENT

Basically you just need lots and lots of books to sell. Ask your members to bring in books they no longer want. Ask family members, friends, church and school members for books they no longer want (and don't forget to invite them to your sale!). Solicit donations of older stock and outdated magazines from retailers. Gather up old collections of comic books, mysteries, any reading materials you can get your hands on.

A gym, cafeteria or hall all work well for a book sale. A facility with lots of tables makes displaying and viewing the books a lot easier. If you can't get enough tables, use large boxes for displaying your literary finds.

Group books according to type ("Mysteries", "Sci-Fi", "Poetry", "Comic Books", "Self-Help", etc.) and make signs to help your customers find what they want.

You'll need a cash box with plenty of change when your sale starts.

MANPOWER

Your volunteers can scour their homes and ask friends and relatives for books they no longer want. Get a committee to contact retailers for donations of old books and out-dated magazines.

As you build a supply of books, sort them into categories by interest area. Use cardboard or heavy construction paper to make table tents or signs for each category.

Several people will need to price books. Pricing each book is generally an overwhelming job. Instead, set price for all books in a category, like: fifty cents for paperback and comic books, one dollar for hardcover books, three dollars for over-sized books, etc. Or, use a colored sticker on each book to give its price: Blue stickers: seventy five cents, red stickers: on dollar and so on.

You'll need volunteers to set up the books, ideally the day before the sale. During the sale you'll need cashiers, people to answer questions and tear down when the sale is over.

Let's get on with it, clear your bookshelves. Remember to replace 'em with some new literary gems from your sale!

BUTTONS & BADGES

You see them everywhere with catchy slogans, art work and photos generating awareness for everything from all over the cultural spectrum. Buttons and/or badges are perenially popular and profitable items.

They can be bought in finished form through wholesale suppliers or your group can buy its own badge-maker and supplies, and make your own. See *Appendix C* for names and addresses of button/badge suppliers and kits to make your own. Use the *Product Order Form* and *Master Product Order Form* on pages 178 and 179 to keep track of all sales.

There are any number of markets you can sell badges to. Let's outline a few:

• *Make buttons to advertise your next fundraiser.* Use a catchy slogan and attention-grabbing artwork (i.e., "D-Day" for Daffodil Day).

• *Holiday and special event buttons are always popular.* Christmas, Halloween, St. Patrick's Day, Valentine's Day, and Easter are times your group can sell badges. In election years, political badges are hot.

• *Buttons with high school mascots or slogans can often be purchased locally.* Check with a nearby badge-maker; they may carry these in stock. You

> **Buttons and/or badges are perenially popular (and profitable) items. ... Humorous buttons are all-time favorites. Everybody enjoys a good laugh, so why not wear your group's favorite joke or quote on your shirt?**

may want to create a badge with your motto and/or mascot.

• *Inspirational badges are popular.* These often have a line of scripture or poetry printed over a tranquil natural scene.

• *Nostalgia buttons are fun.* '50s and '60s be-bop, hippie and protest buttons appeal to a large market today. These sell especially well at dances or activities focused on these eras.

• *Humorous buttons are all-time favorites.* Everybody enjoys a good laugh, so why not wear your group's favorite joke or quote on your shirt? Buttons with pictures of popular musicians and bands are hot items with most teenagers.

• *Photos can also be made*

into badges and are very popular. To maximize your profits with these buttons, find a photo store or badge-maker that does this kind of work and will give you a quantity discount.

• *Photo badges of friends, sports events, plays and other events are fun to collect.* They appeal to large numbers of students in most schools. Make and sell badges for homecoming dances, proms, Valentine's Day or other school holidays.

• *Or, how about taking orders for photo badges from the parents of students in a local dance class or theatre group?* Photo buttons from amateur sporting events are always popular. For example, you could arrange to take instant photos of Little League team members at a game, make the buttons on the spot and sell them to waiting parents. The possibilities are endless.

SUPPLIES & EQUIPMENT

Many of the buttons you want to sell can be made with your own badge-maker kit. Check into what these kits offer. The artwork and slogans you want may be a part of the kit. If not, your group probably has enough creative people to make your own artwork and slogans. Making badges lets you make your buttons as original and as personal as you want. Purchased or handmade, selling buttons and badges can put real money in your treasury!

CHRISTMAS TREE SALES

It's the middle of December and the smell of freshly-cut evergreens wafts through your display of Christmas trees. A steady stream of customers are buying tonight. Ah, yes, the Christmas tree sale is in full swing now.

This event takes planning, lots of work and, done right, can be a good money-maker. Begin by contacting a Christmas tree farm months in advance of the holiday season. See if your group can get trees at wholesale prices. If it's a local farm, find out if they'll let you cut the trees for an even lower price.

You may have to agree to buy trees in quantities of 50 or 100 at a time. In this case, maybe a consignment deal can be worked out. This will protect you from being stuck with unsold trees you'd otherwise have to pay for. Selling on consignment can be the difference between a money-maker and money-loser!

Next, you'll need a place to hold your tree sale. If you can use your church or school parking lot, you'll have a ready market. Send home flyers with school children or church members. Encourage them to "Buy your Christmas tree here; Support your youth group." Tell them that buying from your group is both convenient and supporting a worthy cause.

Make sure you have a variety of tree sizes and price ranges. Group them on your lot by size. Color-coded price tags are convenient for both the buyer and the seller.

In addition to cut trees, you could offer small potted pine trees for sale as an ecology-minded alternative. Get these trees from a local landscape nursery on consignment and return what doesn't sell. Be sure to include instructions for planting the tree after the holidays.

This project could run from the day after Thanksgiving until December 24th. You'll need to have team volunteers ready to run this month-long sale throughout this time frame.

As an added twist, you could put a bow and a tag on each tree with the name, age, gender and clothing sizes for an underprivileged child or forgotten nursing home resident. Include ideas of what that person needs most, for example household items, clothes or gifts. Ask the tree buyer to register the card if they're going to participate in this gift-giving.

You can get the information on needy people from local charitable organizations. They'll tell you what each person needs and where you should deliver the gifts. Some agencies distribute the gifts themselves; others prefer to have group representatives deliver the gifts.

On December 23rd and 24th all remaining trees could be given to needy families who can't afford to buy their trees (get a list from a local charitable agency). Be sure to work out the financial details of this idea with the tree farm when you first purchase or take the trees on consignment.

Since you'll already have volunteers staffing the Christmas tree sale, why not also sell

> *This event takes planning, lots of work and, done right, can be a good money-maker. ... Since you'll already have volunteers staffing the Christmas tree sale, why not also sell wreaths, English ivy, ornaments or fruit?*

continued on next page

RADIO ROUNDUP

Does your group have a favorite radio station? Perhaps you've worked with a station to produce PSAs, ads or a particular fundraiser and everything sort of clicked. And now you would like to do something else with them. Well here's the perfect fundraiser for all that.

Ask the radio station to donate a block of radio spots to your group for this unusual fundraiser. After you have a firm commitment from the participating radio station, your group will sell these spots to businesses in your local area

for the going rate and keep the income. Form a committee of some of your more talented members to write the ad copy (see *Selling Advertising* on page 86). They can also be used in the production of

these spots as the on air talent. Work with the radio station's advertising people to create solid, hardworking ads.

In addition to creating a good selling message for each business, you'll want to identify these businesses as supporters of your group. Using your members in the spots can give a unique flavor to the ads. The radio station benefits by getting a tax deduction for the donated spots and, hopefully, new customers from your ads.

> **Using your members in the spots can give a unique flavor to the ads.**

---

continued from preceding page
wreaths, English ivy, ornaments or fruit ? See *Appendix C* for suppliers. You could buy the goods wholesale and sell them retail or take orders. If you're taking orders for delivery, keep in mind that the holiday season gets very busy for just about everyone, so be realistic about what your group can or cannot do.

SUPPLIES & EQUIPMENT

Your primary needs for this project are Christmas trees and a good, high-traffic location to sell them from.

A corner of your church or school parking lot would be the ideal place to set up your Chirstmas tree sales effort. If you don't have access to a parking lot, contact a grocery store or a strip mall with a large

parking lot. Often they'll let a group use a section of their parking lot for this kind of event. You'll also need twine, lights and extension cords, a booth or stand with a cash box and change, and tags to price your trees with.

MANPOWER

The chairperson of this project needs to contact the tree farm and make arrangements for pick-up or delivery of the trees. If you are picking them up yourself, you'll need drivers with vehicles large enough to hold a good-sized load of trees.

This project runs for about thirty days, so you need to be selective about the hours you'll be open. Keep the tree sales open primarily during peak hours: Monday-Friday 3:30-9:00, Saturday 9:00-6:00, and

Sunday 12:00-6:00. This schedule works out to about forty hours a week. Make sure you have enough firm commitments from your volunteers to man your sales lot before going ahead with this project.

Always have at least two people (one adult) staffing the sales lot. When the weather is extremely cold, be sure to rotate workers every couple of hours and remind them to dress appropriately for the weather. Ho, ho, ho!

NOTE: *For an additional source of income from this project, you could also sell hot chocolate, coffee and small snacks to your tree shoppers. See* Food Stands *on page 127 for more details. In general you'll want to keep your offerings quick and easy as you don't want to overload your volunteer workers.*

COOKBOOKS

Everyone in our family loves Grandma's sugar cookies. All families have their own "special" recipes. Why not combine those of your family, group members and friends into a cookbook? Since most people enjoy a new cookbook, creating and selling them can be both fun and profitable.

To start this project, ask every member of your group to bring in five to ten of their family's favorite recipes. Sort them into categories: appetizers, salads, main dishes, casseroles, desserts, etc.

If you're going to publish the book yourself, you need to first decide what size you want it to be and how you want it to look. Have a brainstorming session with your more creative people and come up with an overall approach to the cookbook's look. To help in this process look at professionally produced cookbooks. Find a few you feel are attractive and useful and use these as your starting point.

Of course you won't be able to afford the glossy paper and color photos, but you can still learn a lot about how to make your cookbook a great one by studying how these cookbooks display ingredients and instructions for recipes and what kind of graphics they use.

> Since most people enjoy a new cookbook, creating and selling them can be both fun and profitable. ... To help in this process look at professionally produced cookbooks. Find a few you feel are attractive and useful and use these as your starting point.

You'll find that photos will often photocopy fairly well. So even if you're printing your cookbook on a photocopier, you'll want to include as many photos of dishes as possible (see *How to crop a photo* on page 55).

It is best to work on either an 8 ½" x 11" or a 5 ½" x 8 ½" sized page (this size page is an 8 ½" x 11" sheet folded in half), which gives you four pages per sheet of paper.

It's now time to go to a local office supply store and see what kinds of things they have to bind the pages into a finished book. There are a number of ways to do this, so explain to the salesperson what you're doing and get his advice. With this all decided, you're now ready to start producing your cookbook (see *Graphic Design* on page 50).

If available, use a personal computer with a printer to handle recipes and other text. You'll find the typing and correcting process to be a lot better than on a typewriter. And your text can be much more attractive because any computer printer— dot matrix (passable), inkjet (great) or laserwriter (fantastic) will give you regular, italic and bold type.

Remember to use italics and bold faces somewhat sparingly (look at the professional cookbooks again). If you spend enough time at this stage of planning to develop a good-looking cookbook of great recipes you may just create a fundraiser for your group that'll sell well for years and years!

To make the recipes ready for publication, check everything twice: ingredients, measurements, preparation, spelling and punctuation, and make corrections each time.

Be sure you identify the contributor of each recipe. Add special comments ("Better make a double batch of this; the first one evaporates as soon as the kids come home from school!") or tidbits of family history to each recipe to give your project more personality.

For graphics you can use photocopied color, black and white photos, drawings or clip art (ask at your local art store). Now you're ready to bring all your recipes, other text blocks, photos, drawings and clip art together so you can assemble the cookbook pages for printing (again, see *Graphic Design* on page 50 for page production tips).

Design a cover with the title for your cookbook, ie: *XYZ Youth Group's Favorite Recipes*. If your group's name is not in the title, make sure you identify yourself somewhere on the cover or the inside page.

Now it's off to the photocopier or quick printer. You can have the cookbook bound by the printer or an office supply store or you could buy the supplies from a wholesaler and put it together yourself.

To make a larger-scale, more professional cookbook, contact a commercial printer and get an estimate on typesetting, design, production and printing costs to have your bundle of great recipes made into a cookbook.

If you want to prepare the pages yourself, you'll be able to save a bundle in typesetting and design costs. The printer will be able to help you avoid costly layout mistakes. He can also give you price breaks on various quantities (press runs) of

cookbooks ordered.

Some printers who specialize in cookbooks are listed in *Appendix D*. Contact them for free information about producing your cookbook.

Another option you have is to contact companies that will put your cookbook together if you agree to let them mention their products in your cookbook. Again, see listings in *Appendix D* for companies that provide these services.

After you have figured your initial costs as close as possible for the cookbook, set a price on it. You can generally figure on a 50% mark-up over your costs.

To help generate cookbook sales, hold a "taste-testing." Choose a date and a time (right after church services is usually good), and give the public a chance to sample various goodies prepared from recipes in your cookbook.

Provide beverages (coffee and punch) and napkins along with the "samplers." Cut prepared items into bite-size portions, and list the name of the item, page number and contributor of the recipe on a small card in front of each item.

Additional sales opportunities are found after church services, PTA meetings, other school or group events. Having a sales table at a larger event can also produce sales.

> *If you spend enough time at this stage of planning to develop a good-looking cookbook of great recipes you may just create a fundraiser for your group that'll sell well for years and years!*

SUPPLIES & EQUIPMENT

Your primary requirement for this project is great recipes! Ask all members, yourself included, to contact immediate family members, aunts, uncles, cousins and grandparents for favorite recipes. Then ask your friends, teachers, co-workers, sponsors and (why not) neighbors to give you some of their best-loved recipes, too.

If you are producing the finished pages for the cookbook yourself, you'll need plenty of photos, drawings and other art supplies, photocopier paper and binders of some sort. See if you can get supplies donated. If not, try to buy them at wholesale.

MANPOWER

Get everybody involved in this project! The more recipes you get, the better your cookbook will be. Be extremely careful when preparing recipes for printing; one omission could be the difference between a fluffy torte or a hard, flat cake!

As you gather recipes, ask your contributors if they'd like to buy a copy of your cookbook. Keep a list of names, addresses and phone numbers of contributors and others who want to buy the cookbook. Also call on friends, relatives, church members and schoolmates when selling your cookbook.

Use the *Product Order Form* on page 179 to take orders. Everyone who buys your cookbook will enjoy *Grandma's Famous Sugar Cookie* recipe!

Who do you know that *doesn't* need to clean out their closets, garage, attic and basement? Encourage your family and friends to sort through their unused treasures and donate them to your group's garage sale! This event takes time and planning, but it can be a real money-maker.

The first thing to do is set a firm date for your sale. Next, decide if it will be "members only," neighbor-hood-, school- or church-wide. The more people you have donating items, of course, the larger the display area you'll need. If you're having a small sale (i.e., members only) you could have it in a member's garage. A school gymnasium or church all-purpose room works well for a school-or church-wide garage sale.

Once you've determined the size and location, begin publi-cizing your sale. Actively solicit donations from family, friends, classmates, teachers, etc. If possible, offer free pick-up service of donated items.

Begin collecting donations several weeks before the sale to give you ample time to sort and price items. Use the *General Donation Form* on page 156 to keep track of donated items. Buy a small receipt book to make receipts for donors who request them. Use a member's garage and/or a spare rooms to store items until the sale.

Publicity is very important for a successful garage sale. Hang up dynamic, copy-intensive posters, hand out flyers and get as many PSAs in the local radio, tv and newspa-pers as possible.

Publicity is very important for a successful garage sale. Hang up dynamic, copy-intensive posters, hand out flyers and get as many PSAs in the local radio, tv and newspapers as possible.

In addition, place classified ads in all local newspapers and area shoppers. In all ad copy you should mention major sale items and categories of goods such as collectibles, sports equipment and others.

SUPPLIES & EQUIPMENT

You'll need lots of donated items to sell. Ask everyone you know to clean out their closets, attics and garages to help with your cause. Buy a large quan-tity of stickers at a discount store to use to price items. Use pens or markers to write prices on stickers. With a simplified price structure you could use different colored stickers to identify prices (i.e. blue stickers=one dollar, red stickers=two dollars, green stickers=three dollars, etc.) If you use color-coded pricing, be sure to display several large posters that clearly show what price each color indicates.

Depending upon the size of your sale, you'll need either a garage, hall, or gym to hold it. If you hold the sale outdoors, you'll want to either have a rain date or have tents and awnings to protect your goods in the event of rain. Tables will be needed to display your wares. Card tables and large boxes work for small events; but if your sale is schoolwide, you should con-sider using the cafeteria or gymnasium with cafeteria tables to display your goods.

You'll need plenty of change and small bills on hand. Go to the bank the day before the sale and get one hundred dollars in ones and fives along with several rolls each of quarters, dimes, nickels, and pennies. Keep track of how much you start with, so you'll know how much cash you've

continued on next page

THEME BOOKS

Does your group have special talents that could be effectively put into a book? Special theme books can focus on holding specialty dinners, craft-making, giving speeches, saving money, hosting parties, household hints, writing letters, providing civic services, environmentally sound hints, etc.

Another approach to finding a special niche for your book is to make it regional or ethnic in nature. Examples of this approach are titles like: *St. Paul's Youth Group's Favorite Recipes* or *Italian Cooking in the Midwest* or *Throwing a Fantastic Fajita Party.*

Maybe your group does a lot with children which might suggest a book about entertaining children of specific ages or maybe a book of crafts

ITALIAN COOKING IN THE MIDWEST COOKBOOK ON SALE NOW!

The overall idea here is to take what your group does best and put it in a book. Start brainstorming and come up with your own great book idea!

or recipes easy enough for the pre-teen set. The overall idea here is to take what your group does best and put it in a book. Start brainstorming and come up with your own great book idea!

Refer to *Cookbooks* on page 170 for specific details about

producing your book.

Once you've completed your book, be creative about selling it. Set up stands at school and church festivals, after church services, even in local grocery stores or malls if possible. Offer your book for sale at school functions whenever possible.

Be sure your book reaches your targeted market. For example, make your book of children's recipes available at local kindergarten and day-care centers. If you have a newsletter, run a full page ad for the book in the first issue after it returns from the printer. Run a smaller ad, a sixth of a page for example, in following newsletters until the book is sold out.

This is the kind of fundraising project that takes a while to produce but done well it can earn your group funds for several years down the road.

---

continued from preceding page
made from the sale.

MANPOWER

You will need lots and lots of donors. Once all the donated items are in one central location, you'll need people to sort them into categories, generally including: clothing: children's, ladies', men's; toys; sports equipment; games; books; outdoor equipment; housewares; accessories; musical instruments; tapes & CDs; etc.

When the items are sorted, you'll next need to price them, either with individual or color-coded tags. Then all sale items need to be presented in the best fashion possible: folded, on hangers, clean, etc.

The day before the sale, get many helping hands to set up tables and sale items. Keep sale items grouped by category, ie.: children's clothing on tables one and two, games and toys on table three, etc. On the day of the event, you'll need volun-

teers to staff the sale. They'll need to take money, make change, help people find items, keep sale items in some kind of order, circulate and help whenever possible.

After the sale is over, you'll need people to box up any items that didn't sell and get rid of them. You could donate these to a local mission, shelter or goodwill. People are also needed to help tear down tables, chairs, and other sale equipment. Let the sale begin!

DAFFODIL SALES

A great way for your group to celebrate the magic of spring is with a fresh daffodil sale. It's also an excellent kick-off for the spring fundraising season!

Contact suppliers of fresh daffodils and find out at what quantities you get price breaks. After selecting a supplier, seek his advice in setting your price structure. When you buy wholesale, you should be able to mark flowers up from 50% to 100%.

Now select a date, the times and place where your customers can pick up and pay for their flowers.

Next organize your sales force and get them selling. Sales can be door-to-door, by mail, by phone, or a combination of all three. In addition, sell to businesses; suggest to managers they give flowers to customers, patients, or clients. Or donate them to their favorite hospital, nursing home, church or other worthy institution.

When you're ready to order the daffodils, group them into cases, half-cases, quarter-cases, and bunches. See *Product Order Form* on page 179.

Be sure to let your customers know *with a printed piece* when and where they're to pick up their daffodils. Order extra for direct sales. After initial orders have been picked up and paid for, market remaining flowers by direct sales for one or two days.

Direct sales work best in areas with heavy pedestrian traffic: shopping malls, downtown business areas (especially during lunch hours) and airports (check with management first). You can either set up a booth or have volunteers sell directly from the box. In either case, display a sign giving the price and who benefits from this flower sale.

Don't limit your group to daffodils. You can also sell carnations, roses, geraniums and small potted bulb plants for later replanting.

> **Direct sales work best in areas with heavy pedestrian traffic: shopping malls, downtown business areas (especially during lunch hours) and airports (check with management first).**

SUPPLIES & EQUIPMENT

You'll need daffodils, order forms, return envelopes for mail orders, scissors and tissue paper to wrap the flowers in until they're sold.

If you have the manpower, you'll increase sales by offering to deliver the daffodils. When offering delivery, stipulate a minimum order and specific limits on the delivery area.

If you opt for direct sales, you'll need a booth with signage. Get your supplier's suggestions on the correct temperature and humidity for storing the flowers to maintain freshness for several days.

You'll also need a place to store, box and prepare flowers for pick-up and/or delivery.

MANPOWER

The chairman of this project is the one to contact the daffodil supplier and work out the details of price, quantities, delivery, storage, etc.

You need as many volunteers as possible to sell the flowers. You'll need people to take orders for pick-up or delivery and for direct sales .

Once the flowers are delivered to your group, you'll need volunteers to package them for pick-up or delivery. If you are selling them on the street, you'll need people to set up a booth and/or create signs to wear when selling daffodils from a box. And don't forget to stop and smell the flowers and the new money in your coffers.

HALLOWEEN TREATS

Want to scare up a great fall fundraiser? Think about selling pre-packaged Halloween goodies for people to give to their visiting hobgoblins and monsters. First you'll need to find suppliers of trinkets and candies in bulk and ask if they'll give your group a donation or the ability to purchase your supplies at a discount.

> **Want to scare up a great fall fundraiser? Think about selling pre-packaged Halloween goodies for people to give to their visiting hobgoblins and monsters.**

Now that you know what kinds of treats are available, you'll be able to determine the

TROOP #17 SNACK PACK

mix of goodies to pre-package and the quanities you'll offer for sale. We've found that lots of two to three dozen work best.

Once you've figured out

what you need, get your Halloween treats and the bags to package them ready to go. For an extra touch, decorate the bags with drawings and/or stickers featuring bats, spiders and other Halloween creatures.

Next set up an assembly line of volunteers to put a predefined assortment of candy, gum and/or trinkets in each bag.

Your volunteers can now go out and sell your pre-packaged treats throughout your school or church membership, or door-to-door in your member's neighborhoods. Remember, you'll need to prepare and sell the treat packages several weeks before Halloween.

GROCERY STORE GIFT CERTIFICATES

Looking for a fundraising product to sell that *everyone* can use? Try selling gift certificates from a local grocery or chain. We all go grocery shopping on a regular basis, which makes this gift certificate one of the most practical of all fundraising products.

To get this project underway, approach a local grocer and explain your group's project to him. If he'll sell you gift certificates to his store at a reduced rate, you can sell them to your customers for their face value and keep the difference. Your sponsoring grocer will benefit by getting an increase in business by the introduction of new customers to his

store. Your group will benefit from selling a very practical "product" for a profit. See

Product Fundraising page 177 for general guidelines on selling techniques.

This project is especially successful during the holiday season, when people do more of both grocery-shopping and

> **Your sponsoring grocer will benefit by getting an increase in business by the introduction of new customers to his store. Your group will benefit from selling a very practical "product" for a profit.**

gift-giving than at other times of the year. Suggest to your customers that gift certificates make great presents or stocking-stuffers and they won't have to worry about exchanges or wrong sizes!

HAND-MADE GOODIES TO SELL

In today's megastore world filled with mass-produced food and gift items it's refreshing to see the growing sales of hand-made goods and home-baked foods in shops and rural malls all across America. With some focused planning and organized effort your group can create a long lasting fundraising niche in this market.

You can sell everything from candy and baked goods to craft items. Seasonal offerings, Christmas wreaths or ornaments, Easter baskets, etc., are always popular and open the door to yearly

> *Ideally what you produce and sell should also help fulfill your group's mission. A group with a strong environmental mission might sell birdhouses every spring to support their work.*

sales campaigns. Ideally, what you produce and sell should also help fulfill your group's mission. A group with a strong environmental mission might sell birdhouses every spring to support their work.

You'll first need to decide what your group can make and sell. When figuring costs per item, be sure to include materials or ingredients, as well as the time and energy needed to cook, bake, sew or build.

The sales end of this project can be an event, complete with booth and signs or you can take orders for later home delivery. In either case, think of a catchy publicity theme like: *Save your dough for our bread sale!*

For a different twist have a specialty sale; for instance, *All Baked Breads* or, *Only Cinnamon Rolls* or, *Just Cookies* or, *Nothing But Pies*. Give out free small samples to boost sales of your goodies.

If you make this project a sales event, do the following:

First, determine a time and place to hold your sale. These events work great at fairs or carnivals, or they can be done as a solo event following a church or school meeting.

Make large, attractive signs that tell what you are selling, the prices and who benefits.

Do an extensive advance publicity campaign for several weeks before the sale itself.

If you decide to sell by taking orders for delivery, use the following procedure:

Give all volunteers order sheets which have detailed information about the items being sold, unit prices and scheduled pick-up or delivery place and time. Use *Product Order Form* on page 179.

Have your sale volunteers approach family, friends, schoolmates, business associates, church members and others. Run a small ad in the newspaper with a telephone number people can call to place their orders. Request payment upon delivery.

Designate a specific date for all orders to be turned in. Allow enough time between order-taking and order-filling so your organization can make whatever it is you're selling.

SUPPLIES & EQUIPMENT

If you are selling candy or baked goods, it may be easier to ask volunteers to make their share in their own homes and bring them to a central place for orders to be packaged and filled. Or, if you have access to a large institutional-type kitchen, you can do "assembly line" style preparing, cooking and packaging. Either way, use the same recipe and ingredients for uniform results.

If you're making craft items, have a committee gather all necessary supplies, then schedule a time for volunteers to meet and assemble all the items. Whatever you make, be sure it's an item you've successfully made before, in order to avoid last-minute disasters!

PRODUCT FUNDRAISING

You open the front door and there stands a smiling young man with a box of products. "Hi," he says in a cheerful tone, "I'm with the XYZ youth group…" You're about to buy something to support a good cause in your neighborhood.

There are two main approaches to selling products to raise funds. The first is to buy items at wholesale and sell them at retail. The problem is you can have a large cash outlay at the beginning. You also risk being stuck with who knows how many cases of candy bars, light bulbs, etc.

On the brighter side, you do have the advantage of no minimum purchase order and on-the-spot delivery of goods sold.

The second choice is to take orders for items sold by companies that specialize in fundraising. With this approach on a specific day your group will add all individual orders together and place one large order with the supplier.

The advantage of ordering items this way is that you order only what's already sold and you don't have a large, somewhat speculative cash outlay at the beginning. The drawback is that takes at least two trips, once to sell the item

> **When you sell products, always sell the best quality you can. People generally like to support a group's fundraising effort, especially if you're giving them premium quality goods for their money.**

and once to deliver and collect for it, for each sale. And there's generally far more paperwork than in a simple, direct sale.

In general it is better to buy inventories of lower-priced fundraising items such as candy bars, light bulbs and other more impulse items. If you're selling

higher-priced things, it is better to take orders first.

In either case, calculate the profit per unit sold. Use that figure to help you set group and individual sales goals. When you sell products, always sell the best quality you can. People generally like to support a group's fundraising effort, especially if they're getting premium quality goods for their money.

Some very successful product fundraisers are the Boy Scouts of America's annual popcorn/caramel corn sale and, of course, the classic Girl Scouts Cookie Sale.

To get your own fundraiser plans rolling, send for information about sale items from our list of suppliers in *Appendix C* or check with local wholesalers. If your group plans to resell items purchased from a wholesaler, use the *Product Order Form* on page 179.

Select the right products, mix with an enthusi`astic sales campaign and the public will be waiting for you at their door!

SUGGESTED SALE ITEMS

FOOD PRODUCTS:

FRUIT: Apples, oranges, grapefruit (or a fruit-of-the-month arrangement)
NUTS: Pecans, almonds, pistachios
PRESERVES, COOKIES, CAKES: Fruit cakes, tortes, cheesecakes
CANDY: M & Ms, candy bars, assorted chocolates
POPCORN *or* **CARAMEL CORN**
CHEESES, SUMMER SAUSAGE, SPICES

OTHER PRODUCTS:

LIGHT BULBS
FIRST AID KITS
SEASONAL ITEMS: Ornaments, candies, decorations, cards, wreaths, candles, etc
CALENDARS, ADDRESS BOOKS
POSTERS, BUTTONS, BADGES, BUMPER STICKERS.
COUPON BOOKS: Good for regional resturants, entertainment, services, etc.

MASTER PRODUCT ORDER FORM

Organization _____ Date _____

Person In Charge _____ Telephone _____

MEMBER'S NAME & PHONE	$	$	$	$	$	$	AMOUNT DUE	AMOUNT PAID
TOTALS								

MAKE AS MANY COPIES OF THIS PAGE AS NEEDED

PRODUCT ORDER FORM

Organization _____ **Date** _____ **Make Check Payable To** _____

Person In Charge _____ **Telephone** _____

Member's Name _____

My Goal Is To Sell: _____

CUSTOMER'S NAME, ADDRESS & PHONE	$	$	$	$	$	$	AMOUNT DUE	AMOUNT PAID
TOTALS								

MAKE AS MANY COPIES OF THIS PAGE AS NEEDED

You've probably seen a million faces, logos and slogans staring at you from the T-shirted crowds afoot in our land today. Printed T-shirts are extremely popular and if your group comes up with a shirt design with wide local appeal, you'll have a hot-selling item.

You can have T-shirts printed with almost anything you can think of. Local sports teams, high school mascots or commemorative shirts for local events are all potentially profitable T-shirt ideas. To have T-shirts available for a specific event, you'll need to start several months in advance.

First you'll have to decide on the topic or purpose for your T-shirt design. Then, when all of that is firmly in mind, bring a couple of your more creative people together and brainstorm your T-shirt's slogan and design. To make this process as effective as possible, read *Graphic Design* on page 50.

After you've settled on a design, you will have to get the the T-shirt art ready for the printer. If your design will be printed in one color, the art (called mechanical art) is relatively easy to do. There may be someone in your group who can either do the art or get it

> *Local sports teams, high school mascots or commemorative shirts for local events are all potentially profitable T-shirt ideas. To have T-shirts available for a specific event, you'll need to start several months in advance.*

done. This will save money.

SUPPLIES & EQUIPMENT

Now contact a wholesale supplier of specialty-printed T's and get a firm quote for the exact type of shirt you want. Make sure your quote includes all necessary artwork and set-up fees. Find out how many shirts you must order to qualify for quantity discounts.

Learn the fiber content of the shirt (people want to know how much shrinkage to allow for) and if the shirts are sized in male sizes, unisex, or male/female sizes. Find out how long it will take to fill your order, then you'll know about when your customers can

expect to receive their shirts.

Once you have determined your exact cost per shirt, set a price for your shirts. This price should be about 50% higher than your cost.

Order extra shirts in large or extra large sizes. There are always some people who'll see your shirt and say, "Gee, I wish I had ordered one of those!"

Put up posters and send home flyers with local high school and college students, since they will be a large part of your market. Make sure all publicity clearly states the price, the order deadline and who to call to place an order.

MANPOWER

Get your sales people out to take orders! Use the *Product Order Form* on page 179. Make sure they get the customers' *size* for each shirt ordered. Set a cut-off date for orders and, at the time of the order, let your customers know when the shirts will be in. Tell them they must pay for their shirts when they pick them up.

If the shirts commemorate a specific event, order some to sell on the day of the event. Also, be sure everyone selling shirts at the event is wearing one—it's great advertising!

When the order arrives, have your volunteers contact your customers and arrange for payment, pick-up and/or delivery. You'll soon see familiar T-shirt images in the mall!

We'd like to thank all of the people, groups and institutions who have shared their valuable suggestions, ideas and insights with us over the years.

APPENDIX

NOTE: *The following business and organization names and addresses are provided for your information. Phone numbers, addresses, and prices are subject to change and should be verified. Inclusion in this list is not an endorsement.*

APPENDIX A:

Vending machines, supplies and prizes.

BIRMINGHAM VENDING

540 Second Ave. No.
Birmingham, AL 35204
1-800-288-7635
vending machines

IMPRESSMENT PLUS

6217 Factory Road
Crystal Lake, IL 60014
1-800-274-2031
Plush toys

MAYONI ENTERPRISES

10340 Glenoaks Blvd.
Pacoima, CA 91331
1-800-345-1183
Vending machines

PLUSH APPEAL

501 North Cortez St.
New Orleans, LA 70119
1-800-899-1869
Plush toys

SUCCESS PLUSH, INC.

10660 Kinghurst Drive
Houston, TX 77099
1-800-396-8888
Plush toys

APPENDIX B:

Information on charities, guidelines for fundraising

ACCOUNTANTS FOR THE PUBLIC INTEREST (API)

1012 14th St. NW Ste. 906
Washington, D.C. 20005
410-837-6533
Helps locate an accountant to assist your organization for a nominal fee.
Also has various publications available on accounting procedures for nonprofits, directory of accounting programs throughout the U.S. and services offered to charitable organizations. Call for list of publications available and prices.

COUNCIL OF BETTER BUSINESS BUREAUS

4200 Wilson Blvd. Ste. 800
Arlington, VA 22203
703-276-0100
Gives advice on charitable donations, CBBB standards, etc. Call for list of brochures and prices.

BOY SCOUTS OF AMERICA

P.O. Box 152079
Irving, TX 75015-2079
972-580-2000
Booklet of BSA general guidelines available for a nominal fee. Additional booklets available. Contact them for list and prices.

COUNCIL ON FOUNDATIONS

1828 L St. NW Ste. 300
Washington, D.C. 20036
202-466-6512
Community foundation information

IRS PUBLICATION 561

"Determining the Value of Donated Property"
Get a copy at your local IRS office or call 800#

IRS FORM 1023

"Application for Recognition of exemption" Under Section 501(c)(3) of the Internal Revenue Code. Get a copy at your local IRS office or call 800#

INDEPENDENT SECTOR

1828 L St. NW Ste. 1200
Washington, D.C. 20036
888-860-8118
"How Much is Really Tax Deductible?" Booklet from Independent Sector, a nonprofit coalition of philanthropic groups. This booklet explains tax rules regarding donations. Call for price.

UNITED STATES POSTAL SERVICE

Guidelines on bulk mailing. Contact your local USPS office for information, application, fee and booklets.

viii • **EARNING MORE FUNDS**

APPENDIX C:
Fundraising products

AMERICA'S BEST
P.O. Box 6380
Montgomery, AL 36106
1-800-633-6750
Seasonal products, wrapping paper, light bulbs, cookies, candies, recipe books, candles, calendars, greeting cards, notepads, flower bulbs, ornaments, first-aid kits, etc.

BADGE-A-MINIT
Box 800
LaSalle, IL 61301
1-800-223-4103
Button-making equipment and supplies

DUTCH-MILL BULBS, INC.
P.O. Box 407
Hershey, PA 17033-0407
1-800-533-8824
Flower bulbs, perennial plants, hanging gardens, garden kits, candies

HALE INDIAN RIVER GROVES
P.O. Box 700217
Wabasso, FL 32970
1-800-289-4253
Citrus fruit, honey, marmalade

MICKMAN BROTHER NURSERIES
14630 Hwy. 65
Anoka, MN 55304
1-800-446-4229
Holiday wreaths

THE POPCORN FACTORY
P.O. Box 4530
Lake Bluff, IL 60044
1-800-541-2676
Popcorn and candy in decorative seasonal tins, mugs, boxes, baskets and gift containers.

PROFIT POTENTIALS
451 Black Forest Road
Hull, IA 51239
1-800-543-5480
Candies, seasonal items, dishcloths, flowering plant packets, first aid kits, light bulbs, pre-packaged snacks, Christmas wreaths, etc.

REVERE COMPANY
P.O. Box 709
Montgomery, AL 36101-0709
1-800-876-9967
Candies, ornaments, seasonal items, wrapping paper, greeting cards, calendars, candles, notepads, first aid kits, plaques, gourmet flavorings, etc.

SPIRIT OF AMERICA
P.O. box 621
Montgomery, AL 36101-0621
1-800-628-3671
Calendars, cards, candies, candles, seasonal gifts, plants, first aid kits, spices, etc.

APPENDIX D:
Printers that specialize in cookbooks

For more information, contact:

CALICO KITCHEN PRESS
1-800-732-4737

COOKBOOK PUBLISHERS
1-800-227-7282

FUNDCRAFT
1-800-351-7822

WALTER'S COOKBOOKS
1-800-447-3274

INDEX

continued on next page

continued from preceding page

INDEX OF RECIPES